From Sheets to Suits

Paul,
Thanks For Your
Support

From Sheets to Suits

Embedded Racism in American Society

John Parker

Library of Congress Control Number: 2015919213
ISBN: Hardcover   978-1-5144-2126-0
               Softcover   978-1-5144-2125-3
               eBook   978-1-5144-2124-6

Print information available on the last page.

Rev. date: 11/18/2015

To order additional copies of this book, contact:
Xlibris
1-888-795-4274
www.Xlibris.com
Orders@Xlibris.com
712103

TABLE OF CONTENTS

ABOUT THE AUTHOR

John Parker is a high-energy, results-oriented, executive public relations consultant and political operative. Parker's experience includes time as editor of a two online newspaper, as well as eleven years as principal of a St. Louis-based, Evolution Communication Group, a certified public relations firm that has the honor of having client relationships dating back to the firm's first year. Drawing on his first-hand knowledge, and how society works in conjunction with the various institutions of the professional world, Parker is an expert on how to project a positive image. Parker has implemented numerous successful campaigns, ranging from grassroots community relations programs to national publicity efforts.

Clients that John Parker has served operate in both the public and private sectors, and are involved in variety of different industry sectors, including economic development, transit, construction, government organizations, professional sports teams, telecommunications, technology, healthcare, real estate and more. He is adept at crafting messages that resonate and communicate complex information to diverse audiences.

He is a renowned national motivational speaker, and a social activist. He is also a radio/television talk show host, and is a twenty-four-year veteran coach of college and professional football. He has a reputation as one of the most inspirational speakers in the country.

Parker is a native of the area of Ferguson, Missouri. He is uniquely aware that, in the eyes of many White Americans, racism and discrimination are no longer a serious and widespread problem in American society, but African Americans face the evils of racism regularly. It is to a considerable degree precisely that awareness led him to write *From Sheets to Suits*. His position is that, to be an African American is to live with racism every day.

ABOUT THE BOOK

Racism refers to a host of practices, beliefs, social relations, and phenomena that work to reproduce a racial hierarchy and social structure that yield superiority and privilege for some, and discrimination and oppression for others. The practices of a White American-led society have not only perpetuated these practices, but deeply embedded unlawful and discriminatory racial policies that affect the everyday way, for all citizens of the United States, and in particular, African Americans.

From Sheets to Suits: Embedded Racism in American Society is without a doubt a controversial examination of the beginnings of racism in this country, originating with the Ku Klux Klan and reaching a pinnacle in the summer of 2014 with the shooting of Michael Brown Jr., an unarmed African American teenager in Ferguson, Missouri, a suburb of St. Louis.

St. Louis, Missouri, is the one of the most covertly racist cities in the United States. Many of the White Americans in the Gateway City are ignorant, don't like to be around African American people, don't believe black people can be educated and go out of their way to prevent African Americans from succeeding. Law enforcement agencies have even gone as far as to intentionally target African Americans in sinister revenue scandals.

Parker examines the forms taken by embedded racism in politics and entertainment, in educational institutions and in everyday encounters. Readers are made to feel the humiliations and hostility encountered by African American people in what remains, to a shocking degree, an embedded racist society.

This book delves into how racism has affected, and has had a hand in shaping every aspect of the society in the United States.

DEDICATION

THIS BOOK IS dedicated to everybody whose mind is open enough for a vision of racial and cultural change. To those young people who are on the front line in the battle against racism, from Ferguson, and coast to coast in the United States. These young people have the leadership and courage to stand up, protest, and show civil disobedience in the fight against this disease that has poisoned and continues to infest our society. I applaud them for the ability to vocalize the injustice in the world, putting their own regard on the back burner.

To the older people who look like myself, and those who don't, who share a vision with me for a future of less racial division and more cultural awareness.

To Rich Pisani, who has become family to me, and many of the St. Louis Ambassadors who have stood up for the betterment of St. Louis, Missouri, and its cultural diversity. Although it has its problems, and a national reputation as "one of the most segregated cities in the country," I do love my city. I don't know if I am going to heaven or to hell, but I do know that either way, I will be going through St. Louis.

Additional special thanks to Jim Allen, my best friend for over forty years. My radio and television partner of fifteen years, Randy Gardner. We have been a perfect example of how two people, from different cultural backgrounds, can become great friends. To Kelly Harris, who has been my good friend, administrative assistant, collaborator, and confidant during this project. Thank you for the support and for always having my back. This book is as much mine as it is yours.

To my daughter, Andrea, and my son, Jordan, the greatest achievements of my life. No matter what happens in my life, you guys always manage to keep your father grounded. My love for you two has no boundaries. Thank you for being who you are. It is with hope that during your lifetime, this stigma of racial divide will fade away and become a memory that is forgiven, but never forgotten, because if forgotten, your own children will be doomed to relive it.

I want you to always have the courage to stand up, sometimes be unpopular, and remain convicted about what you believe in. People, both family and false friends, will turn their back on you, but you hold true to what is in your heart and remember that after everybody walks away, your daddy will always have your back. I love you. Dad

PREFACE

MODERN EMBEDDED RACISM? That alone is a very unique term, as there is really nothing modern about racism. If we talk about it in modern terms, then we must start with the Ku Klux Klan.

The Ku Klux Klan is a many-sided organization. Comprising its creed have been a half dozen or so tenets. To carry out its program based upon these articles of faith, the secret order has used a variety of political methods. Unfortunately, the Klan has left the scantiest amount of documentary evidence concerning its activities. For this reason, no work on the Klan, including my writings, can pretend to be truly comprehensive, but it is the foundation for racism in America.

Racism infects this country in epidemics that rival any disease in the history of man. Trying to understand its origin in a person's life is at best impossible. Nobody is born hating anybody, but somehow it is inevitably learned, which means at some point, either inadvertently or on purpose, it is taught.

It could be through politics, economic development (or lack thereof), law enforcement methods, the judicial system, or even the media. It eventually contaminates lives on a daily basis. The problem is that, much like the common cold, society has never found a cure, and the longtime effects have been more devastating than any natural disaster.

Being from St. Louis, I had the misfortune of watching racism rear its ugly head in the worst way during the summer of 2014. I watched a city, my city, which has already been labeled as "one of the most segregated cities in the country," become a battleground pitting White vs. African American, law enforcement vs. protestor, judicial system vs. citizen and in many cases old friends vs. history.

With the killing of Michael Brown and subsequent protests in Ferguson, Missouri, at the forefront of our minds, and the tragedies of Trayvon Martin, Eric Garner, Freddie Gray, and the countless number of African Americans killed by law enforcement a not so distant memory, race and racism are once again in the headlines across the country. While many people often answer the question "Is everyone a little bit racist?" with a quick "No," this suggests the problem is not so much overt racism but rather unconscious and embedded attitudes that result in discriminatory policies and behavior.

Having been on the scene of and in the mix of the Michael Brown killing in Ferguson on a daily basis, and having been one of the first African American families in that area of St. Louis, I have seen every good, bad, and ugly thing that you can imagine. Racism has been a part of my life for as long as I can remember, from education, to athletics, to my multiple careers. Sometimes it has been blatant, in the form of people openly calling me "Nigger" right to my face, to the subtleness of being rejected for employment because I didn't have the "intangibles."

Many people have called me a racist, or a "race baiter." I just laugh at the accusation, because that is always the defense when someone discusses clear facts about racist behavior with someone that has no clue about racism or racist behavior. I have been referred to as someone who will not let it die, and who continues to "stir the pot" of racism by always talking about it. Well, as someone who considers himself somewhat of a good cook, I have always found that it is imperative that we always "stir the pot." Otherwise, things will slowly burn and eventually erupt.

When you are over fifty years old like myself, I believe something comes over. You begin to see the world in a different light. It started for me long before the summer of 2014, but like an addict, the killing of

Michael Brown triggered something in me that made me significantly aware of the country we live in. A country where young men and women of various cultures can put on the same military uniform, and go off and defend the mythical representation of the American flag.

I say "mythical" because when these same people return home, they are forced to live completely different lives, because of the difference in skin color. That angers me, and both people that look like me and many that don't.

Thus, writing this book has been far from easy.

John Parker

CHAPTER I

WHAT IS RACISM?

Racism is when you have laws set up, or systematically put in a way to keep people from advancing, to stop the advancement of a people. Black people have never had the power to enforce racism, and so this is something that White America is going to have to work out themselves. If they decide they want to stop it, curtail it, or to "do the right thing" . . . then it will be done, but not until then.

—Spike Lee

I AM GOING to answer this question numerous times in this book, with a number of different definitions, but let me start with this one. Racism is discrimination against an individual due to his or her membership of a particular race, and it is a problem across the United

States. Racism can be practiced at an individual level, such as when private citizens make comments or stereotypes concerning others, or at an organizational level, such as if policies are implemented to discriminate against others.

These actions and attitudes may be taken in order to benefit one race, or simply because one race is thought to be inferior to others. In the United States, the Constitution protects individuals from being discriminated against in employment on the grounds of color, race, nationality, religious beliefs, or ethnicity. This is true of discrimination whether it is done on purpose or not, as well as whether it is direct, indirect, harassment, or victimization.

Racism can be obvious or unintended. It can also be on purpose or inadvertent, but wherever racism is in place, it is detrimental to everyone. Discrimination against African Americans makes it acceptable to discriminate against members of any race. Therefore, nobody is protected or safe where racism is alive. Communities, like Ferguson, Missouri, can have a large impact on stamping out racism in their town.

Finding the meaning of racism and understanding its manifestation in a community, along with coming to understand its effects in communities like Ferguson, and dealing with the discriminatory behavior within these communities are all crucial topics that can and should be addressed to be sure equality truly exists for all.

Racism in the public corners of society in institutions such as employment and education are clearly defined in the Constitution of the United States, but racism in informal arena needs to be defined by the actual communities themselves. These meanings do not need to be delusional in grandeur. They don't even need to be written down or articulated, but should be made clear by actions that a community will not put up with racism. Only at the point where every member is clear that the community will not be tolerant of any form of racism, in any situations, will everyone feel equally protected living and working within it.

New urban communities are those that are bringing back the smaller lifestyle that comes from urban living. Communities such as these can be in both the urban or suburban areas of any city, but the main focus of both of these communities is to work toward embracing the opportunity of living as one unified community and constructing a community foundation to enhance the entire community's quality of life.

However, no new urban community can flourish if racism is allowed to take hold. No matter how strong the foundation, racism continues to divide communities all over the United States. Only by making sure that there is equality for all citizens can a community best protect all citizens and make the most of the many talents of the citizens living within the community.

What if racism does occur in a community? How should it be dealt with? Racism should always be met with a quick condemnation. Often members of the communities will desire to speak with perpetrators directly, while others feel it easier to show their support for victims of racism.

These communities should not result to behaving like a "Stepford Cult" and force citizens to behave in a certain way, but community members should know that behaving in an inappropriate way will result in dealings with law enforcement. In no way should any community try and match racist behavior with vigilante behavior of their own. Teaching citizens, instead of punishing them, is the best way to help combat racism or any other form of discrimination or segregation in any community.

Combating racism in the area of a community is crucial to making all citizens feel significant and protected. In order to make this happen, there has to be serious communication between citizens about their stand on racism, and we must realize how racism can divide a community. They must deal with people who continue to speak on a racist foundation or perform actions of racism.

Racism should never be fought with unethical behavior or an illegal action. Communities should begin to educate those who enact racist behavior against others so that everyone begins to learn the importance of both equality and also the detriment of racist behavior.

Sometimes racism or racial discrimination is described at the organizational level, as a system or policy of treating one (or multiple) races unfairly. Racism may be practiced to benefit one race, or simply because one or more other races are thought to be inferior. Unfortunately, racism still exists across the United States, and is deeply embedded and institutionalized.

No single issue or subject is more volatile than a discussion of racism in America. Both sides of the political aisle agree that a sincere and more common-sense discussion about the virus of racism in the United States would go over like a proverbial lead balloon, and for many of White America, who don't believe that racism really exists, or whose lives are completely unaffected by it, the conversation is unnecessary.

Even when they witness events, through the mainstream predominantly White-focused media on a daily basis. It is hard to ignore the killing of Trayvon Martin, Michael Brown, and Eric Garner, and then the multiple accusations of voter suppression, targeted toward minorities, while many in the White American community (and some nonbelievers in the African American community also) refuse to believe in the notion that racism is a major factor in what happens in our everyday life.

Furthermore, they are also unwilling or unable to review the history of this country and see that what is happening today is nothing more than a reenactment of the history of the United States. The only thing that has changed is the technological ability to hide it.

In my case, being born in the 1960s and growing up in the 1970s, during the storms and upheaval of civil rights demonstrations by African Americans for rights and privileges which should have been established a century earlier at the end of the war between the states. The idea that racism does not have modern-day implications is completely absurd to the people, many of whom I have known for nearly three quarters of my life, who truly do not know about the American story that includes genocide, murder, slavery, Jim Crow laws, and the incidents that have affected generations of African American men, women, and children.

Often it is that they know, and truly have no compassion or flatly don't care that entire generations have been wiped out through these acts of violence, like a tornado across an Oklahoma plain. If we truly are to understand the effects of racism and the ancestors of the perpetrators, we must first be honest about history, instead of writing and rewriting it to fit the story that is best for their justification.

Missouri is a state whose birth came on the sweat and toil of African Americans whose very rights as human beings were negotiated and sold away. As stated in the Missouri Compromise of 1820, there was a congressional agreement that was created to regulate the extension of slavery for the next thirty years. Some would say that this very compromise still exists today, and in several cases it does.

Based on this agreement, Missouri would be admitted as a slave state, Maine would join as a free state, and the geographical line of slavery would stay the same latitude as the southern boundary of Missouri: 36° 30′ north latitude would later be known as the "Mason–Dixon Line."

Nearly two centuries later, even with the United States moving toward some kind of racially equal society, portions of the United States are still being used as pawns in manipulating districts to help cut off the African American and Hispanic vote. People still continue to stick their head in the sand when it comes to racism in this country, and it still holds us back from rising to its potential and repairing the damage of the history that has recently been reacquired.

There are many people that reject the idea of racism by saying "Slavery ended in the 1800s." Others are always asking the question "Why don't African American people just get over it?" I like to remind these same people to go back and read the Thirteenth Amendment to the Constitution again. It declared that "Neither slavery nor involuntary servitude, **except as a punishment for crime whereof the party shall have been duly convicted**, shall exist within the United States, nor any place subject to their jurisdiction."

That means if you were convicted of a crime, you were not free. Today, there are more Black men in prison than were enslaved in 1860. Is that by random occurrence, or by plan? Considering that our prison system is mostly privatized, I would say that there is a blueprint being followed.

We, as a country, should realize the fact that we cannot kid ourselves anymore about racism and race relations in the United States. There will always be some measure of anti–African American, anti-White, anti-Hispanic feeling in our country. Some might say whining about it will keep it from going away, while others will find more solid ground from historic events that only through vigilance and finding one's voice will we be able to advance the cause of equality for all people.

Racism is quite often a very strong word to use, I have to say, but there has been a lot of unfairness and discriminations throughout the years in America, which is what has always made me interested in, and maybe obsessed with, this topic. The unfairness people receive from other people because the color of their skin. I myself and some people I know have experienced unfair, humiliating, and in some cases deadly acts because of the content of their skin.

Many people know that racism has occurred in the past when African Americans were treated unfairly, being kept apart from the White American race. But they have also fooled themselves to believe that much of that changed when people began to fight and demonstrating for equal rights by having boycotts, protests, and consistently having those individuals who were racist know that they deserved equal rights as well as they did. Those racist individuals and systemic entities know different, and have chosen to dig their heels in and embed those racist feelings and policies even deeper.

Fact is, until people receive justice, they are going to have their voices heard until they receive justice. We witnessed this in Ferguson, Missouri, with daily, weekly, and monthly protests against the brutality of law enforcement. People, many of them White, don't believe racism still exists. I always laugh. I laugh because it is much easier than jumping on my soapbox and raising hell. Racism does still exist in the United States, and if people would open their eyes, it would be apparent, but you cannot make someone believe something that you, because of how the system is set up, cannot clearly prove.

We need to realize that this country is, and will remain split along racial lines, and the politics of the day reflects such a split. The racist element in America is still strong as recently as the last presidential election, and even the events in Ferguson, Missouri, during the summer of 2014.

I believe this question needs to be asked. Is the problem of racism a political problem, pitting Republican vs. Democrat, or moral issue, setting up a battle between the good-hearted and evil? Racism itself is, at the least, a complex equation. It is problematic to prove, or even to identify or characterize it. It does not land into any one category because of its lengthy implications and factors. However, one thing for sure is that the moral items surrounding embedded racism generate concerns from a social standpoint which can truly only be handled in the political arena.

If the government of the United States' reaction to these issues is below average (like it always is), the moral issues that started the problems will continue to not only survive but also grow exponentially. This is the chemical makeup of racism in the United States. You will never be able to legislate what is in a person's heart or mind.

The silent prejudices of an individual soul are not controlled by any type of law or jurisprudence. Actions are the only things that have the potential to be controlled. So, if there is a law that says that no one will be denied employment because of race or ethnicity, then employers must abide by the law.

Nevertheless, in many employment locations all over the United States, job applicants are carefully examined and scrutinized by calculating interviewers and employers who are schooled on just how to get rid of those potential employees who don't have the intangibles that would best work their business. The same is accurately true for the housing industry. In many cases, landlords, homeowners and building managers, and neighborhood associations work hard to keep their neighborhoods with the right "look." This is another verification of the embedded status of racism.

Are these indications of a moral decay or a simple governmental "I don't give a shit" and neglect? Is there not some sort of process to monitor and account for the hiring methods of employers for nearly every available job in the United States? Is there an organization to stand by American citizens who are rejected from new places to live or homes due to race or ethnicity? Is there a limit to where the moral issue concludes and the political and legislative responsibility and support takes control? One simple realization is that maybe in the United States, made up of a broad range of diverse individuals, people will never be able to exist with each other without prejudging each other and fearing one another. The roots of racism are absolutely identical.

Racism is more than just a moral issue. It has now become an embedded political policy concern. The United States government needs to finally begin to make every effort to assure its citizens that all are allowed to realize their constitutional "inalienable rights." This will take a very long time as the judicial system faces the new challenges brought about by the always-transitioning diversity of the country's population.

Today we face issues like Gay Rights and the Confederate Flag, which have come to the forefront, and have often pushed the issues of civil rights of citizens to the back burner. The needs of the citizens of the United States need to be at the forefront of the legislative process.

The fact is that society does not have a chance at redemption unless it changes its heart as a whole. When the people of the United States learn to see each other through the eyes of God, then and only then will we see one another without discrimination and alienation. Anyone who has a faith in the Lord realizes that he does not show partiality. Everywhere in this world he accepts only those who show fear to him and do what is right to their brothers and sisters.

With that being said, I've also come to the sad conclusion that racism will always exist here in the United States, but its outward expression is not what it used to be. It has now become faceless and nameless.

It is embedded in the very fabric of our lives, and in the institutions of the United States. It's in our boardrooms and small businesses. It is prevalent in law enforcement and the courts system. Racism lives next door to you, and you don't even know it.

However, we as a people can cure the disease of racism, but we need to come together. Although it has never been done in the past, it can be done. We live in a country where people should not have to act a certain way when being stopped by authority or when trying to associate with coworkers. Being colorblind has not and will never work. We as citizens need to end this "we're all the same race, the human race" illusion, and work to understand each other's true CULTURES.

While we should not call every disagreement an issue of racism, it is time to call out the racism that indeed does still exist. Racism that wounds our soul as a nation, and that obstructs the promise of the United States of America.

I am often asked about solutions, but we must first determine all of the questions to be answered. We must truly realize the history of this country and the atrocities that have been inflicted upon the people. We are very big on remembering tragic moments in history. We remember the attack on Pearl Harbor. We regularly recognize the lives lost during the attacks on 9/11. We have memorials for Jewish Holocaust victims, but we fail to understand that we had concentration camps in the United States for over two hundred years, among its own citizens.

The United States has never in its history been held accountable for the treatment of its own citizens. In order for a person, company, or country to move forward in the future, it must be held accountable for its past behavior.

The most difficult conversation to have in this country is about race. It makes people uncomfortable. It forces us to deal with our personal fears and inadequacies. It makes us all vulnerable to attack, and with any attack comes general and personal defense. With defense comes walls, and often behind those walls is violence.

Ending racism is about making people "comfortable being uncomfortable." When that happens, we will finally be on a course to finally eliminating this disease we call racism.

CHAPTER 2

HISTORY OF THE "INVISIBLE EMPIRE"

I wish I could say that racism and prejudice were only distant memories. We must dissent from the indifference. We must dissent from the apathy. We must dissent from the fear, the hatred and the mistrust . . . We must dissent because America can do better, because America has no choice but to do better.

—Thurgood Marshall

WHILE IT HAS definitely never been the elephant in the room, the subject of the Ku Klux Klan always raises the juices of the racism conversation.

The Ku Klux Klan, sometimes referred to as the "Invisible Empire," was an organization that was born out of anger over the abolition of slavery, a fear of changing an embedded way of life and from the very basis of racism: hate. After the Civil War ended, the Southern region of the country was left decimated, and the people of the South were hit with the feelings of frustration because of the bad conditions and the drastic changes in the political and economic structure they had grown accustomed to.

The South was ruined. Cities and landowners, which had once known prosperity, were now looking at a bleak future for some time to come. Southerners were less than compliant in conforming to the new laws that were coming down the pike. The people of the South were facing hunger and poverty. It would be similar to living in an occupied country and the new "Reconstruction" government not only challenged, but in many cases altered and destroyed the authority of the southern White rule. The intention of the United States (Union) government was to destroy the power structure of the South.

The Freeman's Bureau which was established to protect the interests of former slaves. The plan was to provide schools, hospitals, and housing for people who had once been owned and were being given their natural-born rights for the very first time. The change became the backdrop of the mid-1800s for the rise of the "Imperial Empire."

In all actuality, the Ku Klux Klan was not originally created to be a violent hate group. It was intended to be a secret society, founded by a group of individuals who were more bored the concocting. The original members would travel through the streets, riding horses, wearing white sheets, and simply raising hell with the locals for pure entertainment.

The KKK began to attract sinister attention and appeal because of their secret society and image, and it spread very quickly throughout the South. In 1867 many of those who had a loose allegiance with the Klan gathered in Nashville, Tennessee, with the intention of gaining oneness, and to begin to construct a proper authority structure and chain-of-command hierarchy.

It was at this meeting that the KKK made a decision to change its creed. Their actions turned from ridiculous pranks to violent, brutal, and murderous acts against freed Negro slaves. This transition of actions came soon after, the first Reconstruction Act of 1867. This was the first Reconstruction Act that displaced and destroyed state governments and divided the South into military districts, five to speak of, as well as gave Negro men the right to vote after the ratification of the Fourteenth Amendment.

This was the act that allowed for Southern states to rejoin the Union, but only upon ratifying the Fourteenth Amendment and guaranteeing adult males voting rights (Negro males in particular). President Andrew Johnson immediately vetoed the bill, but the Radical Republicans voted and repassed the bill on the same day.

As Negroes gained the right to vote and their first real voice and degree of influence in Southern politics, the KKK put into motion their plan to destroy the Negro political effectiveness by driving out its vocal leaders, who were both White and Negro, and to taking over the reveling political impotence and social and economic subordination of the Negro of the South.

The foundation of the KKK that was born then, and still survives today, is first and foremost White supremacy. "Night Rides," as they were referred to, were used to intimidate and place terror in the lives of Negroes, these same Negroes whose only ambition was to exercise and enjoy their brand-new life with their new rights and freedom. The rule of the Ku Klux Klan was to keep Negroes from voting and further bring down the political system that had been for decades, and continues to this day to be, advantageous to White males and White Americans in general even today.

In the years that followed, Klan members often wore White cardboard hats and covered themselves in White sheets, rode the countryside, and murdered both Negroes and White Americans who showed sympathy to the plight of Negroes. White immigrants, Italians, and Germans were also targets of their attacks, these immigrants were wrongfully blamed for the election of the Radical Republicans. The Empire epidemically spread through the South, solidifying the White power hierarchy in the local governments. In some counties, the Klan became the assumed de facto law that state legislators had no real control over.

Congress passed something called the "Anti-Klan Law" in 1871. Based on how this law read, Southern governments no longer had authority over such crimes as assault and murder. It also stated that the President had the power to declare martial law in states where violence that was associated with the Klan occurred or continued. The laws decreased much of the luster of the Klan. However, it was not enough to dissolve the Klan.

The Whites of the South retook control of most of the state governments before 1870. They also found that the South did not need the enforcement tactics of the Klan anymore. These horrific tactics were very successful at stopping Negro voters from exercising their constitutional right to the polls. In addition, these tactics included Negro officeholders being hanged or beaten, which sent a real message to other Negro supporters. The Democrats of the South were victorious in elections in the "one-party" system. This also gave them the ability to pass laws immediately that took away many rights that Negroes had gained during the Reconstruction Era.

The Klan completed its plan of total White dominance in the South. It soon after dissolved as an organization by the mid-1870s, but even though the Klan stopped operating as a unified organization, the violent acts toward continued until the era of rejuvenation for the Empire in 1915.

William J. Simmons, a Spanish American War participant and dreamer gave a sort of rebirth to the Klan. He claimed he had visions of bringing back the organization since he was a little boy. When *The Birth of a Nation* opened in 1915, it was just the jump-start Simmons needed. He used advertisements for the movie to promote his dream of creating a new Invisible Empire.

On the night before Thanksgiving in 1915, Simmons and a small group of members from various other fraternal orders met on top of Stone Mountain, Georgia. This is where they burned a cross to represent the rebirth of the Klan from its docile state to begin a new mission for the good of the human race. A local newspaper from the Atlanta area carried Simmons' formal introduction of what he called "The World's Greatest Secret, Social, Patriotic, Fraternal, and Beneficiary Order."

This rebirth quickly gained its required ninety members and a constant stream of respectable middle-class members. Robert Ramspect was one of their first members. He was a soon-to-be congressman from Georgia. Later came Paul Etheridge. He was a lawyer and longtime member of the Fulton County Board of Commissioners of Roads and Revenues.

This enthusiastic and newly formed version of the Klan was developed by Simmons as a sort of "Ponzi scheme" to make money and rip off members. How it worked was that the new members were charged membership fees, and in turn they would sell life insurance policies for Simmons.

Simmons would collect not only the membership fees but also a residual income off of the policies. The new Klan stressed that its members were 100 percent American and loyal to the supremacy of the White race. All this meant that you had to be sure that you would always keep the Negroes of the time in their place.

The Klan's membership numbers weren't very high by the 1920s. Statistics put it somewhere between eight hundred and only a few thousand. This is until William Simmons met two people who were very powerful in Southern politics. Edward Young Clarke and Elizabeth Tyler were in charge of the Southern Publicity Association. The Southern Publicity Association collaborated to promote the Klan in exchange for 80 percent of the profits brought in by the organization for payment of dues.

The list of enemies and institutions the Klan was against began to grow expeditiously and soon included not only all immigrants but also nightclubs and establishments and such behavior as premarital sex. These newly established tactics gained an immediate success. This was in part due to members combing the countryside and instigating fear among citizens. The enrollment in the KKK grew to almost one hundred thousand people by the summer of 1921. Simmons's goal of making exorbitant amounts of money paid off as each member was required to pay a ten-dollar membership fee.

Edward Young Clarke continued to increase the profits of the organization when he created various business ventures. He developed both a manufacturing company and a publishing firm. He also invested in real estate. The organization grew so much that eventually it needed to incorporate as the Knights of the Ku Klux Klan, and The Gate City Manufacturing Company of Atlanta became the sole manufacturer of Ku Klux Klan attire and paraphernalia.

As the Klan expanded, so did the concerns and issues of the organization. While their officials discussed plans and ideas like some college fraternity, their associates in other parts of the country started living up to the rhetoric the organizers were using to rack up initiation fees from new members.

Violence was all the rage, and it quickly expanded out of control as the terroristic tactics of whippings, lynchings, rapes, murders, and other violently gruesome occurrences happened. Often, Klan members would use such acts as pouring acid on Negroes to brand the letters "KKK" on their foreheads.

Regularly, law enforcement, judicial, and political figures turned their heads to the hidden violence that was openly committed. The group began to splinter when news stories and newspaper articles began to be published in newspapers from coast to coast that shined a light on the violent acts of the members of the Klan.

They also showed how the organization was manipulative when it came to finances. This led to many members becoming discouraged by the truth about the organization, but that number paled in comparison to the number of new members that had already decided to join soon after the articles were published. It was found that certain newspapers also aided the Klan by inducing Congress to investigate the organization. As it ended up, the result was that Congress gave the Ku Klux Klan the best promotion they ever received. In a sense, the Congress of the United States eventually made the Klan.

The organization continued to grow, even with a rift that led to Simmons being removed from power. Hiram Wesley Evans stepped into that smoothly. Evans was a dentist from Texas. He took over as leader of the organization in 1924. Under his leadership, the Klan began to promote itself as a group that was dedicated to defending the morals of the country. The contradiction to this dedication was that the organization used violent and terroristic methods to punish those whom they felt to be less that moral. While Evans was at the helm, a wave of terror supported by lynching's and murders swept over this country in a large number of communities in the United States were firmly in the grasp of the Klan's terror.

As these violent acts grew, so did the Klan's grasp on the political landscape of both the South and the West. The Klan created a chemistry between violence and politics. These became two methods of maintaining White supremacy. Earl Mayfield, a longtime member of the Invisible Empire, was elected to the U.S. Senate in 1922.

He was victorious over two competitors who happened to be Jewish. He won due to the strong support from his fellow Klan members. The organization has also been identified with helping to elect governors in various states, including Georgia, Alabama, and California.

Politics was always an important piece of the foundation of the Klan's powerful alliances. It allowed them to reach the goals and objectives of the organization without drawing the negative attention of extreme violence.

These great achievements in politics discouraged racism, and as the KKK became more entangled in politics, for a short period, it became less associated with violence and vigilantism and more interested in controlling the legislative process. Politics for a period was a new way for the Klan to spread its White supremacy viewpoints. Too bad it did not last.

In states like Alabama, Mississippi, and Georgia, the Klan achieved great political power. It even became necessary for a candidate, if he intended to be successful, to be in great favor with the organization. This is if he intended to be elected to office.

Bibb Graves was elected to Governor of Alabama, and Charles C. McCall achieved the seat of the state's Attorney General. Both of the men were full members of the Klan and had their full support of the organization. The Klan was generally credited with generating have of the vote needed to win any election.

They controlled the political process and much of a state's employment. The Klan was successful at influencing a state's most prominent officials, because it maintained the memberships of almost every political official and law enforcement officer in any given state at this time. In the state of Alabama, the Klan had over fifty thousand paying members in 1925, which created a strong and supportive voting base. In 1926 Hugo Black benefitted from this support and was elected to the U.S. Senate.

In the early 1920s the Klan was at the helm of the judicial system and all law enforcement in the state of Louisiana. They were worse than J. Edgar Hoover of the FBI. The Klan watched phones, read personal mail of citizens, and even searched out strangers to the community, and when the Democratic governor of a state in the South had to ask a Republican administration to help preserve law and order, that was a sign that the Klan had completely taken over. In most cities in the South, the postmaster, sheriff, deputy, prosecuting attorney, and police force all became members of the Ku Klux Klan.

By the mid-1920s the Klan began losing much of its power due to local candidates taking a stand on the KKK issue. Henry Fuqua was a Protestant from Baton Rouge who won in the runoff for Governor of Louisiana. He based his entire platform on shutting down the Klan. He got three main bills out of the state House and Senate passed.

These began to curtail the power of the Invisible Empire. One of these bills required the Klan to annually file a membership lists. This virtually took the secretive shroud off of the organization because it would be forced to identify its members.

The other bill that was passed read that there would not be any wearing of masks in public on occasions other that Halloween, school affairs, minstrel shows, and Mardi Gras. This meant that if the Klan paraded around in their hoods and sheets, they could and would be arrested. The kicker was the final bill which made crimes such as threatening people, if the person threatening was wearing a mask, a felony crime.

Ironically, even with a large number of Klansmen in both the House and Senate, these bills passed overwhelmingly. The national headquarters in Atlanta moved quickly and kicked out all the representatives who voted for the passage of the bills. This included two highly important members who held the positions of Grand Titans in the organization and the Speaker of the House. After the passage of these bills, the power and control base of the Klan became extremely limited in the state of Louisiana.

In other states such as Arkansas, the Klan was credited with electing a large number of its membership to a broad range of political offices including to the United States House of Representatives in Washington. In Little Rock, Arkansas, in the mid-1920s, the Klan held nearly every political office. Another perfect example of politicians forming alliances with the Invisible Empire in order to gain the necessary support to win elections.

By the late 1920s the endorsement of the Klan had become so valuable that they were able to have their own primary elections to decide which of its members or close associates would have the support for the Democratic Primary. Through the political process, the KKK was able to govern over a number of states in the union. The Klan continued it terroristic tactics over the Southern region. They did this through both the political process and its usual violent tactics. This lasted up until the time of World War II.

After the war, the Klan again lost its luster, but it did however leave its ideals behind in the culture of the South. The next rebirth of the Klan took place in the '50s and '60s because of the rise of the Civil Rights Movement.

The Klan has been the focus of numerous violent attacks, with many of them quite famous. Let us not forget the tragic events in May of 1961 at the Trailways Bus terminal in Birmingham, Alabama. The longtime CBS radio reporter, Howard K. Smith, was on the scene of the "Freedom Ride" tragedy.

He reported that White Americans grabbed the passengers and dragged them into alleys and corridors. Many of the "Negro" passengers were pounded with pipes, key rings, or simply with fists. Photographs of the day showed passengers were beaten and kicked until their faces were a bloody pulp.

The attackers were members of the Ku Klux Klan who absolutely were opposed the "Freedom Rides." Both African Americans and White Americans elected to ride on buses and trains together in the front and the White Americans in the back. This was the opposite of the times of the day. It was noted that while this violent attack took place, there was not a policeman in sight.

Years after the attack took place, there was testimony before Congress, and it was revealed that there was a previous arrangement made between the local Klan leaders and the Birmingham police that the attackers would be given ample time to freely assault the passengers. The police agreed to delay intervening. The Klan had once again worked its way back into the state governmental system. This also set them up to be free from the prosecution of local law enforcements.

In 1964, in the small town of St. Augustine, Florida, an attorney for the KKK proclaimed, "We White Americans are due more rights, not less. When the Constitution said all men are created equal, it wasn't talking about Niggers." Attorney J. B. Stoner then proceeded to lead nearly two hundred marchers, all White, who were accompanied by the state police with dogs, through the Negro ghetto, inciting an incident with the people living there.

Once again a secure relationship was being built between the Klan and local law enforcement. Not too long after, a Southern Christian Leadership Conference demonstration was attacked by over eight hundred Klan members. It was even reported that they ripped the clothes from a thirteen-year-old Negro girl, and the same reporter from Newsweek stepped in to protect the young girl. The next day after the attack, Governor Bryant made a decision to ban all marches. He chose to do this, instead of stopping the KKK.

The Civil Rights Act helped to ensure total equality in not only the polling booths, but in other areas that were suffering from the ills of segregation such as the classrooms, factories, and in the basic everyday public amenities of hotels, restaurants, and movie theaters. The passage of the Civil Rights Act had no real effect on the violent acts of the KKK.

Three Civil Rights workers, Andrew Goodman, Michael Schwerner, and James Chaney, were active in trying to get registered Negroes to vote and working on Negro political activity. These three young men were arrested for speeding in Neshoba County, Mississippi, and were never seen alive again until their bodies were found in a landfill.

Sheriff Lawrence Rainey, along with his deputy, Cecil Price, made the claim that the men were held in custody for only a few hours, but were then released. These men were trained workers, and were instructed to call in regularly. When the men were reported as missing, the FBI were ordered to investigate the incident. Over two hundred Navy officers spent several weeks searching for these missing men. In late summer, the bodies of the missing men were located in a nearby dam, where they were buried after being shot.

There are a number of loopholes in the law, and because murder is a state offense, it was up to the Prosecutor for the State of Mississippi to get a conviction of Sheriff Rainey and Deputy Price.

In the end, the State of Mississippi decided to take no legal action. Deputy Rainey and sixteen of the others involved in the murder were indicted by a federal grand jury. The charge was "conspiring for the deprivation of constitutional rights to life and liberty."

It was a verdict that was the equivalent of a slap on the wrist. Nobody ever went to jail for murder, and it proved another reason for the African American society to lose faith in the judicial process. Many believe that President Johnson got the FBI involved because two of the victims were White. That would be a fair assumption.

What was never reported is that while searching for Goodman, Schwerner, and Chaney, the bodies of over forty African American men were found in the lakes and rivers, while they were being dragged. Those forty men had families and loved ones also. Who grieves for them?

During the '60s the Klan was extremely and adamantly violent about keeping Negroes from voting time. Negroes at that time only interested in their human rights guaranteed to them in the Constitution. Klan violence and political influence to achieve their goals was at an all-time high. While in recent years its membership has dropped, today, this group and the foundation of its beliefs are still around. They still are focused on White supremacy, and they intend to keep America a "White man's country."

Although it is sad that this is their belief, the fact is that the KKK has been an embedded factor of the Southern political system. They are responsible for just about everything that has affected the history of White voters in the Southern region of the United States. The KKK has backed the White political machine by showing their support for the Republican Party.

Over the last twenty years of political battles, it is clear that the Republican Party is trying to fight the perception, in a painful manner at times, that their party is the foundation for racist voters with old memories of times gone by and how life used to be. Their reputation is that the GOP honestly has no regard for the concerns, issues, and tribulations surrounding the African Americans in the United States.

Right in the middle of many African American politicians moving through the ranks of the Republican Party, it has to be noted that those suggestions are not necessarily true. The Republican Party's mandate, including the association with the Ku Klux Klan, explains why the GOP is often looked at as being an extension of the "Invisible Empire."

Just about the time when the Civil Rights Movement was at its apex, it became a legitimate threat to many

White members of the Republican Party and of the Southern states. Because of this, the Klan's power became significant. It also transitioned into working to segregate the White Americans and Negroes.

This would stigmatize and polarize both communities for generations to come, as we have seen. The Klan worked with White voters in the South, to think about defending White supremacy when they were thinking about casting their vote.

Many younger voters today are quick to associate the GOP with a racist political party. What they don't realize is that there was once a very strong association between the Democratic Party and White supremacists in the South. That transitioned in another direction soon after the national Democratic Party began to champion with a number of civil rights issues and stood in solidarity with Negroes who were fighting for equality.

The KKK began soliciting White voters to center on casting votes against democratic policies, bills and laws that would help Negroes. This encouraged White voters to look beyond their political affiliations and move toward politicians who supported segregation and oppose anything else that would treat Negro people as equals to White Americans.

The effect the KKK had on political results was supported by the fact that former Democratic voters began to get behind Republican candidate Barry Goldwater in the election of 1964 and later, a third-party candidate named George Wallace (Alabama's Governor) in 1968. Wallace was a staunch supporter of segregation, including standing in the schoolhouse doors to keep Negroes from attending school.

The voting record of a number of counties confirms that there is a strong correlation between where the KKK recruits its members and voter turnout. It also controlled the behavior of both voter turnout, and their behavior. The Klan led the charge by encouraging White Southerners to think White supremacy first. Areas with a large, embedded, and active KKK chapter were found to be likely to support Goldwater and Wallace.

Despite the fact that fraternities of the Klan were often born in towns with established homeowners and a high percentage of African American residents, areas that were considered less prosperous, where White Americans had to compete with African Americans, usually housed the most active hate group participants.

Given that there were various road blocks in place against African Americans in 1964 that kept the right to vote out of their reach, this supports the fact that there was high support among White voters in counties where White Americans were most concerned about disrupting the political structure. By the beginning of the 1970s, many White Americans in the Southern states felt loyalty to the GOP, because their beliefs were more in direction with the interest of those same associates opposed to civil rights than with the Democratic Party.

There also began a major increase in GOP voting in areas that had active KKK chapters compared to counties that didn't have active chapters of the White supremacy coalition.

Even though the Republican Party's economic views have never been and will never be in the favor of working-class people from the South, most have remained loyal to the party based purely on the KKK's beliefs and support. They continue to ask for White voters to insure that no "Nigger-loving" politician runs for office. This support has been trumpeted in the polls by those who supported White supremacy and the Klan.

The KKK reared its ugly head after the Civil War. It has been called "America's first true terrorist group." Since its inception, the Klan has seen an ebb and flow in the life of the organization. At times it has been more extreme than other hate groups. Regardless of the levels and surges, the KKK still maintains today its infamous heritage of hate, violence, and brutality.

In the beginning, the KKK centered its actions on African Americans only. It soon began inflicting its wrath on White Americans who stood up for them, and against the government that supported the rights of African Americans in this country. Additional rebirths of the Klan, which typically emerged in times of controversial social change, or national racially charged incidents, added more enemies of the Empire's list. This ranged from Hispanics to Jews, Catholics, homosexuals, and various groups of immigrants to this country.

Obviously these enemies were groups that came into direct economic conflict with the lower-class White Americans that formed the foundation of the KKK. In the past two decades, the prestige of the Klan began to fade, being surpassed by emerging neo-Nazi groups.

By 2005, these neo-Nazi groups had begun falling from grace, with many groups dissolving or beginning new associations with other emerging hate groups. This fall has helped create an increase in other hate groups rising to the top of the racist food chain. There is currently a rise in racist skinhead activity, but this has also provided a modern birthing opportunity for a KKK reincarnation.

In the early 2000s, many communities in this country began to experiences a significant influx that has virtually changed the face of the United States. African Americans, Hispanics, and other foreign immigrants began moving into neighborhoods that have been solely White communities. The immigration issue of the United States has done little more than create fear and anxiety about immigration in the minds of many Americans.

Many KKK groups have attempted to take advantage of that fear and uncertainty, using anti-immigration sentiments for recruitment and propaganda purposes, and to attract publicity. The Klan has only had one direction in their movement. They have set down in stone the goal of complete segregation between the races, and to dominate through violent tactics to achieve White supremacy.

Today there are nearly fifty various factions of the Klan in the country, and over one hundred chapters of the organization. Although they had over a hundred thousand members in the early 1900s, their current membership levels are sitting around five thousand.

The Klan has impacted nearly all areas of society, from African Americans to people of the Jewish and Roman Catholic faith. Really any group of people that were not in line with the organization's White Protestant way of looking at things was considered an enemy. There were a selected few factions that were spared from the wrath of the Klan, but nevertheless they still saw on a regular basis, the heinous attacks committed on those others.

The Klan had about four separate quarters of history where their activities were highly noticed and the actions were the most intimidating to African

Americans. Understandably, this was right after the Civil War until about the late 1880s. This was a time of not only reconstruction, but also restructuring a way of life they had lived for nearly two hundred years in this country already.

The early 1920s was the most powerful time for the organization because it was able to gain significant political power. The "War to End All Wars" had come to an end, and society had been strapped with a level of boredom. The United States, like many other societies, has a war-based mentality. We prosper economically as a country when we are in a military conflict somewhere in the world.

We also have this ridiculous patriotic instinct to proclaim to the world that "America is the greatest country in the world," which gets fueled when we are at war. But when Americans, and in particular, White America, is not off terrorizing some country by forcing them to live the "American" way of life of baseball, Levi's jeans, and McDonald's hamburgers, they turn their attention to terrorizing minorities in this country even more.

I believe we are going through that phase with the terrorizing tactics of law enforcement individuals in this country, inflicted upon African Americans and other people of color. The late 1940s to the early 1970s and the late 1970s to the early 1980s. The 1920s time period was probably one of the most influential.

After World War I, the people of the United States were looking for something to do. Without violence, the people were bored. They became extremely patriotic and wanted to place blame on someone for the causes of the war. For this they turned to the minorities in the country.

The KKK has attacked many Americans. For years, discrimination, violence, and segregation have been problems surrounding African Americans, and it continues today. During the 1920s the Klan helped impose their views on a large number of American citizens. Through lynching, beatings, whippings, and murders, the KKK got the point across that all African Americans were inferior to them.

The Klan has gone through what I refer to as an "invisible transformation." No longer is this group, born of hate and terror running around the countryside burning crosses and publicly lynching African Americans. The organization is now hidden in plain sight through embedded racism, in the form of housing practices, law enforcement, politics, and something viewed every day, the media. The KKK, therefore, has now come to speak for the great mass of Americans of the old pioneer stock. I believe that it does fairly and faithfully represent them, and the proof lies in their support.

If you are seeking a true comprehension of the Invisible Empire, you first get a true feel of the mind set of what I refer to as "Old School" White Americans. This is a group of White Americans that sometimes is referred to as the 'Master Race," but is in fact a mixture of variations of the White race (Germans, Nordics, Irish, etc.). They want to be known as the creators of the true White race, and the Ku Klux Klan caters to the needs of this "Master Race."

These White Americans today have an uneasy and insecure feeling when it comes to present society. They are dreaming of the 1950s when basically White men were in complete control of our society. Women had no place except in the home; African Americans were barely even considered human beings, being corralled into segregated areas from restaurants, to public transportation, to, of all things, sporting events. They hate our current government, especially the leader of the so-called "free world" being a person of color.

They believe in a very streamlined society of traditional roles for the sexes, and are flipping out over things from African Americans protesting over police brutality to Olympic Champion Bruce Jenner becoming a woman. They truly want the "good ol' days" back, and regularly fight for systems to bring back those times.

These White Americans believe that our country has gone through a moral metamorphosis for almost fifty years. They are fixed on the feeling that traditional

(White conservative) standards are crashing on a daily basis and nobody honors any of them anymore. The Protestant Church, the Nuclear family, and the changes in how they are able to educate their children in what they have referred to as "fundamental fact" have been changed.

Myths like Columbus discovering America or that the forefathers of this country were great men have been replaced with the actual truth, and although they are trying to maintain an old status, like a dog hanging on to an old bone, the meter of society continues to run and today's world is passing them by.

These White Americans are nothing more than paranoid about society, and when anyone gets a feeling of paranoia, they begin to encapsulate themselves with their beliefs, and like-minded individuals as allies. In addition, they have revived and actually increased their long-standing distrust of some of the most political factions on the country. They will immediately attack religion, and first on the list is always the Catholic Church.

Many White Americas with these beliefs, whether they are truly associated with the Ku Klux Klan or not, are often coupled and described as having racist and prejudicial tendencies toward African Americans and other minorities. The one thing the Ku Klux Klan has done is given this faction of White America a microphone for their beliefs. The Klan gives them an outlet to reinforce their racist foundation about this country, through a group that has a racist history.

The variations of the Ku Klux Klan among the makeup of the organization is immense. It could be the corporate CEO, who hates the pressure of Affirmative Action, and would like to keep his corporation all White. It is a farmer who loses a crop year after year. He watches Fox News and jumps behind the rhetoric and blames the African American President, who in his mind controls the weather that grows his crop. The trend as of late is to recruit the loner student by using words like *patriotism* and *Americanism*, and plays to the racial instincts of White America.

These racial instincts are perpetuated by the Ku Klux Klan in order to manipulate the process of building an America that seeks to complete the foundation of the organization. They believe in the patriotism of America and do not believe that the true patriots of "real" America are African Americans or minorities of any kind.

The Klan believes that these are the true and loyal feeling of the White race and to embed the seed of White supremacy by playing to the conservative traditions of White America. The Klan believes White America should be Native (but not Native American) and White, and if they are Protestant, then that closes the deal.

Today's Klan is more than some sheet-wearing organization of hell-raising, Nigger-hating Rednecks. They have transition past those days of raw exposed terror because of the legislative system never prosecutes much of the obvious. It has transition into the corporations, boardrooms and courtrooms of the United States.

It is now a developing army of the top political leaders who have only one focus. That is to cater to the beliefs White America. The Klan is still alive, well, fully in active, and looking toward the future where they believe it will once again pick Presidents of this country, and you can bet your ass that none of them will be African American.

Today's Ku Klux Klan has surpassed the days of public lynchings and night rides. They have become significantly more technologically advanced and have moved into the world of social media. They have Facebook pages with thousands of followers. They have Twitter accounts and regularly send out tweets. They have YouTube, Instagram, and a number of the popular social media forums.

They are regularly recruiting White American kids, many of which are loners and absent from the regular youth world of the country. These are a very vibrant recruiting area for America's youth, many of them being lost.

But there is also a trend that has been developing. That is the fact that a number of corporate and business executive leaders, who have kept their membership in the Ku Klux Klan private, have begun coming out of the closet. If this trend continues, the United States could soon expect a strong public resurgence in the organization and although it may not be public knowledge, there are number of corporate leaders that fully support the message of the Invisible Empire.

CHAPTER 3

POWERFUL POLITICAL
POSITIONS FOR RACISM

*Standing still is never an option so long as
inequities remain embedded in the very fabric
of the culture.*

—Tim Wise

MUCH OF PRESIDENTIAL history is shrouded in trivial stories and fiction. George Washington chopping down cherry trees and good old Abe Lincoln never telling a lie. That one is funny because as everyone knows, all politicians lie. Politicians hide behind the cover of two lives on a regular basis. By day President Calvin Coolidge was the most powerful man on the planet, as the ruler of the free world, but it should also be noted that he was a well recognized member of the Ku Klux Klan.

The Klan had numerous members elected to positions of political leadership and as with most politician, they were almost never convicted of any crimes. It has be verified that President Coolidge publicly had Klan cross burnings on the steps of the Capital building in Washington D.C. Coolidge was also the first President to allow and support parades and rallies for the Klan.

The organization was truly set up to be a secret society that understood and promoted American values. They promoted American patriotism and recruited other White Americans to vote for Klan members who were running for public office. This led to a significant division in the United States because of a difference of opinions.

American patriotism of the time did not include minorities. It also did not include women in positions of leadership. Women like Marian Ferguson. Ferguson was the first female governor in Texas, and set out, though unsuccessfully, to rid the State of Texas of the Ku Klux Klan.

By this time, the Klan were donning the White sheets and hoods as their ceremonial uniform. The sheets were to signify purity and innocence of White America. They used the sheets to promote the foundation of the Klan's beliefs of White supremacy and dominance. It was early in this century that the KKK began to segregate and discriminate against anyone who was not Protestant, most notably, African Americans.

The Klan began to commit violent acts against everyone that did not fit into the classification non-Protestants. Many of these violent acts were horrible at best. Whether it was a lynching, cross burning, hanging, or a murderous execution, these acts set a precedent for the future reputation of the Klan.

The KKK created to an unrecoverable division in the United States. Its hateful violence toward anyone that was not a pure White was spread throughout America by many new technological inventions of the era. People, White Americans, supported the organization because they were manipulated to believe that the Klan promoted strong family life, decency and American patriotism.

The Invisible Empire became an integral organization that added to the disruption, and in many cases the destruction of the reconstruction of the United States in favor of the beliefs of the South. The Klan had one belief of a United States where there was one White race, and they promoted tis belief through discrimination, segregation and extreme violence.

The Klan makes the claim that they are not racist. They claim to be more of a "racialist" organization. To the Klan, they claim that they do not hate any particular race, which is the way most hate groups go about spinning the true feelings of their particular organizations, but that they love the White race and have something called "White pride." This is the foundation for their belief, but people should realize that the honest foundation of the Klan is for the White Race to be the only race on the planet.

And with most hate groups, they often have some interpretation of religion and the bible, and they believe that the White Race is the irreplaceable headquarter of America, and believe that the Christian faith, and the high levels of Western culture and technology need to be controlled by the White race. They believes that the only way to achieve the ultimate goals of this country is to have a United States with only pure, White Americans are living in it, leading it and there should be absolutely no race or culture mixing.

A belief that White America is the victim of society today, and is being heavily discriminated against is also spewing from Klan propaganda. Their organization's "quicksand" foundation is based on the premise of equal rights for all, and special privileges for none because this is how they recruit new members by making them believe the organization has a legitimate foundation.

But in all actuality, the Klan is against all integration and equal opportunity programs such as Affirmative Action programs or any other government programs that aids Africa Americans in anyway.

They claim that by giving the African Americans in particular jobs and accepting them into the institutions of the United States, White Americans would be discriminated against. The Klan considers this to be a mythical systematic process they have created called "reverse racism." Many in White America have used this term to support this issue and in many cases, inadvertently support the Klan.

Among their other beliefs, the KKK believes that the United States should stop trade with countries that do not have firm and strict laws regarding the environment. They believe the use of the military should be put in place to keep illegal aliens from entering the country. They also support the belief that all anti-gun laws in the United States should be done away with so every American citizen can protect themselves, and that the budget of the country should be balanced.

That last one is not all bad, and they even believe that one way to achieve this is to institute a flat tax to contribute to the funding of community, state, and federal projects, and all those who can physically work should work. That is a pretty good idea. No wonder some politicians and big business leaders of the modern age often distance themselves from the KKK. Heaven knows they would never want to pay in taxes what the everyday citizen pays.

The KKK has many ways that they spread these ideas and beliefs to the public. One of the easiest ways is to make themselves seen through public rallies and protests. Recently, the KKK and other groups associated with the KKK began protesting the Martin Luther King, Jr. holiday. They are against this holiday because they claim that Martin Luther King, Jr. was a communist and anti-Christian. Another reason the KKK is against the holiday is because Martin Luther King, Jr. urged integration. The KKK also stages rallies and protests outside of public courthouses. Since courthouses are well-known visible places, the KKK knows that they will get media coverage and they can get their message out.

This leads to another way that the KKK thinks that they can get their message of White power out to the general public. Using the media to inform the public of your ideas is one of the easiest and most effective methods. The KKK uses all forms of media to get their message out, including radio and print advertising.

However, the most common form of media that the KKK uses is television. Members of the KKK make their own videos talking about the White Rights movement, and what the KKK stands for, etc. They then distribute these videos or play them on a public access television channel.

The Klan has its own brand of literature and has an established distribution process. This process has aided the organization in letting the public know who they are in addition to getting their beliefs communicated to that same public. They more than often leave their literature in the mailboxes and driveways of predominantly White neighborhoods.

In the St. Louis area, they often target the St. Charles area, where the majority of the residents are White, and moved to the area to escape living in an area where there were "too many" African Americans.

Besides being a writer, I am a public relations professional. Public relations is a way of moving the reputation needle in the directions that best fits your organization, and without a doubt the Klan has taken advantage of this industry.

The fact that no PR firm worth its salt would ever take on the Ku Klux Klan as a client. The Klan has begun to train their own members to do the job of promoting the organization. Klan members are making appearances on television programs, and being guest on nationally syndicated internet radio shows. They are making themselves more accessible to answer questions from media outlets and citizens.

Often they are sought out by fledgling newspapers or even young journalist who are starting out or trying to make a huge splash with an exclusive interview or feature article. It also gives the public a misrepresentation of the organization as having civic qualities, by getting away from spewing their historical rhetoric of hate messages, and heinous crimes against African Americans.

The Klan is trying to enter into the political realm under the same shroud that they have always operated by. They are infiltrating the political sector by using "sleeper" members. These are usually members who have chosen not to make any association with the Klan public. This makes it easier to integrate into the political party of their choice (mostly Republican).

The process is not an "all or nothing" system. They do not initially want to take over the world. They start out gaining small positions at the local or municipal level. This then sets the stage for members to begin moving into State level politics.

David Duke started out just this way. He was elected to the Louisiana House of Representatives. Duke was a State representative and served on several committees. He then ran from governor of Louisiana and received overwhelming support (700,000 votes). He allowed access to the media, where he actually held rallies for the Klan. He made the television talk show rounds and gained significant clout. At the writing of this book, Duke is still involved in the political arena in Louisiana. He is the chairman of the Republican Parish Executive Committee of the largest Republican county.

The Klan believes in conveying its message of re-educating the teachers of this country. They believe the education process in their real tool to educate young White youth about the basis of their movement. A movement that is based solely on hate. The Klan believes that because teachers have direct access to young people on daily basis, they can be a real support and recruitment tool.

The Klan has designed workbooks and teaching materials for educators. Their intent is for teachers to talk about the Christianity of the United States, and to attempt to educate students based on the beliefs of the Klan.

These materials include brainwashing mostly poor White kids, and attempting to convince them that there is a war going on for their minds and their lifestyles. They usually prey on the lowly intelligent "loner" type kid that separates himself or herself. "If you have no friends or family, we will be both" is the thought process, and it readily works on the self-esteem of a young person.

Hate has not been ignorant to the technology of the times we are living in, and hate groups such as the Ku Klux Klan have taken full advantage of the internet waves to get their message out. The simplicity of finding information on the World Wide Web has made both messaging and recruitment of members easy. There are hundreds of Web sites and thousands of pages where you can find Klan and other associated organizations posting rhetoric, and anyone with a computer has access to this information. There are even merchandise sites for the sale of clothing supporting the group.

This advanced technology has catapulted the political process for candidates, and it has provided the Klan with an avenue to propel their hate campaign, in the same shrouded way it has always operated. It also provides a way to recruit without involving the well documented violence that the Klan is known for violence.

The end goal for the organization is to position themselves among the political ranks, gaining both power and momentum, and eventually implementing and ingraining their beliefs into the laws of the country. Their affiliate groups are growing. This, among other reasons makes the Ku Klux Klan a significant threat to the sovereign society of the United States of America.

The Klan's thinking is that if the organizations are against immigration then we can make "Joe Six-Pack" against it too. They have always had the plan of gaining a foothold in the mainstream White community. Ninety percent of KKK members will never commit a crime, but their rhetoric will influence the one in the group who may go off and do something extreme.

Today, the secret society of the Klan has several thousand members nationwide and has gained hundreds of new members over the immigration issue.

Its exploitation of opposition to gay marriage, its fear of crime, is their foundation, and nothing can help get their message to the air of paranoia like the sitting of the country's first African American President.

It has expanded in parts of the country including the Great Plains and the West Coast where it used to be inactive. In one example, the Klan attempted to recruit members in Iowa towns such as Denison and Storm Lake where immigrants from Hispanic countries have settled recently.

The KKK fits into the broader picture of right wing militant groups that sprang to prominence after Timothy McVeigh, and the Oklahoma bombing in 1995, but they have been divided and weakened by dissension. In addition, they have also developed a close relationship with many of the law enforcement officials and local governments throughout the United States that enabled them to spread terror in major cities in the country.

Most visible KKK members no longer wear White sheets and instead frequently dress like racist skinheads and neo-Nazis at meetings with whom they cooperate. The problem now is that in many cases, you are unaware of where they are. Now KKK members where $1000 suits, police uniforms and doctors coats. They are now found in corporate boardrooms, small businesses, and nonprofit organizations. Klan members remain identifiable at meetings with other groups by the Klan symbol, and they have become unidentifiable because they are embedded in the very fabric of everyday life.

There have been many members of influential government status that have been member of the Klan, including the office of the President of the United States. A known group include President Warren G. Harding, President Woodrow Wilson, President McKinley, President Calvin Coolidge whom we have already mentioned and President Harry S. Truman.

President Warren G. Harding was actually sworn into the KKK in a ceremony conducted inside the White House by the Imperial Wizard. Harding's membership history gives a detailed account of many secret swearing-in ceremony in the White House based on claims of private communication in 1985 from journalist Stetson Kennedy.

The 1920s Republican Party platform, which expressed President Harding's political philosophy, called for Congress to pass laws combating lynching. Harding was the first American President to publicly denounce lynching and did so in a landmark 21 October 1921 speech in Birmingham, Alabama, which was covered in the national press.

Ironically, Harding also vigorously opposed an anti-lynching bill in Congress during his term in the White House. While the bill was defeated in the Senate, such activities would be in direct conflict with Klan membership. President Harding regularly received members of the KKK while in office.

President Woodrow Wilson and President McKinley were members of the KKK, but little is known of their membership. There is at least one book that documents they were actual members, but it only mentions they were members, that's all. President McKinley was a Union officer, but many Union men joined or were affiliated with the original First Era KKK during the Radical Republican's anti-White Reconstruction Era. General Hardee of the Union military was another one who later joined the KKK. President Wilson would have been a member of the KKK under the Command of Imperial Wizard Colonel Simmons.

Most of White America would never believe that many of the leaders of the "free world" were members of the Ku Klux Klan. Take President Harry S. Truman. He was a minor ordinary Klansman in the early '20s. Truman started out as a judge in the small area of Jackson, Missouri. He was running for his second term when his protégées Edgar Hinde and Spencer Salisbury suggested to him that he become a member of the Invisible Empire.

The KKK had significant political power in Western Missouri, and two of the men who were opposing the future President, already had the Klans reigning support. Truman, being the admirable man he was, was opposed to the idea of joining the organization, but eventually put up the membership fee of ten dollars, and became a member.

It is true that Truman became a member, but never really became active in the organization, only using them more too secure votes and support from the organization.

One of the reason he never fully committed was because the Klan demanded that Truman commit to not hiring any Catholics or Jews if he was successful in his reelection. Truman, being as stubborn as he was known to be, adamantly refused to be controlled by any outside entity and because most of the men he had commanded in World War I had been local Irish Catholics, not to mention, the Pendergast family, who were Catholic and operated the political machine of Jackson County, were his patrons

There were two groups that were supporters of the Democratic Party. "Goats" and "Rabbits." These groups were in a constant state of political warfare, with lines being drawn when Truman appointed Goats, and put them on the county payroll. The Klan only wanted voters to support "100 percent pure American" candidates, which was opposite in the thought process of the Catholic Pendergasts family.

The Klan made a decision to side against the future President, and align the organization with the Rabbits. With this realignment, the KKK issued instructions for

White Americans to vote Republican in the election. Truman ended up being defeated. Truman later made claims that the Klan had leveled death threats against him. He even attended a number of their rallies where he stood up publicly and dared them to make an attempt. This story is probably more fable than fact, as Truman had a habit of writing his own historical account of circumstances.

Many observers of Truman often saw his association with the Klan as some type of temporary fascination. It is a fact the Harry Truman's term as President signified the first real change of the government's ledger toward Civil Rights since after the Civil War.

Truman's two year membership with the Klan was actually somewhat lacking. This led eventually to having a major falling out with the organization. He later severed all ties with the Klan and openly repudiated them. Some often say that this is where the phrase "give them Hell Harry," came from. Truman's family has attempted for decades to deny his Klan affiliation ever since, but they have failed miserably, since it is well documented history.

Supreme Court Justice Hugo Black was a member of the Klan. His sheets were found complete, with his name embroidered in them in an old Klan membership Hall in the '60s. Justice Black was successful in defending E. R. Stephenson in the national trial for murder of a Catholic priest.

Because he believed it would help is political career, he joined the Klan soon thereafter. Justice Black ran on a Senate ticket as the "people's candidate." He was under the belief that he would require the votes of KKK members for a victory. Judge Black would later admit that associating himself with the Klan was a major mistake on his part, but he admitted that he would have committed to any organization if it would have gotten him elected.

Gutzon Borglum was the man that climbed thousands of feet in the air and carved one of our greatest monuments; Mt. Rushmore. He was also the architect behind Stone Mountain, and portions of the base of the Statue of Liberty. Few know that he was a life-long member of the Klan. He was a member of the Imperial Koncilium, but like many members of the organization, because of intense scrutiny, he eventually denounced the KKK.

Chief Justice Edward Douglass White was a member of the Klan and attended the White House screening of the movie "The Birth of a Nation." in 1915. As was Democratic Senator, Theodore G. Bilbo of Mississippi a member of the Klan. Senator Bilbo, in an interview on the radio program *Meet the Press* once said, "No man can leave the Klan. He takes a solemn oath not to do that. Once Klan, always a Klan."

The former Governor of Alabama, Bibb Graves, was defeated in his first Democratic campaign for governor in 1922. He had the secret endorsement of the Klan and was elected to his first term as governor. He later became the Exalted Cyclops of the organization, a position President of the Montgomery chapter.

Edward L. Jackson, a Republican, who was the former Governor of Indiana was a member of the Klan. Jackson was later involved in a number of scandals that eventually brought him down. He was brought to trial on charges of bribery that were related to his activities associated with the Klan, but he was never convicted because of the loophole of the statute of limitations.

George Gordon, a Congressman from the 10th district of Tennessee became one of the Klan's original members. He became the organization's first Grand Dragon, and composed something called the "Precept." It was a book describing the Klans organization, purpose, and principles.

Robert C. Byrd was a staunch recruiter for the Klan early in his career. The Democratic Senator from West Virginia rose to the position of both "Kleagle" and "Exalted Cyclops." When he left the group early in his political career, Byrd spoke out in support of the Klan.

He once composed a letter to the Imperial Wizard in which he made clear that "The Ku Klux Klan is needed in today's world like never before, and I am anxious to see its rebirth here in West Virginia." Byrd appealed to the Klan again in his bid for the United States Senate campaign in 1958.

Byrd has made history on other occasions. In spite of the fact that he was the only Senator to vote against both African American United States Supreme Court nominees Thurgood Marshall and Republican conservative Clarence Thomas, and he also filibustered the Civil Rights Act of 1964. Since then, Byrd has stated publicly that becoming a member of the Klan was his "greatest mistake."

Surprisingly, the NAACP managed to give him a 100 percent rating on their issues and concerns during the 108th Congress. This was however contradicted, when in a 2001 incident, the Senator repeatedly used the phrase "White Niggers" on a national television broadcast. This just goes to prove the statement "Once Klan, always Klan."

David Duke has headed up the growing list of candidates who have considered or are now considering a bid for the GOP presidential nomination. A former grand wizard of the KKK and Republican executive committee chairman in his district until 2000, Duke continues to have a significant following online. His videos regularly go viral.

He once launched a tour of the country to explore how much support he could garner for a potential presidential bid. Although he hasn't considered running for serious office since the early '90s, he did win nearly 40 percent of the vote in his bid for Louisiana governor. He has always described himself as someone who advocates the civil rights of White America.

Former and current neo-Nazis, Klan members, neo-Confederates, and other representatives of the various wings of what is called the "White Nationalist Movement" are showing trends for attraction for both large and small political office. They also spread their paranoid propaganda by pointing to rising unemployment, eight years with an African American President, and rampant illegal immigration as part of a growing mound of evidence that White Americans need to take a stand.

Most aren't winning, at least not yet, but they are drawing attractive levels of support that surprise and even alarm groups that keep tabs on the White supremacy activity. Jeff Hall, of the National Socialist Movement showed up in the headlines after a tragedy. He was allegedly murdered by his ten year old son, but before his death, he had campaigned for a low level water boarding of illegal immigrants position in Riverside, California.

Hall was a plumber who often patrolled the United States border in a paramilitary-style uniform, wearing a swastika. He was also able to gain about a third of his community's vote. That is a respectable amount of the votes for a person running openly as a Neo

Nazi, but because Hall's political life was cut short, we should assume and expect more White supremacist hopefuls in future elections.

After the election of President Obama, there was a significant rise in the number of hate groups in the country. On the contrast, there was also a spike in the number of African American children born. Many in White America had an immediate reaction of rage (and outrage) when President Obama was elected. Hate groups such as the Klan began to change their attitude.

They felt that if an African American man can get elected to office, then we should stop fighting progress, and begin researching exactly how it worked, in order to get someone in that position who represents the interests of pure White Americans? Shortly thereafter, David Duke assembled supporters in Memphis, Tennessee, to begin strategy sessions to determine an exact process.

In the next election of 2010, this country saw the largest electoral push by a field of White supremacists in the last fifty years. You also saw these same White supremacists publically running for offices that had never had competition. This has now become a common practice and is not likely to dissipate in future elections.

The reality is that nearly none of these individuals are successful in their campaigns, mainly due to their extreme views on issues. Nevertheless, the fact that there has been such an increase of White supremacists who are openly running for these public offices is a clear indication that White Nationalism is on the rise in the country.

Loy Mauch, a neo-Confederate, won a seat in the Arkansas House of Representatives. James C. Russell, who denounced all interracial marriage, received over one-third of the vote in his competition for the New York House of Representatives. Some candidates benefited from a new umbrella organization.

The American Third Position was launched in 2010 by a handful of weird-looking professors and corporate lawyers. Their plan was to represent the political interests of "pure White Americans." One of their political hopefuls, Atlee Yarrow, filed paperwork to run for Florida governor in 2014. The "A3P" is nothing more than a hate group, but it is distinguished by the fact that it has open membership. This is very similar to the NAACP.

When they became disappointed with Ron and Rand Paul and other leaders who they believed are close, but not close enough, to their views, the A3P began fielding candidates like Harry Bertram. Bertram ran for the West Virginia board of education and received 14 percent of the vote. Bertram's platform is conservative like the Tea Party, but with a more racist tone.

The numbers for these candidates are small, but not exactly laughable, especially for a new group explicitly running on a separatist White-interest ballot. They are just beginning. These group's platforms include a complete moratorium on immigration. They are beginning to fill a vacancy that many White Americans are desiring to have filled.

There is no surprise that many White Americans are supporting a clown like Donald Trump. He is telling this faction of Americans exactly what they want to here. They really don't realize that they have more in common with the African American person working next to them, than they have with an arrogant billionaire, who is more famous for filing bankruptcy that for foreign policy.

Undoubtedly, there are hate-filled candidates who are already filling out paperwork for upcoming elections. Many KKK members are emphasizing the rhetoric that White America needs to wake up to the fact that they are becoming a minority in our country. A former organizer named John Abarr filed to raise money for Montana's lone U.S. House seat. He has no worries or cares that the Republican Party isn't backing him because he does not believe public opinion is all that much against the KKK. He believed Montanans were independent thinkers, who would side with "pure Americans."

He describes the KKK as a Christian organization that focuses on the civil rights of White Americans. On the other hand, Abarr publicly glosses over the brutality that has earned the group its bad reputation. He says he does not agree with lynching anybody for any reason, but adds that it was a different time in our history. He believes, like much of White America, that since we already have an African American president, he's not sure when we'll have another pure White president elected again.

The list of these people goes on and on. Billy Roper, who was another self-described blue-collar, pro-White candidate is a member of the Nationalist Party of America. He had a long career in the neo-Nazi organization. He also failed at his bid for Governor of Arkansas in 2010. Roper, along with another "White Aryan" Vice Presidential candidate, promised to continue the fight for the civil rights of Americans of European ancestry.

"Stormfront" is a precinct for politically minded White-rights activists. It is the nation's largest White-supremacist website, where thousands of "racial realists" can discuss topics from home-schooling your children to working to unite all of the like-minded hate groups into one unified front.

Don Black, the Stormfront founder and radio host, says that the strategy is to start from the ground up. He believes it's impossible to get into the Senate or

Congress, but state legislatures or smaller offices can be beneficial. Black says the Tea Party's influence spurs hopes among his ideological soulmates, but that the initial excitement gave way to a real sense that the Stormfront crowd will have to go it alone.

Many Stormfront followers are involved in the Tea Party, but much of their leadership is skittish when it comes to talking about racial realities. The Tea Party is a healthy movement, but many are too conditioned to run like scared cowardly rabbits when called racists.

No office is too small. Sergeant Harriet Paletti of Wisconsin is head of the National Socialist. She is an upbeat working mom with three kids who only takes off her swastika clothing when she's at work. Hopefully it will never happen, but if or when she is ever elected, she says she'll represent everyone in her mostly White district, regardless of color. No right-minded person of color will ever believe that. She just doesn't believe in intermingling in private life, part of what she in her very small mind calls a "natural law of self-segregation."

The United Klans of Tennessee has several mayors and county commissioners serving who do not openly identify as KKK members. They insert themselves into the infrastructure of other established parties due to the bias against hate groups and the difficulty of third parties getting ballot access.

Unlike other neo-Nazis groups, these have hair, no ink, no piercings, and increasingly are college-degreed. They are the "suit and tie" executives in corporate America and do not favor bomber jackets. Because they have changed their attire "From Sheets to Suits," this faction has become unrecognizable. They have quietly been joining national campaigns and offices to start sharpening their political teeth. They absolutely have people working with the most recent incoming class of freshmen in Washington and most in the federal government don't even know it."

A David Duke like candidacy could have a galvanizing effect on American politics. Duke has been living in Europe in recent years, but maintains a high profile, and stokes his fan base online. Duke says there is nothing wrong with a White political block. "I have no hatred of anyone," Duke says. "It is just a love of my heritage and values." Spoken like a true racist hiding in plain sight.

CHAPTER 4

AMERICA GETS AN AFRICAN AMERICAN PRESIDENT

People in the media say they must look at the president with a microscope. Now, I don't mind a microscope, but boy, when they use a proctoscope, that's going too far.

—Richard Nixon

WHEN PRESIDENT BARACK Obama was on the verge of becoming the first African American to receive a major party's presidential nomination, racism and potential security issues emerged as factors in the race to the White House. The role of race in the Democratic primaries was heavily discussed, while racist caricatures and jokes about threats against Obama's life were widely condemned, they seem to reflect an undeniable element of racism that still exists in the country and would play an unknown role in a general election.

There was the question that the possibility of violence directed at presidential candidates, especially Obama, was a major concern, as was described by the media's careful coverage of the issue. There was a hypersensitivity about this issue, and in one sense, obviously there should have been. During the presidential campaign of 2008, Hillary Clinton made comments about the 1968 assassination of Kennedy and caused friction among those who believe that the candidates wanted to talk about the security issue surrounding Obama.

I can remember catching a flight at Lambert International Airport in St. Louis that year when an African American woman told me that Obama shouldn't run. She said, "They're going to kill him," and polls verified that perception. Fifty-nine percent of Americans said they were concerned that someone might attempt to physically harm then Senator Barack Obama, especially if he was voted the Democratic nominee for President.

The controversy centered on a depiction of Obama in an assassins cross hairs of a rifle that appeared on the cover of the Roswell Beacon newspaper in Georgia. The controversy focused on the image that was printed, and the story, which included interviews with several White supremacists. These people felt threatened by the future Presidents candidacy, but their true feelings reflected a deeper reality. A reality that is very apparent in American society.

Many racist who wished to remain nameless, as if that is something new in the country we live in, were repeatedly spouting the same rhetoric that "some idiot out there's going to put a bullet in that silver-tongued Nigger and then there'll be a race war." There are many in this movement who are preparing for war, and in some cases, even praying for it.

The Beacon was heavily criticized for the image, and other local businesses denounced them and elected to stop doing business with the paper. The newspaper's publisher, John Fredericks, defended the story, saying "Good, bad or ugly, we tell the truth."

When people, mostly African American, begin to discuss race and racism in the United States, it is automatically "blood in the water" for the sharks of the media. White Americans follow by asking the question of "What racism?" because they believe just because we elected an African American president, that the issue of racism should be put to rest

So let's just all pump the brakes here for a second. That seems to be a habit of society when talking about race in America. Here a few things that need to be remembered.

In November of 2008, this country accomplished something, that no matter how many times it has been attempted, no other country on earth has ever elected a person to lead, that was a minority in a country with a different majority race. The fact that the United States of America was able to elect an African American man to run this country was both astounding and a curse at the same time. Astounding, because we live in arguably the most racist country in the world, and we were able to accomplish this feat. A curse because this feat would give people the impression that racism fails to exist in the United States anymore, and we might begin giving up the fight for equality for all.

When I was growing up, and teachers asked me what I wanted to be, I once said I wanted to be President of the United States. My first-grade teacher quickly responded by telling me to "rethink my ambitions because the likelihood of a Negro becoming President was nonexistent."

There was a feeling of pride among Americans in 2008, and even among many White Americans. They felt when President Obama was elected, that this country had finally turned the corner on race relations. When we swore in President Obama, that made the majority of Americans in this country feel very good about themselves.

President Obama had one of the highest approval ratings in history immediately after the Inauguration, which obviously meant that even some of those who voted against him were impressed by how he was handling his job at the beginning.

Not all Americans, mostly White, were enthusiastic about having an African American holding the highest political office in the land. Let me be crystal clear. Just because you are White, and you disagree with history's lone African American President, it does not make you a White supremacist or even a racist. I have a large number of my conservative Fox News watching buddies who like President Obama on a personal level, but do not agree with his political views. I personally do not believe that these people are racist, and it is okay to have a difference in opinion.

Most importantly, and this should be realized, that there is a fanatic of hard- line racist White Americans. These people are supremacist at the very least. They did vote against putting an African American in the highest office of the land. They did this on the sole basis that he is African American. Like most cowards, they try and hide, but they often hide in plain sight. This is what inspired the title of this book; *From Sheets to Suits*. This same group of racially motivated White Americans are angry about the path that they feel this country in headed down. They have never supported any type of racial equality in this country, and will never be brought around to that way of looking at the United States.

Looking back in history, their political representatives voted against both the Civil Rights and Voting Rights Acts of 1964 and 1965, and most have never ever waivered from it. The most prominent broadcasters on the right-wing airwaves are addressing their audience with blatant racist rhetoric messages. The Limbaughs, Becks, and Hannitys of the world have been riding this wave for years.

This was clear, and if you witnessed the televised town hall meetings when President Obama was campaigning, you would have felt the same way. If you were paying attention, you could see signs of that underlying racism at the most heated town meetings surrounding the election. Of course not everybody who attended, or even was mad about health care or the government at those meetings, is a racist, because most of those people weren't, but many of them clearly were. There were blatant signs of racism at some of the town meetings and, indeed, many signs that carried overt racial messages.

It was not hard to get the true meaning in the racial sub-texts when the level of animosity ratcheted up against President Obama. The animosity was not ratcheted up because White America disagreed with the President. It became intense in a mean and vicious nature because President Obama is African American. The type of racism and disrespect that the President, like many African American citizens feel on a daily basis is based on plain and simple hate of the African American race and culture.

Let's be honest. The "birthers" movement was based on nothing more than hate, and I might add that most of the White Americans who were involved in this nonsense should go back to the ninth grade and take a civics class. They would then realize that if either of your parents are American citizens, it does not matter where you are born. You are a United States citizen. Birthers made an attempt to question President Obama's citizenship just before speaking to the nation's school children about studying and working hard. Senator John McCain, President Obama's opponent was born in Canada, but I heard nobody questioning his citizenship.

Disrespect toward President Obama was made even more blatantly public when a White Congressman from the South shouted a rebel yell of "you lie" against the President on the floor of the House of Representatives. This same Congressman went on to raise hundreds of thousand dollars in funds, based on this blatant disrespectful act.

As much as we see it, racism is not the end all reason for every social problem we have in our society. Therefore it truly is unnecessary, and in some cases inappropriate to play the "race card." Believe me, we have all been privy to this card being played, warranted and unwarranted. Contrary to popular belief of White America, Barack Obama has never played upon the race card during his time in office. I am sure that he wanted only what every man who sat in the chair before him wanted. To be judged as the President of the United States, and not as the first African American leader of the "Free World."

Racism is still a significant factor of American society, and the fact is that no matter what we think about society, or how much we think the world has changed, there will always be a faction of White America, who are hardcore fundamental racist. They will never become accustomed to the fact that African American citizens of this country are in the few positions of power, especially in the political world. And they will never be able to stomach the fact in their "patriotic" minds and hearts that, in their words, a "nigger is running this country."

Senator Dick Durbin received information that caused him concern over Obama's safety in April 2007. He approached congressional leaders to discuss Obama's security situation. He knew the crowds would be large, but some of the other information given to them raised concerns among many of Senator Obama's party. Homeland Security Secretary Michael Chertoff authorized protection of the future President. It consisted of three shifts, working eight hours each to cover Obama 24, hours a day.

As the first African American president, Barack Obama received more Secret Service protection at the earliest date ever in a Presidential bid, and because of the millions of threats to his life and the life of his family, President Obama has had the largest Secret Service detail in presidential history.

Barack Obama superseded the Republican expectations on his way to becoming the country's first President of color, but he has fallen victim to a regularity of racial taunts and racial innuendos that have made their way to the social media world of the Internet. He has been attacked in e-mails, in cartoons and in newspapers from New York to Los Angeles and everywhere in between.

President Obama has been attacked in both a way that has been subtly shrouded in a cowardly manner, and in a way that left absolutely no doubt what the meaning was and clear whose mouth it came from. He has had a broad range of critics and offenders that ranged from the unknown lunatics, who you would expect to attack the President of the United States, to elected officials, some within his own party.

Even many Obama allies, have had to issue an apology after apology for what some feel to be offensive rhetoric while discussing the leader of the free world. The public illusion that most of White America claims is that they have not judged Obama's presidency based on the color of his skin, but that concern has always been mentioned in Obama's presidency.

Obama image has been depicted in print to resemble a broad range of assorted characters including a Zulu witch doctor. They have shown no mercy on his family either including attacking the First Lady. White America has never been comfortable the idea of having an African American family in the White House.

Somehow there is this idea that the first family would cover the beautifully painted interior walls of the White House with wood paneling, and take all the pictures of past, slave owning Presidents down and replace them with black light posters of half-naked African American women with big afros. In the beginning of President Obama's term, there was even such sensitive scrutiny by some that even simple gestures like a high five or even a fist bump were analyzed for the possibility of some type of racial meaning.

Although the race of the President has become less of a factor for most of White America, there are still those who refuse to let it go. Just as there are those who are still hanging on to the support of the Confederate Flag, there are those, many the same as the Flag support crowd, who will go to their grave believing that African Americans will never be welcome in seats of political power, especially the office of the President.

Giving the past Presidents of the United States a hard time, by making fun of them has always been an American rite of passage. Everything from George Bush's "C" level grades to the fact that Bill Clinton had a difficulty keeping his Johnson in his pants. They have all had bull's eyes on their backs, and been a target for every comedian a critic. The fact the George Bush

II was a "C" student is way more fact that humorous anecdote.

But for many reasonably minded Americans, criticism based solely on the color of Obama's skin crosses a line. Some of the attacks the President has taken have been unusually harsh for any American President. As expected the vicious and racially charged insults, that have never stopped and continued to grow even to this day among a small minority of people, who always use the President's skin color as a way to lash out against his policies, or they call him names like Communist, or Marxist, or Socialist because it would show their true colors if they just called him what they really wanted to; "Nigger."

You've always had the kooks, nut-jobs, the bat-shit crazies and those buried in racial paranoia that think "Black people are taking over the world." You're always going to have these lunatics. I don't think that changes, and I believe the people who focus on race and express animosity and antagonism toward him based on race won't go away.

Despite any understanding or inroads that were gained in regard to Presidents Obama's own racial identity, poll numbers have showed a major slipping of confidence in progress for African Americans overall. A recent poll found fewer Americans believe President Obama has helped race relations than when he took office.

Another factor to understand is that when Obama first became President, the country was experiencing one of the worst economic crisis since Herbert Hoover. Unemployment percentages in the country were driving toward the nine percent plus range, and George Bush (II) departed office, leaving a whopping projected deficit of over $1.2 trillion dollars.

President Obama and the new administration were like the character Dalton from the '80s movie *Roadhouse*. In one scene of the movie, Dalton, the lead Bouncer has been hired to clean up a nightclub in a small redneck town in Missouri. After one evening, the club owner makes the statement, "We had a good night. At least nobody got killed," at which Dalton responds, "It will get worse before it gets better." They were far more correct than they realized. During President Obama's first quarter, the Dow Jones industrial stocks plummeted to less than eight thousand.

But since the election of the first African American President in history, the unemployment rate in the United States fell to below six percent. The stock market has risen in double digits. The inflation factor has diminished. The automotive industry was rescued as was the banking industry. We stopped looking for weapons of mass destruction, killed Saddam Hussein, and ended the war in Iraq, and for the first time in the history of the United States, we have the ability to provide health insurance to every citizen of this country.

There is absolutely no doubt that President Obama saved the U.S. auto industry, and probably saved Michigan from a new Great Depression. It was no accident that he visited a Ford assembly plant near Detroit regularly.

I am by no means saying that President Obama has been a perfect leader of the free world. Quite the contrary. He has had his battles with congress and public relations situations. I have felt that sometimes he just needed to be like a bull in the china closet, and actually be the "HNIC" (Head Nigger in Charge), but he has done his best to handle his statue with the adequate decorum associated with the highest office of the land.

But in saying that and given his accomplishments, people from other countries often assume that our current President has been hugely popular and achieved "rock star" status. Not in this country. A country that still looks at African Americans as second-class citizens. President Obama is still the target of a steady stream of bigotry and disrespect. Congress has regularly fought him at every opportunity like no other President in history.

Most of White America will never come to terms with it, and continues to deny the reason is because he is African American, and they still don't respect any African American person with his status, especially one with the educational sheepskin that he has. It has long been stated that the most dangerous person in the world to White America is a highly educated African American man. This is one reason that it was a crime to teach slaves to read. There is only one reason for all of this. Racism.

I cannot "prove" that racism is the reason for many of these occurrences. I also can't prove that Denzel Washington is a better-looking man than I am either, but I know perfectly well that if people compare me to him, there is a pretty good chance that I will fall a bit short. Maybe it is because of the Academy Awards he has received, or being named the "Sexiest Man Alive" more than once, and me not even being the "Sexiest Man in Ferguson, Missouri."

The question that White America regularly gets, and they refuse to truthfully address is does the race of President Obama play a part in how people, both White and African American people in the country look at him? Yes, there are select White Americans who look at him and only see an African American who should never have the seat that he does.

Likewise, there are select African Americans, who truthfully only voted for him because he was African American. Neither group gives a rat's ass whether the man was qualified for the position.

Racism is much like pornography. Most people know it when they view it. But, much like pornography, having an African American President was not everybody's "bag of nuts," and although his popularity has fallen in some polls, he has had to deal with a rising racial climate like no President since Lyndon Johnson.

President Obama has been blamed for everything from rising (or falling) gas prices, the Ebola disease scare and the war in Afghanistan to VA hospital abuse, not attending a police officer's funeral in New York and the social uprising in Ferguson, Missouri. One thing you can't blame him for (and many have tried) is racism. Every President has faced these same reductions in popularity at the end of their terms. That is just a sign that eight years is a long term for the office.

It was an absurd notion all along that President Barack Obama, as the nation's first African American President, could somehow miraculously suppress racism in America, simply by using his White House bully pulpit.

President Obama has spoken about racism in this country on numerous occasions, many since the killing of Michael Brown Jr. on August 9, 2014.

He has also put racism in its unpopular place in our society, especially since that fatal day in Ferguson, Missouri, and the many incidents that followed.

President Obama has been the subject of constant criticism on race, but how can you honestly blame the President for Grand Juries who fail to indict police officers who kill unarmed African American men? And how can you blame President Obama for a police culture, that systematically and on record, targets African American men?

Redditt Hudson, a former St. Louis police officer, told CNN that the St. Louis Police Department is "deeply racist." He also said many White officers don't want to participate in cultural sensitivity training seminars because they consider it a "waste of time." President Obama can put policies in place to deter police from firing at African American men, but he can't ride in every patrol car every night, and stop cops from pulling triggers.

White Americans have a hard time dealing with the concept of racism. Many of them I have heard say that racism "ended in the '60s," which could not be farther from the truth. I attended the weekly "dog and pony" show, popularly known as a Ferguson Commission meetings. This is a commission that was created by Missouri Governor Jay Nixon to examine the root causes for what happened in Ferguson, and the societal efforts surrounding the city of St. Louis. Truthfully it was the Governor's public relations make up, for not deploying the National Guard to protect the city of Ferguson, on the November evening of the Grand Jury reading.

St. Louis is a city that had 159 murders in 2014, and at the printing of this book in 2015, was on course to exceed the 200 mark. There was a survey where it was asked "In what time frame do you think the racial climate in the St. Louis area will change?" The answer selections were "A. one to three years, B. three to five years, C. five to ten years, D. ten to twenty years, and E. Never."

The overwhelming majority answer to this question was "A. one to three years." Now on this evening, the majority of the audience was White. This should give people a clear indication that White citizens, of the St. Louis and surrounding area, are completely clueless to the depth of racism in this community, and across this country.

This isn't going to be solved in the next one to three years, not overnight and not in mine or my children's lifetime. This is something that is deeply embedded in American society, and it has been embedded for over four hundred years will not be removed in five.

In order to eliminate racism, it would require a persistent attack at every level when it rears its ugly head. It would take a true dedication from society as a whole. It would require a monitored and measured progress, and we all know that typically, progress is in small steps or in miniscule increments.

We also have to remember that regardless of how the incidents that are happening in the country, the shooting of unarmed African Americans, racial profiling, red-lining in real estate, it in fact cannot compare to the hell that my parents and grandparents faced over the past one hundred years.

My mother has faced some unbelievable atrocities in her life, but has remains open hearted toward White America. She regularly tells me that things are better than they were. The times are past when, by law you could not go to certain areas, or live in certain areas. She is not naïve by any means. She realizes that in some cases things are better, but by no means are they great. With that, she always tells me to just "keep on living." We must always recognize the progress being made.

It is not the job of the President of the United State to enact and create laws. He only has the ability and responsibility to propose policies. President Obama faced a Republican-controlled Congress, whose only focus it seems was to put a crashing halt on the first African American President's legislative agenda.

As his term in office comes end, I believe Obama, has done the best job he could have possibly done, considering the position he walked into. He will go down in history, regardless of what White Republican America thinks or feels, as a phenomenon. There will be no doubt that his election to the office of

President of the United States was truly the most historical moment in American politics up to this time.

It has brought forth and truly solidified a feeling in this country, especially in the minds of African Americans, that the myth we were told as kids that "you can be anything you truly want to be in this world," a belief that, up to this moment in history, has been tested in the minds of many African Americans who have felt segregated in just about every aspect of American society.

Obliviously, that brief feeling of inclusion has suffered major blows. Historically, and recognized more so since August 9, 2014, African Americans been openly and publicly discriminated against, killed by the police, and regularly assaulted and raped by the judicial system.

Today's reality is that day after day, race relations in America is getting worse, and the judiciary process is not even helping matters. Take a serious look at the Trayvon Martin case. Martin was a seventeen year old, African American teenager who was shot dead by George Zimmerman. Zimmerman was the coordinator of the neighborhood watch organization in the gated community where he was renting a house. The six female jurors acquitted Zimmerman.

Being heavily involved in the incident in Ferguson, Missouri during the summer of 2014, I was hit in the face again with the fact that not much progress is being forged in racial or cultural understanding. The shocking judgment on Michael Brown's killing found the Grand Jury rule that Darren Wilson, a White Police Officer who shot Michael Brown Jr., would not be indicted, even when the six gun shot wounds on Brown's body suggested otherwise. New York citizen Eric Garner's case followed suit and generated much protest.

Although the officer in the case was indicted, the Tamir Rice case is ongoing and following the judicial principle or conclusions that, Tim Loehmann will most likely be acquitted. This is not a good story for American judicial system, and it just keeps getting worse day after day. The picture being painted every day is that the police, many of them being White, can continue to shoot unarmed African Americans, many of them youths, without being held accountable and prosecuted.

African American youth, especially men, are twenty-one times more likely to be shot dead in America than their White counterparts. African American people in general are arrested ten times more often than White Americans in this country, but contrary to the popular opinion of many White Americans, African Americans don't commit ten times more crimes.

President Obama's time in the Oval Office has helped to expose the fact that the United States still has a great deal more to do to combat racism. Of course, this country has made strides from the civil rights era to now. Martin Luther King had a dream, and many people get stuck on his "dream" and forget that Dr. King's life was a mass of civil disobedience because of the reality of the time. Nevertheless, a lot is yet to be done for Martin Luther King Jr.'s dream to be completely fulfilled.

My mother, bless her heart, always tells me this; "African Americans are not where we want to be, not where we need to and should be, but by the grace of God, we are not where they use to be."

CHAPTER 5

RACISM IN THE MEDIA

This country cannot keep turning our backs on African Americans. I have fought too hard and too long against discrimination based on race and color not to stand up against any discrimination based on race or culture.

—*John E. Lewis*

ONE OF THE issues associated with racism is stereotyping people. I believe that not all stereotyping is good, and at the same, not all stereotyping is bad. But one thing for sure is that a stereotype comes from something that society has seen regularly, has associated with a group or culture of people and it helps generalize these same groups or cultures in order to make sense out of a complex situation.

White American society has developed a class system of value and power in the United States. This has in turn given White America a sense of order and a belief that White Americans in this country are perceived to be more dominant than African Americans. This is a reason that White American society has always segregated people into different races.

Race is not a medical term used in any form of diagnosis, but White America has regularly segregated all Americans based on genetic traits of skin color, hair color and texture, and facial features. These segregations have done very little more than perpetuate this class system. White American society has trained itself, based on this system, to believe that people are defined by racial boundaries.

These boundaries are carried over to every aspect of society, including politics. They have socially constructed and have expanded past race to include religion, nationality, heritage, and cultural practices.

When you look at the world from a racial point of view, you have no psychological choice but to develop negative stereotypes of many of the various cultures that are different than your own. Because of human psychological factors, it is natural for the human ego to drive the human thought process. This means human beings naturally believe that their associated culture is the focus and center of everything (that is good) in society, and all other groups fall short in comparison to it.

These negative stereotypes are often coming from a place of prejudice. They are almost always negative judgments based on bigotry, because they associate only negative assessments and qualities with these designated groups. For instance, Jewish people are always associated with being cheap, Italians with organized crime, or African Americans with dealing drugs.

The damage caused by this constant exposure to negative stereotypes also brings stereotyped people to believe, and in fact, live up to the stereotypes. It creates low self-esteem and low expectations, and in addition, this type of stereotyping does nothing more than contribute to the list of problems that regularly plague the African American communities of the United States, including high unemployment, low educational achievement, and criminality. The problem is that because these stereotypes are often based on a small grain of truth, they are quickly enshrined as the gospel truth.

The repetition of racist stereotypes has been used to enact some of history's worst atrocities. Consider Germany during the 1930s. Hitler's hatred of Jews could never have been propelled into the murder of over six million men, women and children if the feelings of anti-Semitism didn't already exist in the country. Hitler, although he was truly a monster, was a genius in the fact that he had the ability to play on the emotions of a country and propel himself into a recognized leader of the world.

But before my White counterparts get on the bandwagon of "John Parker supports Hitler, the murderer of over six million people," let me reiterate that Adolf Hitler was a MONSTER, and the world should have gotten the satisfaction of watching him hanged by the neck until he died like the animal that he was. I hope that clears up that.

Let's not forget that during World War II, Americans were quick to demonize enemies. Remember the atrocities inflicted upon the Japanese Americans who were living in the United States. Somehow White America chose to forget that we placed thousands of these citizens of the United States in internment camps, because of simple fear and racism. White Americans have long believed that these actions were justified, because of the negative stereotyping of enemies the United States before the war.

What these and most all stereotypes have in common is that they tend to reduce people to an exaggerated depiction of what makes White America comfortable. Truth is, society today is becoming more sensitive to issues of culture and gender than it once was, but the common misconceptions about cultures and various races of people continue in our society, and don't look like they are going away anywhere too fast. Identifying criminals by race and inaccurate societal portrayals has significantly affected how the citizens of the United States perceive, relate and associate with one another.

As a polarizing institution of our society, the media play a critical role. They provide us with definitions about who we are as a nation and as a country. They attempt to reinforce the values and normalcy of our society. They give us concrete examples of what happens to those who go against the norms, and most importantly, they perpetuate certain ways of seeing the world.

The media continues to provide us with images of description and remedy. They tell us how society and the world see us and at the same time tell us how to behave in society. This was nowhere in time more prominent than during the protest in Ferguson in 2014.

The media promotes a notion of consensus and a belief that there is a core group of society, of which we are a part. This core group continues to define the social order, and suggests that it is in our interest to continue to maintain. Through coverage of the people that deviate from the consensus, we are constantly presented with the threat of the picture of a lawless society, where chaos could reign.

This notion of consensus, that there is a common value system supposedly binding us confuses the hierarchies that are present in other societies. The national media tends to portray all groups as having equal power or equal cultural capital. The mythical notion that everybody in society is equal in the eyes of said society, and that everybody possesses the same equal access to society's institutions helps to lock in our brains the belief that our society/nation is a liberal state.

Most inequalities, and yes, they exist within this mythical notion, are translated into the responsibilities of the people. In other words, if one cannot get a job, then it is a reflection of that individual's inability to find employment. Within this imaginary system exists the true and very real barriers of racism, sexism, homophobia, and class that are all translated into individual actions. Social institutions that perpetuate these restrictions are presented as being innocent of these actions. In fact, they are often represented as being too liberal in their intent.

At the same time, the media sees themselves on a higher rung, reporting on issues of concern to the citizens of the nation. They defend their position by claiming neutrality, objectivity, and balance. They are there to present the so-called "facts" as these are seen and developed in any arena of social life, as being objective by virtue of their distance and supposedly nonpartisan relations. They also claim that they provide balanced coverage, by presenting various sides to an issue.

They also claim that they provide the best possible explanation of issues that occur in society, when it is clear that issues and incidents are open to interpretation, especially when it comes to issues of race. When viewed in that light, they take from society and attempt to return to society, their views of events and issues that make sense.

At the same time, the media tend to report most directly the comments, statements and arguments of other powerful institutions, the government mainly. The definitions that are articulated by these social institutions are seen as credible and less open to interrogation. The positions of the elite, in this case powerful institutions, gets perpetuated over time and becomes part and parcel of our definitions of social reality. Hence, the behavior of law enforcement is usually not exposed, because the media does not want to destroy the American myth that police officers are our "friends."

The media does not stand alone from society on what information they report. In fact, they are an integral part of society. They utilize the same stock of knowledge that is part of that common-sense pool that informs all of our lives. It is common sense to expect punishment if one has committed a crime, but apparently, according to more tragic events, there is an exception to that rule if you are a White law enforcement officer.

It is common sense to have a system of law and order, except if it is a system that is set up to abuse minorities. It is common sense that some people will make more money than others. This pool of common-sense knowledge is a reservoir of all our unstated, taken-for-granted assumptions about the world we live in. It is filled with historical traces of previous systems of thought and belief structures.

An inherent part of that historical legacy is the way in which the media has positioned and represented people who were different from what was considered acceptable in American society. That difference has covered the entire span of people, from Native Americans, African Americans to other people of color. In the view of White America that is regularly perverted by the media, any difference is always constructed as a negative sign and imbued with connotations of threat, invasion, pollution and the like. People who were different are positioned as "others." They are viewed as the criminals. "They" are dirty, unkempt, causing trouble and bringing disease.

"They" have to be kept out or contained in a separate area, away from "civilized" society. Critical to the media discourse of our time is the opposition between "them" and "us." What "they" are, "we" are not, and vice versa. Scholars have identified the presence of an underlying "moral economy." Within that order, Native Americans and African Americans are consistently portrayed in negative terms. In contrast, White Americans always rate high in terms of positive media coverage.

Clearly, the economic structure of the United States news media makes them subject to the pressures of powerful interest groups. In 1967, a national report attacked the mass media for their bad handling of the daily coverage of racial events. This report charged the media with not properly communicating about race to the majority of their viewing audience.

It was a belief that White America at the time needed to hear more about the actual conditions of African Americans in the United States. Let's be honest here. Only when these events are associated with concern or directly affect the White American public do they truly become newsworthy anyway.

The face of the media is predominantly White in the country, and with such, truly only caters to the same race. White America should be honest again. It does not care about African American problems or issues unless it directly affects their world or vision thereof. Only the symptoms of these conditions which inconvenience White America. It is only events that actually fit the criteria for the press that receive real and honest coverage.

There are various reasons for the media not covering the real and deep-rooted causes of racial stereotypes in this country. The main reason is because White America does not truly pay attention to these stereotypes, unless it affects their lives directly. When it affects the operational procedures of their world, whether it be from a family standpoint or the corporate culture that has been manifested over years of segregated oppression. Events like boycotts of public services, like the Montgomery (Alabama) Bus Boycott, picketing of businesses and corporations, civil rights demonstrations like we saw in Ferguson, Missouri, in 2014, and the racially sparked violence that often follows such demonstrations are the situations that get the real attention of White America. It is not surprising that the White-oriented media seeks to satisfy the needs of their White audience, and reflect this pattern of attention to these selected events.

In my research for this book, I found that most serious crimes in our major cities are not committed by all African American kids. Quite the contrary. Heinous crimes (rape, murder, assault, etc.) are in fact committed by a very small proportion of African American youth. Even though the statistics are below ten percent, African American men under the age of twenty-two are regularly stereotyped and labeled as the criminal menace.

Because of this stereotype, our country has set these young African American men up as targets, and it has now become common practice for law officers to stop young African American males, to harass, brutalize and in certain cases, murder them because America has jumped on the anti-African American male bandwagon. The negative stereotyping has a long lasting effect on African Americans, because it will have an effect on their ability to prosper as a community.

Even though biologically, medically and even biblically, there is no such thing as race, the social construction of race as a category is alive and well today. The classification system which racializes different groups, and typifies them according to their skin color and other defining features has a long history dating back to the invasion of Europeans upon the New World (where there were already people living). Where racism was truly born was under a period when various groups were subjected to domination, in the name of building a nation.

Under those circumstances, it fit White Americans and legitimized how they looked at African Americans as being less of a people that required domestication, containment, and if need be, extermination. With the advent of colonialism, racism was born and shined a light on the different and negative valuations attached to skin color. However, the system was also used to rationalize the large-scale genocide of African Americans.

The press uses its power to convey its understanding of African Americans and other minorities as being beneath White America in every way and being inferior. In other words, racism is a systemic happening. It reinforces the behaviors of the dominant faction of society. It is a phenomenon which permeates into the everyday world of people in the United States. People must also realize that it's not confined to individual people of our society. It is present in the fabric of every aspect of our way of lives.

When we as a country choose to generalize people of color, we disregard their contribution to society. White America then moves to a process of institutionalization, where it assigns values to both the accurate and inaccurate differences between White Americans and African Americans, in order to solidify the rights of privilege.

White America will never get onboard with the fact that the media does perpetuate racism, because it regularly accentuates, exploits, and reinforces the racial boundaries that permeate society. This also helps White America feel confident in these boundaries by focusing on the so-called problems and the inferiority of African Americans. This in turn solidifies the foundation of their inequity, creating more and more exclusion.

Mediated racism functions in several ways. The most obvious is the association of particular groups of people with specific actions. Numerous studies have pointed out that on the whole, African American people tend to be absent from the media in general with one exception. They are conspicuously present in stories dealing with crime or with problems in their communities. Their presence in certain categories of media coverage tends to underline the assumption that only African Americans commit crimes, and that African Americans are a the problem.

This suggests that the only resolution available is to ensure that African Americans don't move into White American neighborhoods, or that African Americans are not allowed to continue expression of their cultural heritage. In fact, the recent trend to attribute actions to particular cultures marks a change in the traditional ways in which racism was communicated.

What seems to be in place now is a more modified form of racism which has been referred to as "cultural racism." This is when the various cultures of a particular groups are deemed as being problematic, and as causing a variety of the society's ills in the United States.

As I already stated, stereotyping is one very common and effective way in which racism is perpetuated. Thus, there is an abundance of representations of these groups within categories such as athletics, entertainment, crime, and so forth. These stereotypes are one-dimensional at best and they only highlight specific characteristics. They are often used to typify whole groups of people.

Other elements that are regularly absent from the stereotypes are similarly and amazingly absent from media coverage. This leads to a situation where assumptions are made about African Americans on the basis of stereotyping. These assumptions can perpetuate exclusion and in extreme cases, are used to justify brutality.

From print to electronic media, the racialization of African Americans continues in a number of different ways. Primary among these mechanisms is the identification of racial background when these are simply not warranted. Take for instance, the statement "The suspect was an "African American male." Or, "the suspect is a Chinese man."

Another technique used frequently by the media is the heavy reliance on official interpretations of events concerning or involving African American people. In these cases, the people themselves are often not allowed to talk. Instead, an official, who is usually White, like a police spokesman, speaks on their behalf. The repeated positioning of African Americans as victims, unable to speak on their own behalf, lends to the perception that they are passive, unknowledgeable and ignorant of English language skills.

In some cases, the media turns to particular individuals within the communities, and positions them as spokespeople. I will apologize now because I have been this person. This often stereotypes the community itself as monolithic, and that one person chosen by the media is seen to represent a community's opinions. But, these communities are not monolithic entities but highly diverse in the range of opinions and interpretations that exist, and are often negated by mainstream media in the United States.

For the media, the focus is on getting a story out and doing it in the most expedient and sensational way possible. The problem is compounded by the reality that newsrooms across the country are largely White American and male. African Americans constitute only a little over two and a half percent of the total number of people employed by the major media in the United States.

When African American people are allowed to speak, their words are often surrounded by quotations, or preceded by words such as "alleged." The implication here is that their stories or perspectives are dubious. Take for instance, the accounts from the witnesses of the Michael Brown shooting. The quotations around terms like "distraught" or "emotional" lead the reader to believe that witnesses are not distraught, but are using an emotional appeal in an opportunistic manner.

Several other mechanisms are used to communicate the negative valuation of African Americans in the print media and electronic media. A common technique is to position different stories dealing with African Americans on the same page.

There may be a story about a particular government program designed to aid immigrant minorities. Right next to it may be a story about an African American man being arrested for some crime. Following this, there may be a story about a Third World country in which it highlights its poverty or lack of order.

Taken together, all these stories communicate certain representations about African Americans. These are false representations which indicate their inferiority, lawlessness, and their inability to progress without having a helping hand from the dominant societies.

These stories legitimize a paternalistic attitude. They communicate that African American people are not like "us" and that "they" need the help of White Americans. It keeps perpetuating the belief that African Americans are inherently incapable of governing themselves.

So I guess the question that needs to be asked is should the media even report on different racial groups? Even so, this really isn't the issue. The real issue seems to stem from the practices of the actual reporting. Reporters all know that it is what gets left out of the story that is often the most crucial.

Presences and absences of information play a critical part in the construction of meaning in a story. What is said has definite implications on what is omitted or not said.

The problem with images depicting African Americans is not so much the existence of an image, but rather the absence of an adequate explanation of why they are suffering in society. This absence opens the door to all manner of mythical interpretations emanating from the individual common-sense view of the world.

Consequently, racist and ethnocentric 'explanations' are inevitable amongst an audience with preexisting assumptions about African Americans and about the superiority of White America. This lack of an adequate explanation resonates with this country's preconceived notions about African Americans, and culminates in the reinforcement of racism at all levels of society. This is particularly so when the society of the United States itself has a history of racism.

As I have spoken about, the national media of the United States often has preconceived determinations, when it comes to speaking about African Americans in reporting news. More often than not, the media always makes up their mind and is rarely objective anymore in their reporting. One technique that seems to be a common practice among the media in this countries literal reporting of something politicians call the "Racial Number's Game."

We often hear about the government having to revise its policies in the face of so many immigrants and refugees. This kind of revision automatically evokes an image of hordes waiting to invade the country. It invites a response which condones the government's stance.

In addition to this, a government's action or lack of action on a certain racial issues communicates its position loud and clear. The media, by reporting this, also cultivates that same impression.

When this separation process is put into motion by the mainstream media, White Americans tend to see African Americans as a victimized race, but still more favorable among other minorities groups. They are represented as lazy people, who don't work and choose to sit home, receive welfare and other benefits for the government.

In addition, through this process, the government is looked at as the African Americans' "Sugar Daddy," sponging off the federal tax system, and living off of the sweat and toils of White America. In the eyes of White America, African Americans are the reason the federal government has put into place protections, so that they can carry on their cultural traditions.

Media outlets seem to always cover laws and law makers in a way that conveniently covers White America, and it tends to often focus on how White American is being screwed over by these laws, especially White men. White America is regularly bombarded by rhetoric about how minorities and in particular African Americans are ruining their lives, taking their jobs, moving into their neighborhoods and turning their White American Protestant and conservative institutions into a society that is being infested with liberalism, as if it is a plague taking over the country.

The foundation of this is the myth that has been pounded into White American, is that everybody is on level playing field, and has equal accessibility to the same advantages of our society. Because White America has had this embedded into their DNA for so long, there is truly no real understanding of the notion that special programs should be created for African Americans, or any other minority class to compete and become successful.

The most ugly thought process is the belief and conclusion of these same White Americans is that most African Americans don't have the qualifications or the "intangibles" as it is sometimes put, to move into positions that have been generally and historically held by White Americans. They are simply not qualified enough to assume the positions they may occupy.

This group of White American's assumptions are often combined with another belief, which is that African Americans, which usually is spoken in the ridiculous term "Reverse Discrimination" or that "Niggers" are stealing jobs and putting "God-fearing White Folks" out of work.

The mainstream media, often in a covert manner, places the aim on African Americans in the United States and the cultural issues, long before pointing at the racism factor and considering the fact that some of these issues center around racism and skin color. They don't do this because if they did, they would create a factor with substance that can clearly be identified.

When racism has the potential to be identified, then there is a potential to create a circumstance where legislative tides can begin, and potentially be defended in a courtroom. In addition to creating a situation which would require demonstrations, protest and the possibility of boycotting businesses and products, as well as the possibility of a protest or boycott from organized groups.

All of this is born out of a ridiculous belief in this country that we have a nation of tolerance, and racism no longer exist. You would not believe how many of my White American counterparts believe that racism ended in the sixties. I almost laugh at the belief, and then I realized that it truly is no laughing matter. This belief is understood by people who are not only more intelligent, but who also have common sense.

Because of this, I have found numerous accounts in all forms of the media, including the trio of newspapers, radio and television that make a great living off of sensationalizing the sometimes raw culture of African

Americans in the United States. This has carried over to the situation comedies that blanket our television airwaves, and has ultimately made it to the silver screen of motion picture production.

The sensationalism follows the stereotypical emphasis on what White America assumes the lifestyle and culture of African Americans are. The lifestyle of living in small run-down apartments while driving a Cadillac Escalade with five-thousand-dollar rims and tires on it. I could go on forever about this.

Walking around with hats on sideways, "Mr. T" gold chain starter kits around the neck, and "Gangsta" Rap music being blared with lyrics that refer to African American women as nothing more than "bitches and hoes."

In comparison they almost never talk about the abuses and torment that occurs against White American women in this country, because that is not what the corporate control entity wants to hear about. You will never hear them acknowledge the obvious lack of equal treatment of men and women, and it would be completely unheard of to discuss racial discrimination and situations shrouded in racism in the country.

So when an African American person commits a heinous crime, it is only seen as a result of the stereotypical lifestyle that they lead, with no consideration for the factors that surround the individual. In a sense, it is summed up as "if they didn't act that way, then those things wouldn't happen," never taking into consideration factors such as depression, isolation, etc. Essentially saying "Niggers! Would you expect any different?"

African Americans have at times raised hell about how the media presents issues surrounding them. Their recommendations have often asked for more positive coverage of situations. This was clearly evident in the coverage of the events in Ferguson, Missouri, in 2014. Every major news outlet was more than ready to report every negative aspect from tear gas being thrown, to rubber bullets being shot at protestors, and even old people being carted away by the abusive police forces that were enlisted for crowd control.

The media often feels that what is positive has to be seen in light of what dominant society values as being positive. If positive means coverage that highlights our contributions, than it may be a valid demand to make. However, if positive simply means that we are shown to act like or appear to be like the dominant society, then it takes on an assimilationist tone.

Many writers have observed that within cinema, the ethnic or racial minority member is only acceptable if her/his cultural or racial characteristics can be bleached out or "White washed." In other words, if it is completely downplayed or removed from the scene.

If this is the only gateway to acceptance, then it means that African Americans have to distance themselves from their cultures, and their realities. For an integral part of that reality is the burden of racism, especially since it impedes an individual's life chances in the area of employment, housing, services and everyday interactions.

The media is in a position to put a clear definition on racism. They often present it in a personalized form because they choose to only report on the most extreme situations that play directly into a particular stereotype. This type of reporting is perpetuated because it often involves characters that fit the stereotype (uneducated).

The media in this way deflects attention away from the systemic nature of racism and how it is truly embedded in the media fabric of the United States. It rarely discusses African Americans in positions of corporate power and access to resources. The media would never bring attention to "elite racism." This is the kind that is practiced in society every day at the corporate level and has historically ruled over and controlled the decisions and policies that affect African Americans.

Finally, when you look at racism from this point of view, there is a notion that the White American–oriented media can be made to unlearn their embedded racism. With an increase in coverage and a truly objective way of reporting the news, the media can realize that African Americans are no different from White Americans.

They must understand that racism is based on fear, and African Americans are perceived as threat to White American. The media must get to a point where they are not the manager of that threat. Racism must be translated as simply an "emotional phenomenon" that really has no basis for existence.

Media organizations are the most difficult to challenge and raise claim to in this country. They often hide behind the camouflage of claiming to be balanced, which anybody who has ever seen a news report knows is a bunch of bullshit. There is a significant misappropriation of balance, which more often than not leads to sensationalism in order to achieve ratings.

Balance in the media is like trying to have control over a volitle situation. It is an illusion or even a myth if you will. Are racists and anti-racists equal? I tend to doubt it.

Does any one person have the exact credibility and access to media as any other person or any an institution? Cleary they do not. How a story is interpreted depends highly on how the same story is told by the media. How many times have you seen a story told from numerous angles in the media?

Fox News is notorious for spinning stories to fit their viewing audience. It is usually spent on the basis of the bigotry of the network itself, which to say the least is thick and well known. When it comes to one of their Host, Bill O'Reilly, I could write for days. O'Reilly had the ignorance to say to an African American guest on his show "Say you're a cocaine dealer, and you kind of look like one a little bit" because he was dressed in a business suit, and presented himself in a professional manner.

He has regularly makes the comment of African American guest "he speaks so well" or "he is so articulate." Someone needs to wake up Mr. O'Reilly and let him know that neither of those statements are of a complimentary manner, and that just because an African American man is wearing a suit, contrary to popular belief, he is not a drug dealer or a preacher. But that is the type of ignorance exemplified by Mr. O'Reilly on a regular basis on his show.

Fox News has regularly edited shows and reports to sensationalize situations, while being caught on numerous occasions doing so. Their Boston affiliate decided to edit the chant "Kill a Cop" into some footage during the problems in Ferguson in 2014, in an attempt to reduce a favorable public opinion of the protests and the protesters. They were caught doing so and were forced to apologize in a public manner, but no real news coverage of this incident was ever followed up on.

The Fox network has also had their own issues with African American employees. An African American worker named Harmeen Jones was fired because he filed numerous complaints of racial harassment. Jones' claim stated that jokes were made at the expense of African Americans, Women, Muslims, Jews, and other protected classes.

Every African American, in a mostly White American working culture has always been given the same advice, and several African American coworkers gave Jones this same advice to "keep his head down and not say anything," and when Jones decided to step outside of the comfort zone of the oppressive climate of Fox, by complaining to Human Resources, he was promptly fired.

Bill O'Reilly is not the only host of a Fox program to either insult or completely disregard the race and culture of minorities in a public manner. Megyn Kelly, another lily White American host, and proclaimed patron Saint of the network, has also show her true colors on numerous occasions. There was an episode when she and others on a news program declared with conviction that Santa Claus was a White American man.

This is in opposition to the proven evidence that Saint Nicholas was actually born in Turkey, which is located in the Middle East. Just like every host on the network, when faced with evidence such as this, to the contradiction of her conviction in a debate with a show guest (who is usually African American), she immediately changed the subject, and attempted to transition into another argument.

The idiocy of most of the network's host is also without sensitivity. Todd Starnes, a columnist for the network, once voiced his complaint about the Miss America Pageant when he publicly stated that the judges show a "lack of integrity" because they would not select Miss Kansas as winner because she had a tattoo on her body of "The Serenity Prayer."

Starnes accused the judges of being too liberal and disqualifying her, saying, "Christianity is of course an inherently American trait and the judges were obviously too liberal and un-American." This is the kind of ridiculous "journalism", and I use the term loosely, that is being promoted by Fox News.

While I myself am a Catholic, the fact that Starnes considers Christianity the "religion of the country" when according to the Constitution of the United States, all citizens have a freedom to any religion makes absolutely no sense at all. Starnes also attacked CNN for the blatant racism that exist in the social media world.

This came after there were racist remarks posted on Twitter after Miss New York won the pageant. Miss New York just happened to be a Native American. And as always, when question on his statements, he also took the network pledge by claiming the win on the fact that the judges were doing the politically correct thing, playing to liberal America, and that they were "just plain wrong."

Fox is not unlike many racist organizations in this country in that it adamantly refuses to accept, and in fact, denies that racism is still alive, well and living in America. This is one reason is gets away with the numerous racist mistakes or "slip ups" during both live and taped programming. They make the attempt at trying to fight this racist foundational belief by bringing a few African Americans on air in order to say to the public "see, we do like African American people." Most of the African American guest that are "privileged" enough and are often paid to perform in this dog and pony show regularly denounce the network at their first opportunity.

The resident ruler of the Fox Network is Rupert Murdoch. He once had the balls to accuse President Obama of making a "very racist comment." He truly has set the mode of operation for the network because when Murdoch was asked about what his comment was, not only did he not respond, he made a sad attempt at deflection.

The Fox network is notorious for this type of behavior, and it goes on and on, because they have also shown no tolerance, and at times have even attacked homosexuals. They have shown no signs of letting up in their attacks either

These attacks are not rarities. The agenda of the Fox network is one of deliberate action, and unfortunately the majority has been aimed at the first African American President in history. Let us not forget when they have used terms like "terrorist fist jab" and "Obama's baby mama" when talking about President Obama's family.

Also, there was a clear racial motive when Bill O'Reilly made a joke about not attacking the First Lady's credibility by saying that he didn't "want to go on a lynching party."

The list goes on and on. Glen Beck is a host on the network, who has gotten emotional on camera at times in his disdain for President Obama, and even calling the President "a racist with a deep-seated hatred for White Americans?" The lunacy and insensitivity of this man clearly has no bounds when he decided to hold a rally in Washington D.C., on the anniversary of Martin Luther King's "I Have a Dream" speech, for no other reason than self-promotion. But let's remember that this is a network that claims they are "fair and balanced."

Some people might wonder why the Fox News Network would risk alienating a potentially significant portion of their audience. Well, let's be honest about their viewership. The African American segment of viewers of Fox News in primetime is barely over one percent. That compares to nearly 20 percent for MSNBC, and nearly twenty one for CNN. These numbers are much closer to the African Americans in the population of the United States as a whole.

Due to the growing media influence, racism has evolved from African American and White American in the past to the total minority-cultural issue it is now. Racism is no longer a national problem but one of a global issue faced by countries all over the world. In this country, it is seen as a serious issue that has caused social unrest and moral panic in society.

Racism is the basis behind hate-crimes, and the Fox New Network should be taken to task on occasion for such occurrences. White conservative commentators from the network, Rush Limbaugh in particular, often use hidden racial messages and bigoted innuendo to fire up the undereducated and sometimes "redneck" White American audience to reject our government and President Obama.

They undermine his policies, and are regularly spewing the rhetoric "birther" conversation. The 2016 Presidential candidate, Billionaire, and egomaniac Donald Trump has made a living on Fox News winding up White America about the President's birth certificate. Again, they should all go back and take an eleventh-grade civics class on American citizenship.

You also have what African Americans refer to as "Uncle Toms" when speaking about Supreme Court Justice Clarence Thomas, former congress member Allen West and Presidential candidate Ben Carson. These men have compared affirmative action to slavery. This ranks right up there with saying "we never landed on the moon."

Don't get me wrong. I am not a fan of Affirmative Action, but I understand why it is needed. Because, as human beings, we inherently "do not do the right thing," and the "ol Boys" network is still alive and well, and living in the United States.

It is obviously clear that Fox News has no concern about offending the African American segment of the television viewers, that don't watch their programming. Put that together with the clear agenda to kill liberalism and devalue Democratic votes and any type of liberal power. If you follow this, then the strategy of fanning the highly ignitable racial tension, that already exist in this country, doesn't seem so bad in the warped perspective of the network, and by God, they do a hell of a good job at fanning the flames.

This should explain why the Fox News Network persists in putting clearly racially offensive features on, and why they think they can always get away with it, without facing any real penalties whatsoever. They have nothing to lose from a money standpoint, and everything to gain by playing to the cloaked racist and the redneck demographic.

They regularly play to the personal feelings of not only White corporate America, but more so the lower-middle-class by perpetuating that essentially African Americans are the reason you are poor, you don't have a job, your taxes are too high, etc. This keeps the animosity between White America and African Americans alive and well.

This probably makes decent hearted people sick, but to the Fox News Network, it is just business as usual, and more importantly, it plays well on the political stage. They have a huge following and making a steady diet of it all.

What the Fox News Network will never talk about and refuses to acknowledge is the fact that beginning around the mid eighties, the percentage of African American families, with incomes of a least $50,000 more than doubled. The median income of African American families in which both husband and wife worked rose from $28,700 in 1967 to $40,038 in 1990, an increase of more than forty percent. By comparison, the median of White American family incomes with two wage earners increased nearly twenty percent during this period, from $40,040 to $47,247.

Although there are significant variations in school dropout rates from community to community, nationally, the dropout rates for both African Americans and White Americans have decreased since the 1970s. The proportion of African American high school dropouts fell from twenty four to thirteen percent over the last twenty years.

When family income and other background differences are taken into account, African American youths are no more likely than White Americans to drop out of school. For many African American youths, staying in school has not improved their prospects for full or part-time employment. In fact, unemployment among this group remains at more than twice the rate for White youths.

The consequence of racially biased media coverage like the Fox News Network is to maintain racist stereotypes in today's culture and to keep us in an increasingly dysfunctional society. As I have said to many of my supporters, the Fox News Network has an agenda of nothing more than keeping that wedge between African Americans and White Americans, and given that the Fox News Network is staffed and controlled almost exclusively by White Americans, it follows that the reinforced popular consensus is that of the racist subculture, that exists in the United States today.

The dysfunctional side of this comes to the forefront when it is made clear to the viewing public that the realistic concerns of African Americans are dismissed by the Fox News Network, as not only irrelevant but also threatening to White America.

The media have always and will continue to portray a self-serving negative stereotype of the African American community. The societal and economic factors of racism have become more than just a bias. It is also a profitable industry, in which the elite will continue to suppress the lower class in order to maximize profits.

We need to remember that one percent of upper echelon of the United States holds on to almost sixty percent of all America wealth. This means that the media, racism, and unrealistic stereotypes will continue to be employed so that those in the upper echelon can be sure that they will continue to cash big checks.

Finally, in regard to the Fox News Network, people need to realize that Fox News and the "Commentators" on the channel all have one agenda. That is to be sure that White America remains afraid and stand-offish from the African Americans. They promote a so-called "fair and balanced" reporting process that in reality, is targeted not only toward the White wealthy one percent conservative Republican, who has no interest in the idea of redistribution of his wealth, but also toward the low-educated but hardworking White person who believes "Black people are okay, I just don't want my daughter around them or dating one."

How many ethnic minorities host their own show, or how many has Fox had or will ever have? How many episodes of shows have we seen where there was a minority guest that was unable to finish a sentence because of an overbearing host like O'Reilly, Beck, Hannity, or Kelley?

Lastly, I listened to Mr. O'Reilly one evening spout his racist rhetoric on his show, where he stated that "young Black men commit homicide at a rate of 12 times the rate of White American men." Seeing that the population of African Americans in this country is only slightly larger than 12 percent, I am wondering what part of his ass Mr. O'Reilly pull this statistic out of.

He has asked, "Why hasn't Jesse Jackson or Al Sharpton ever done any promotion for young African American girls to not get pregnant?" Finally he spoke about the city of Detroit, where he supposedly went and asked people "what has been the downfall of their neighborhood?" He just happened to be in an African American neighborhood, and he stated, not the people, that the problem was "young African American men selling drugs."

It is both amusing and irritating how Mr. O'Reilly believes he has such a pulse on the African American community. Amusing, because he has never spent serious time in the African American community, because he knows very well that he would never be welcome there.

Irritating because he knows that the people actually bringing these drugs into the country, that are subsequently destroying Detroit and cities like it, ironically look just like him, because I don't know any African American people with planes and the capability to fly drugs into this country, and this scenario has been happening in the United States for decades.

He also knows that if there is no quality employment available, then people, any people, will revert back to the very words that resonate with every living being: Self-Preservation.

I suggest this to Mr. O'Reilly. If he is that concerned or torn up about "young African American girls" getting pregnant out of wedlock (which happens to many girls of all cultures), he should feel free to not wait on Al Sharpton or Jessie Jackson. He should pick up the torch and use the bully platform of his "fair and balanced" program and help out all of these poor and pitiful young African American "chilrren." He should do this before these babies, with no apparent father in the picture, grow up, make money, buy planes, and start flying in the drugs to Detroit.

CHAPTER 6

RACISM IN THE ENTERTAINMENT INDUSTRY

When you have a system where you probably only see three movies with African-American leads in them a year, they're going to be judged more harshly, and you're really rooting for them to be good a little more so than the 140 movies starring White Americans every year.

—*Chris Rock*

THE HISTORY OF the treatment of African Americans in this country is one of oppressiveness and humiliation. African Americans were forced to come to this country against their will, for the sole purpose of being slaves and serving the needs of White Americans.

Somehow, even after being subjected to four hundred years of tilling fields, serving to the total needs of a White American society, that stole this very land they call America, and becoming the very foundation of which this country was built, African Americans have been labeled with the worst stereotypes of lazy, cowardly, and irresponsible. African Americans are labeled as sub-human, and believed to have the behavior of wild animals, that can only be controlled if they can be contained.

The entertainment media has done nothing less than solidify these ridiculous stereotypes through the type of television programs and motion pictures they are producing. Although African American roles have had some type of prominence in the film world for over one hundred years, the ironic thing is African Americans were not even cast to pay themselves in early roles.

The film industry chose to keep African Americans out, and allow White American actors and actresses dressed in what they called "Black Face" to portray those characters.

When Hollywood decided to go the "Black Face" route, it did nothing more than breed and reinforce these stereotypes. The one other thing that needs to be remembered is that African Americans were not only in the usual stereotypical roles, but they were also casted in roles that were completely subservient to White Americans.

With movies and motion pictures being the influential form of media in this country, this set the tone on how African Americans are view in this country,

The problem with these portrayals is that there are people out there who have little to no encounters with African Americans, and these depictions give the perception that African Americans behave like these movie characters.

Because of the influence of media entertainment, White America makes its determination of African Americans based on what they see on television every day. Even after over one hundred years, the negative depiction remains embedded in the fabric of our country, and until the media and entertainment industry decides to make definitive changes, changes that have the possibility of reducing revenue to the industry itself, African Americans will remain in the thought process of White America as an accumulation of second-class citizens, that really have no use at all.

The media entertainment industry has come a long way since the beginning of the 20th century. The first African American to have the leading role in a motion picture was Sam Lucas, for his performance in *Uncle Tom's Cabin*. At this same time, another film also gained a place in history as one of the most polarizing motion pictures of the time it was released. It was titled *The Birth of a Nation.* It was a movie that was made to support the efforts of recruitment for the Ku Klux Klan.

The National Association for the Advancement of Colored People (NAACP) was so very much against the playing of this movie because it depicted African Americans as animals that needed to be controlled by the secret society. The NAACP publicly protested, and worked hard to have the movie banned.

This movie was so significant to the history of the entertainment media industry, because it launched the birth of "race films" that had a sole foundation of bigotry. These films made an attempt at portraying African Americans in a much more positive position in our country. It also tackled concerns and issues that African Americans were facing in the United States.

Up until this time, African Americans or "Negroes" as they were referred to then were looked at as nothing more in this country than jive talking, tap shoe dancing, ignorant beings, who were just lazy good for nothings. They appeared to be unteachable animals, but that all changed when "race films" came on the motion picture screen. Negroes began to be seen as intelligent, respectful people who came from a very dignified race.

Negroes of the times were intelligent enough to know that if they were going to reinforce these traits they would have to take up their own charge, stop relying on White America to recognize those traits and begin promoting themselves by making their own movies.

Native Missourian, Noble Johnson, was a pioneer in the "Negro" film industry. He was both an actor and a producer who had a plan to achieve something in the motion picture industry that had never been achieved. He achieved the creation of the first Negro owned motion picture company in the country. It was called the Lincoln Motion Picture Company.

Released in the summer of 1916, his first production was titled "The Realization of Negro Ambition" and it featured Negroes in dramatic roles, that did not have the ridiculous stereotypes of the time attached to them. The story line was of a college graduate from a Historically Black College in the South, saving a White racist man's daughter, and the same White man giving him a position in business in the North.

The Lincoln Motion Picture Company did what it needed to do, through the motion picture industry, to promote the true and accurate life of African Americans. They attempted to show that African Americans were more unified to the beliefs of White America than White America wanted to realize. They were also trying to fight off the stereotypical labels placed upon them by White America.

The Lincoln Motion Picture Company also marketed their films successfully. The marketing was the responsibility of Noble Johnsons brother, George. George Johnson sought out to market the films of the company to both a wider and "Whiter" audience.

This was difficult to say the least and they were ultimately faced with showing these films in schools, and maybe a few of the theaters that were around that catered to "colored" crowds.

The movies produces by the Lincoln Motion Picture Company became so popular that they started a trend in the motion picture industry that still exists today. They set into motion the process of releasing multiple movies at a time without concerns of the reviews of success or failure for the previous productions. Eventually they attracted the attention of White America and the financial backing by a man named P.H. Updike. With Updike's financial support, the company would not only produce pictures that were entertaining to the African American community, but also to White America.

Even though this was ambitious, it was about eighty years to early. White Americans were not ready to see African Americans as intelligent equals. It was safer in their thought process that African Americans remained "shiftless and shuffling" little animals.

This would eventually sentence the company to death, but the Lincoln Motion Picture Company had established its place in the history of the motion picture industry. It laid a foundation for the creation, by Oscar Micheaux, of the Micheaux Film Corporation.

The Johnsons brothers had actually spoken to Micheaux some years earlier about purchasing the film rights to his first novel "The Homesteader." Like the Johnson brothers, Micheaux sought out to change the depiction of African Americans portrayed as negative and in stereotypical roles. Micheaux produce the film himself, and it was financed by fellow farmers, many of which were White Americans

Over the next twenty plus years Micheaux produced films that addressed a number of issues facing African Americans, even attacking the injustices of "Jim Crow" laws. Like the Johnson brothers he gave the world an accurate picture of African American life without any of the indignities of stereotypes.

Micheaux rejected the typical Hollywood roles that were pigeon holed for African Americans. As the entertainment media industry began to transition, "race films" began to die out and Hollywood looked at this as an opportune time to start making movies that were suited for African American audiences of the time.

Both the Lincoln Motion Picture Company and Micheaux Film Corporation left a lasting mark on the film industry. Their films were independently made and inspired other African Americans to be independent. They truly inspired a new generation of White American producers who saw a niche in the business and jumped all over it. Paul Sloane who worked at Twentieth Century Fox was one of those White American producers. Sloane produced the first of these niche films, casted with only African Americans. It was titled "Hearts in Dixie."

The movie attracted White audiences, and introduced these audiences to what is now one of the most stereotypical characters in African American film history. His name was Stepin Fetchit. Fetchit typified what White America thought about African Americans of the era, as being lazy and good-natured slaves, who would never work, and was always forgiven for his behavior, because he was an "ignorant darkie Negro."

Fetchit played into these stereotypes by allowing himself to be abused by his White boss. After the boss would kick him in the ass, Fetchit would grin broadly and wink his eye always drawing a big laugh from the audience. Fetchit was a clown in the eyes of White America, and what they called a "good nigger;" one whom they could control and abuse, but knew that he would always remain loyal to them. This gave them a sense of security because Fetchit "knew his place."

It was a degrading and undignified portrayal of African Americans, because Fetchit's performance depicted African Americans as being lazy and foolish, but truly meaning no harm. And again it gave White Americans that had never had any interaction with African Americans, the wrong impression of the race. Stepin Fetchit was immensely talented and generally used by White film makers to reinforce the stereotype of the lazy, stupid, good-for-nothing "darkie Negro."

While he was an extremely talented entertainer and a true pioneer in the film industry, most African Americans had a tumultuous relationship with Fetchit. Many felt like he did nothing more than solidify the stereotypes White Americans projected as African American behaving like buffoons.

Eventually, Hollywood gained some sensitivity and stopped the casting of African Americans in Fetchit characters and roles in films, because they were offending African Americans, but realized that this was a revenue stream that they did not want to cut off. Although it was commendable to finally get to this point in the entertainment industry, it is a disappointment that this thought process was ever in place.

The Stepin Fetchit character has been revitalized in Hollywood and lives on today. I have watched the movie "Nothing to Lose," and it reminds me of the antics of Fetchit. Like so many others, in the comedy "Nothing to Lose," starring Tim Robbins and Martin

Lawrence, it is made abundantly clear that Hollywood has yet to abandon those negative stereotypes of African Americans, which were first created in the early 20th century.

Tim Robbins plays Nick Beam, who's portrayed as a nice advertising executive, who loves his wife dearly. He is the quintessential White guy who is square, straight and narrow. His co-star Martin Lawrence plays the wise-ass, street-smart African American guy. One day, Nick comes home from work to find his wife in bed with another man. Distraught, he drives the streets of Los Angeles aimlessly, until he finds himself the victim of an attempted carjacking by Lawrence.

This movie shows a White American guy lecturing the African American character about the immorality of committing a crime. Robbins is constantly repeating to Martin Lawrence "You are a bad person," and Lawrence fires back at Robbins about not standing up for himself, and for not handling the situation with his wife "like a man." This is a perfect Hollywood example of the White character getting the opportunity to be upstanding and virtuous, while the African American character gets to show his buffoonery by "being cool." From beginning to end, Martin Lawrence plays the part of the clown sidekick to Robbins' aristocrat, upstanding traits of dignity.

In a sense, actors like Lawrence are the modern day Stepin Fetchit, with lines like "My ass done fell asleep.

I "dint" know an ass could fall asleep!" after he leaps from a car and dances around comically screaming. This Fetchit type character perpetuates the negative stereotypes of African Americans that White America relishes, because it makes them more comfortable to see African Americans as buffoons, and that African Americans don't seem to notice or mind.

These types of negative stereotypes of minorities in films can be found in Hollywood epic blockbusters also. In "Star Wars: Episode I - The Phantom Menace" many of the characters have unique ethnically tinged caricatures. For instance, Jar-Jar Binks mimics a Rastafarian man with dreadlocks. He had a wide nose, bulging eyes, fat lips and speaks in a Caribbean-style Pidgin English. He was a character who achieved successful status by stupidity and chance. He is portrayed as a good-for-nothing sidekick to the all-important and king-like Jedi Knights.

Even when Jar-Jar is there when the Jedi Knights most need him, he is portrayed as a no–account who happened to accidently fall into his heroism, which is looked at as being more humorous than heroic. The other issue that is created is that he does this all without any awareness of his own safety, but for the benefit of the Jedi Knights, knowing that the Jedi's will go right back to treating him as a second class member of their organization. This legacy is still practiced today in Hollywood films.

It loves to continue employing the stereotype of the lazy, loyal, stupid, bumbling, African American buffoon (Kevin Hart, Mike Epps, etc.). Hollywood executives are subconsciously obsessed with this stereotype, because it makes them and all of the White movie-going public feel safe. The most dangerous thing on the planet is an African American with a conscious mind, and with the reinforcement of negative stereotypes of African Americans and likewise, the ultra-positive stereotypes of White Americans on the screen, Hollywood clearly has no intention of ever abandoning the "dumb nigger" role in their films.

However, progress has pushed forward the way in which African Americans are portrayed on television. The world should declare that television is the greatest technological and influential device ever created in history, especially when we discuss its influence on children. It has caused numerous changes, especially in the new millennium. But, despite these changes, there are still challenges that must be conquered before the world is where it needs to be.

These challenges include most importantly the executives at the top, who decide on programming for television. Until these challenges are met, all progress will remain for the most part nonexistent. Television produces far too many shows that portray African Americans in negative ways, or in some cases, like the show Friends or Seinfeld, don't show African Americans at all.

How can you possibly have a situation comedy on television, which is shot from a New York location standpoint, and not have an African American cast member or for that matter, ANY minority cast member at all?

American Pop Culture and the television industry have walked hand in hand. Both have been defined and characterized by the innovations surrounding technology and culture. Television provides information to billions of people on this planet, in a way that is match by absolutely no other form of technology.

Mass media has become increasingly entwined with television, and less so with newspapers, magazines and other print sources, and as a direct result of this, we now are able to have a 24 hour news cycle and other forms of acquiring information like no other time in history. Television, gives people insights into a world that is unfamiliar and vastly different from the one they might be living in, regardless of whether it's the news, sitcoms or dramas.

The reality is this. Television is the only exposure that some people have to other parts of society. The portrayal aspects of individuals on television are extremely important because they influence the thoughts and beliefs of the world. This is important to remember because over two-thirds of all television viewers are children, who most often have no frame of reference.

Recently, public concern has arisen over the issue of media diversity, when it comes to child viewers. Film and television provide many children with their first exposure to people of other races, ethnicities, religions and cultures. What they see onscreen therefore, can impact their attitudes about the treatment of others.

It has been said that only two years of viewing Sesame Street by preschoolers can be associated with more positive attitudes toward African and Latino Americans. In addition, White American children that have never had interaction with African American, or who are exposed to a negative television portrayal of African Americans, will develop a negative attitude toward African Americans.

This illustrates the importance of the social responsibility that each and every member of American society has to ensure that television portrays African Americans accurately, and without bias. Because television is such an integral part of society, it is imperative that the wrong ideas and values do not go across the airwaves, and into the homes of unsuspecting young children.

Studies have shown that television teaches stereotypical attitudes and preconceptions about people and lifestyles, that they would have no contact with, outside of watching the way these people are shown by television. Unfortunately, in a time where children spend more time than ever watching television unsupervised, the television becomes the teacher.

Because they have not developed full mental capacity, children are less likely to distinguish a stereotype from reality. When they watch The Cosby Show, they see an ideal African American family on television, in a perfect home with no money problems. They may wonder why they don't have the same. Of course, the whole revelation of Bill Cosby in real life has ruined that image.

If they see things on television that they do not have a comparison in real life to, the television image will be the reality to them. When images and ideals presented at a young age take hold and are reinforced. Over years of viewing, these images become reality. They may feel inadequate in comparison to the lives some seem to lead, and superior and hateful to those portrayed in a negative way, even though that portrayal is not true.

Once these stereotypes and misconceptions become ingrained in the psyche of American children, they become self-perpetuating. Being unable to combat the effects of this phenomenon, we could essentially be creating an environment that is every bit as hostile as "Jim Crow" America and the segregated South was in our history. With the understanding that these are extremes, without changes in the media, there is the plausibility of such a disaster.

African Americans are the casualty of a media war. It perpetuates social stereotypes and ethnic homogeneity. Television continues to promote social stereotypes even in this age of multiculturalism and diversity. The media has too long flourished in a White American world, looking out of it, if at all, through the eyes of White American men and a White American perspective of the world. Studies consistently point to a pattern of news selection and coverage that represents the views and values of the world of journalists.

Through studies of television network news and weekly news magazine coverage, it has been observed that news supports the social order of public, business, professional, upper-middle-class, middle-aged, and White American male sectors of society. These enduring values of this social class ethnocentrism, responsible capitalism and moderate behavior as the values that are propagated through news coverage.

Essentially, what is going on is the entertainment media is portraying a biased view of society. It is not promoting the aims of presenting the public with an objective coverage of the news, or the production of diverse films, instead the bottom line is ratings, clicks on a website and ticket sales. Therefore the objectives of a network or a film studio is to cater to an audience.

This results in a newscast or a film production that is geared toward the White American majority. This leads to the embedded racism that has been found to exist in newscasts and movies across the United States, and around the world.

This same problem occurs in the sitcoms and other shows that fall into the realm of entertainment. The only way to make money in this industry is to ensure that people watch the shows. The critical equation for any segment of this industry is ratings equal earnings. Like the news telecasts, and the movies, these other shows cater toward the majority, at the expense of the African Americans.

The United States is one of the most culturally diverse nations in the world, but the media and entertainment industries tell a different story. While improvements have been made over the last several decades in the way race, ethnicity, gender and other social issues are portrayed in the media, the entertainment industry still has far to go in its attempt to reflect society's changing demographics.

For instance, a study discovered that ethnic minority groups make up a mere sixteen percent of prime time drama casts, even though they represent over twenty five percent of the population. Twenty six percent of major characters in movies are women, although they comprise over fifty percent of the population.

When people of color, women, seniors and other social groups are portrayed, activist groups contend that these images are often stereotypical, inaccurate and not reflective of the individual diversity that exists in real life. African Americans are not only underrepresented on television, but are segregated into specific types of content, and rarely engage in cross-ethnic interactions.

For every "Cosby Show" or "Fresh Prince of Bel Air," there is a "Good Times," "Sanford and Son" or "Cops" to cancel out the positive effect that the show may have. "The Cosby Show" clearly had the effect of broadening the American television public's perception of the African American family and African American economic status.

Shows like "Sanford and Son" and "Good Times" showed a lot of different stereotypes, with Fred Sanford always having crazy schemes and being presented as a lazy Stepin Fetchit type "Nigger" and J.J. from "Good Times" as a cartoony street wise and lazy "jive-talker."

Until we successfully decrease the number of "bad" shows that air for every "good" show, we aren't really making any progress. Television, in the past two decades, has made major gains in terms of casting diversity and the portrayal of African Americans in differing roles. From being scarcely visible in the 1950s to being portrayed as wealthy Attorney's and doctors in the 1990s, television has made great strides and taken steps to change the way it portrays African Americans.

Despite those exceptions to the rules, there still remain numerous shows, movies and newscasts that shine a negative light on African Americans in this country. Unfortunately, we are able to see that the gains are still not all that significant.

It has been found that from the 1950s to the 2000s, African American representation has gradually increased and negative stereotypes have in turn decreased. African Americans have slowly become more likely to be portrayed positively than are White Americans, and the truth and fact is they engage in proportionately less violent and criminal behavior in the real world.

An exception to this general pattern is the newly popular genre of reality based programming, which frequently casts African Americans in criminal roles. Latinos are also less visible in prime time television than they were in the 1950s. Their portrayals have not improved markedly since the days of Jose Jimenez, Ricky Ricardo and the Frito Bandito.

The entertainment industry has always had its focus on making people laugh. They have made little to no changes in how they show African Americans on television. In fact they are showing African Americans in even less respectable roles. This cannot possibly bode well for the future of African Americans in television.

Often African Americans don't do right by themselves, by being more pro-active in the roles that they play on television. African Americans in the television industry should apply themselves more to taking on roles of respectability, and deter from the path of White American expectation, in the roles of drug dealers, rap stars and sports figures.

Producers like Tyler Perry made a choice because of the discrimination he face in Hollywood. This is difficult, because African Americans rarely have this opportunity because of a lack of credibility. Perry used his own money, and in fact his own house to produce his movies. Hollywood was aggravated by this fact, and even more by the fact that Perry has been unbelievable successful

Even though television has made changes, the results have been less than spectacular. The entertainment industry has become a "bottom line" business, run by CEO's who really have no interest in the entertainment factor of the industry. They are only interested in the billions of advertising dollars, and if the people from the top of these networks are not pushing for wholesale changes in the industry, there is probably no chance of controlling this truly uncontrollable industry.

Change must be initiated by the top executives in the industry. Only then can it trickle down to true visibility, and subsequently alter and improve the casting opportunities for African Americans on television. Most people who watch television don't even understand who is in charge of what is aired on television.

At NBC's news division, there are approximately six hundred and fifty employees. But in this department, there are only sixteen African Americans. You are talking about a news division that is responsible for reporting news from around the world, about various cultures of people on this planet, and yet this department, of one of the world most renowned networks is over 96 percent White American?

Because of this fact, it is virtually impossible to get any type of multi-cultural programming on to the network. Television is not much different than White American society as a whole in that just like society, it will cast people and create roles for people, who look like them, in roles that are looked at comfortably and positively.

These are the roles that are mainly casted with White Americans. African Americans of course, mainly get casted in roles that are negative. This is the trend that lends itself to racism in the industry.

The issue of casting African Americans is not where it needs to be, and both the changes and the walls that keep the industry corralled must be torn down, and be viewed clearly. These walls will keep the industry from progressing. We must always ripple the waters of change and wash the evils of racism away, in order for the right thing to come to pass.

Changes will never take place until there is mandated diversity in the industry. There are a few shows that actually show African Americans in positions of legitimate power and regular life. No, you can count shows like "Empire" or "Power" because those do nothing more the play into the stereotypes that are expected in African American society. Yet, the number of programs that place African Americans into inferior roles far out-number the ones presenting a positive image.

Television has rarely been truthful about the society that we live in, and can be a corruption for the young and impressionable minds that follow it. Change is slow, but hopefully the wheels of change will continue to turn.

African Americans have rarely had the opportunity to speak about their own lives in the television and film industry. White America has had complete control over the industry, and has subsequently always chosen the images of African Americans that the public would see.

This has seldom altered, but in the early 1970s, a phenomenon called the "Blaxploitation" film was created. They were directed toward ghetto youth in African American urban areas. They were stressing the movement of "Black Power" which was meant to place them in a mindset to stand up and fight alongside the Civil Rights Movement against racism and the treatment of African Americans in White American society.

Many African American filmmakers often believe that their actions are helping the African American community, by exposing faults and showing them a better way, but because of the large crossover audience of today, they only contribute to the dominant negative stereotypes. African American filmmakers and entertainers must be mindful that the messages of their movies are not lost in these stereotypes.

Many great African American filmmakers have been born as of late. This is happening simultaneously with an increased desire by African Americans for films, that don't portray them in the stereotypical roles that are expected by White America. This new selection of films is more appealing to a broader audience including more progressive thinking White Americans who have become fatigued with the stereotypical violence of African American casted films.

In the comedy entertainment arena, African American comedians today are in a position to change many of these ridiculous stereotypes through the method of humor. African American comedians should make an effort to build bridges between the White American and African American communities through their comedy. The problem is that often their means of connecting White Americans and African Americans only contributes to more negative stereotypes of African Americans.

The most glaring example of this is the comparison between African Americans and "Niggers," which many comedians direct at the White members of his audience. African American comedians often define "Niggers" as those African American people who create problems, not taking care of their children and committing crimes in not only the African American community, but in society as a whole.

While many African American comedians' intentions may be to explain that not all African Americans fit the stereotype of criminal, they only really succeed in strengthening the stereotypes that they are trying to dispel.

Most White Americans understand that not all African Americans are ignorant and violent because almost every White American person knows at least one African American person who is an upstanding citizen, but they still believe that the majority of African Americans fit the stereotypes.

Some African American comedians reject the popular sentiment that the media is to blame for many of the negative stereotypes associated with African American people. Many say that they are not afraid of being robbed by the media, but by "Niggers." Without thinking, by doing this, they themselves become part of the mass media that perpetuates these negative images

If an African American comedian's audience were strictly made up of African Americans, there would be no problem with this type of comedy, because African Americans have an easy time laughing at other African Americans. The vast majority of African American people realize that those African Americans who commit crimes, and thus validate these stereotypes, are of a small number in their community.

Unfortunately many of the White American members of the same audience only know of African American culture through what they see in the media, and some African American comedians. While these talented individuals are trying to eradicate certain stereotypes, they only seem to validate them through their ill-conceived humor.

In contrast this type of humor which often demeans African Americans, other African American comedians use their position as a comedian and entertainer to erase certain stereotypes and expose social problems. There are movies produced and comedic stars that do just that. While these are not exclusively African American movies, they do subtly expose how racism and drug arrests are related to the African American community.

Because the police are constantly suspecting African American men of trafficking drugs, they are already easy villains to the judicial system, that often quickly proceeds to sentencing African American men to prison terms. These are the like of today's headlines. Drug dealers are often easy targets for corrupt police in our society, because they have been villainized as the cause of all crime and problems within society.

The entertainment industry regularly depicts the stereotypical drug dealers of today as young African American, "thugs" who are ready to kill at any moment. Because they are depicted as villains, it is very easy for people to believe them to be killers. These filmmakers are able to make their point without attacking anyone, who can really fight back.

These African Americans therefore serve a social purpose by explaining how innocent people can get in trouble very easily, and by contradicting the images of African Americans, that many members of White America believe to be true. These filmmakers therefore chose a great film to make and be a part of, and they should be commended for doing so.

The "Blaxploitation" films of the 1970s provided the Civil Rights movement with a great foundation for sending its message of change to the world. These films served their social purpose well, and seemed to become obsolete by the early '80s. There have been a few good "Blaxploitation" movies since then, but the ones of the 90s seem to glorify the violence of murderous acts more than they cause awareness of African Americans in today's society.

As much as it is true, African Americans cannot totally blame the entertainment industry for constantly enforcing such a stereotypical image. Especially when the creators of these films are African Americans themselves, whom also claim that this is an accurate portrayal of urban life.

The negative message of these films is that young African American men, who are in criminal circumstances should get out as quickly as possible, in order to prevent becoming like their friends, or getting killed because of them. In other words, "if you lay down with dogs, you will wake up with fleas."

If young African American men do not leave the deadly behavior of all of their friends behind, they will end up as a statistic, attached to so many African American youth. That is either suffering death or ending up in prison.

The problem with this somewhat truthful layout is that the "gangsta" culture has become as popular in the African American community through such media as "gangsta" rap that many of these films of the 1990s had huge crossover audiences. Surprisingly, many of these audiences were composed primarily of young White American kids.

The only true exposure that many of these young White Americans get from African Americans is through these movies and the "gangsta" rap music. Therefore, their view of African American culture and African American people is skewed by these, dare I say it, "horrible" movies.

African American filmmakers and music makers are left with a huge dilemma, then, about how to reach their target audience of inner-city youth without giving credence to stereotypes.

John Singleton, a great African American filmmaker has had a great amount of success in depicting inner-city life in a manner that does not glorify violence or reinforce negative stereotypes. Singleton often depicts the lives of several young men at pivotal points in their lives.

There is always a protagonist in his films. This is a "Theo Huxtable" type kid that has the best family situation of all of the characters in the movie. His parents may even be separated, but his father still plays an active role in his life.

This contradicts the common stereotype that African American fathers are deadbeats, who do not support their children financially or emotionally. The other character in his movies plays the role of the kid who has a real future They earn awards and scholarships through athletics. Both of these characters hopes to escape the dangers of the ghetto, to become successful members of society. This is the scenario of Singleton's epic "Boyz N The Hood."

There is the stereotypical picture of an African American urban youth, who has a criminal history. He plays the role of redeemer through his devotion to his brother and his future. The audience sympathizes with this type of character, because there is nobody who love or cares about him.

While the many characters in movies like this seem to fit certain stereotypes of young African American males as "thugs," which incidentally has become the alternative word of White America, since it is politically incorrect to use the word "Nigger" anymore. They solicit the sympathy of the audience in such a way that the audience cannot hate them.

The villains in the film are those who try to hurt the main characters by almost forcing them to turn to violence as a means of defending themselves and their families. A White American audience can then see that the African American men fear are only a small minority within the total African American community.

African Americans also benefit from this portrayal of urban life because although the athletic character usually dies a heinous death at the hands of other criminals. The Protagonist always makes the right decision, and sticks to the morals, that his parents have instilled in him.

He does not avenge the death of his friend, and he is able to continue with his life instead of ruining his future by committing a criminal act that would land him in prison for the rest of his life. In contrast, the dead characters criminal brother usually carries out the execution of his brothers murders.

Movies such as this empower African American youth, who feel like they are stuck in the same situation. A situation where many of their friends are criminals and they feel like they are being sucked into that same life. There is always one that sets a great example for these young men to follow, because he does not give into the pressure to become a criminal.

Being a great filmmaker, John Singleton makes a successful attempt to portray life in the ghetto accurately. He does this without stereotypes, and shows urban youth how to fight the negative influences that surround them, in order to rise above their circumstances.

As more and more African American entertainers come to the forefront of the American film industry, African American films are becoming more and more popular with White American audiences. It is becoming more important than ever, for African American entertainers to be responsible to the African American community, in the images that they choose to portray.

Even when they think that they are helping to eliminate stereotypes, they must be mindful of the fact that many White Americans might not understand the context, in which their social commentaries are made.

When dealing with race relations in America, they must concentrate their efforts of emphasizing the positive aspects of African American culture and properly identifying African American criminals as the minority within the African American community, while also showing the causes of these social problems.

In order for African Americans to make progress in breaking down stereotypes, they must all work together to ensure that they do not commit the exact same errors in depicting stereotypes as White entertainers do.

Movies, television and the news are all guilty of what most people would consider racist beliefs and acts. Despite the progress that has been made in the industry, three decades of reforms should produce results significantly more substantial than those that we have witnessed.

When movies like "Homeboys from Outer Space" can air on the television, it is apparent that networks are not heeding the objections, cries and protests from African American or White communities. Instead, they are glaring at the "bottom line" which is whether or not the show runs in the financial red or black.

It is extremely difficult to apply pressure to the major networks and film producers, when their shows, newscasts and movies continue to make money. This, of course, can be attributed to the positive portrayal of White Americans and the negative portrayal of African Americans. The White American culture is so large that it can sustain its own market niche, thus enabling the industry to post profits, even without the support of the African American coalition. As in any industry, the bottom line is money.

Although we would like to see quicker and more significant changes and reforms in these industries, one cannot help but think of the fable of "The Tortoise and the Hare." Though the rabbit was speedy and conniving, the slow and steady tortoise eventually proved to be more successful in its endeavors.

Patience is a virtue, and this remains true for the changes that will eventually encompass the entire industry. However, these changes will not be effective if African Americans cannot refrain from perpetuating and utilizing the same stereotypes that our opponents have made us famous for.

African Americans need to take an introspective look at each other and realize that in order to achieve the eventual outcomes they are pursuing, they must not give in to the monetary benefits of producing self-disparaging movies and television shows. Only when African Americans have accomplished this, will the status as second class citizens begin to evaporate.

CHAPTER 7

ECONOMIC RACISM

When African Americans are unemployed, we're called lazy; when White Americans are unemployed it's called a depression.

—*Jesse Jackson*

PEOPLE IN THE United State are under the impression that the disease of racism has been around since the dawn of time, and they would be sadly mistaken in believing that myth. In reality, it was a system that was created in the late 1600s. It started out as a way for White America to come to terms with the reality of enslaving African Americans.

Slavery was the business of the time, and although it has been around for a very long time, several centuries in fact, and although it lasted for this of a long time period, it has differed among various cultures of people.

A fact that various cultures understood, but both White Americans and African Americans don't know is that prior to the early 17th century, African Americans were almost on the same social level as their White American counterparts. They lived their lives in a somewhat guarded harmony. Some African Americans worked as indentured slaves, but had the opportunity to purchase their freedom. After which, they would continue in society as landowners, and yes, many of these former indentured slaves even owned servants of their own.

This however took a turn sometime around the mid-17th century when policies were put in place to confiscate their land by White American landowners. African Americans were eventually labeled as aliens of the lands they were formally in possession of.

Racial inequality and economic disparity have always been brothers of the same mother. To many, there is the belief that slavery is the offspring of racism, and this is simply not accurate. Racism was something that developed as a result of slavery. With regard to United States history, racism has always been seen as a way for White America to keep control of the economic status quo.

African Americans could be bought as property, were discouraged to own property and were racially targeted for toxic loans when trying to do so. Amazingly enough, whether it is believed or not, this economic system is still alive and operating in banks and financial institutions in the United States today.

African Americans have been shafted by the system in ways that are too great to count. The fact that this system has been so embedded in society, has led to decades upon decades of racial injustices that range from discriminatory hiring practices and lower quality of educational opportunities, to illegal housing practices and voting procedures that have once again curtailed the ability for African Americans to have a say in who their legislative leaders are.

African Americans have been, and remain to this day in an unemployment crisis of epic proportionality. The unemployment rate of African Americans have always been twice the level of White Americans, and White America has always failed to admit the association between racism and unemployment for the last half century.

Because of this century old systemic racism disenfranchisement, African Americans have been thrown to the wolves of economic disparity. The difference in wealth disparities between African Americans and White Americans has reach double digits figures. White Americans maintain control of more than thirty times the levels of most African Americans.

Attempting to beat this disparity figure will always be more of a task than African Americans will be able to complete. A total recovery will require a plan that addresses the past racial and economic systems, the current state of the discriminatory system that is currently operating in this country, and must incorporate a plan or a process that includes some type of infrastructure, to address the issues of education, health care and employment.

African Americans should have the opportunity to level the economic playing field, and deserve the opportunity to develop wealth-building strategies.

There is another phenomenon that is a factor in racial disparity. It is known as price discrimination and it is very closely related to economic discrimination. Price discrimination is a scenario where businesses (usually ones that have a monopoly on a product) vary their prices for the commodities and services, and charge consumers based on their willingness to pay.

When we discuss bias and discrimination in the United States, the conversation must always include both price and economic discrimination. In this regard, White Americans are offered higher wages because they do not identify with the negative attributes that some business owners consider uncomfortable.

For example, if an African American person, who is new to the community, or comes from a particular religious or cultural background, would be offered lower pay than the pay offered to White American workers with the same skills. This was a usual practice because the White American worker was favorable to the business owner, meaning that the White American worker was the right age and more than anything else, he was a White American, which is the desirable ethnic background.

An additional phenomenon of economic and price discrimination is directed at the consumer side of business. This is when the business owner offers goods and services based on the neighborhood or surrounding area the business is located in. For example, people always talk about health and wellness. It is a real trend in today's society, but is you look very closely, very rarely do you find any type of health club or fitness facility in the African American community.

Furthermore, when it comes to grocery store chains, you have a different level of various providers. You have the higher end grocery chains that have a high selection of products that are of great quality. This is never the case in the African American community, because African Americans can rarely afford to pay for the higher quality products, because of the unemployment rate and the economic discrimination that exist in these communities.

Insurance companies may be the absolute worse when come to this phenomenon, because they tend to narrow their scope of consumers that fit into the factors that they are looking for in race, age, gender and neighborhood that they live in. Many also assess higher rates based on factors of race, age, or gender. Insurance companies consider the ideal customers are highly likely to pay costs that are considerably higher, than those consumers that the business is looking to trade with.

Businesses also be victims of economic discrimination. In this scenario, the gender, race, and religious preference of the business owner may be a factor in what type of prices the business pays. This means that a business owner who is a member of a minority race and religion in the area, and is not the typical gender for owners of that type of company, may pay more for the same business services offered to owners who are considered more desirable in terms of gender, religion, and above all, race.

In America, there are laws that help to minimize the amount of economic discrimination that occurs. But even with regulations against this type of economic activity, instances do still occur, although they may be more difficult to prove. When an instance of economic discrimination is identified, it should be reported to government authorities immediately.

This is where African Americans feel they have no voice, because in most cases there is no trust, because the person they are reporting to does not look like them. They feel that just because they have on a suit does not mean they are not a racist. That racism has become embedded.

Economic discrimination is fully connected to social discrimination and racism as a whole. We see blatant racism in society everyday but we often overlook institutional racism, which is at least as important as its counterparts. It you do nothing more than focus on the area of poverty, it is clear that African Americans are not close to any type of equality.

Almost one half of African Americans in the United States lives in poverty. One out of every eight African Americans in this country lives in a phenomenon that is referred to as "deep poverty." To put this into simple terms that pretty much everyone can comprehend, one quarter of all people in poverty in the United States are African American.

I did not write this book to point out the various racist systems that exist in this country. These systems have been well recognized, well examined and clearly validate the economic costs of discrimination against African Americans. I wrote this to show the tangled webs of discrimination that exits between opportunities, jobs, our illustrious judicial system and its for-profit prison and penal process.

I wrote it to identify systematic discrimination such as the ghetto tax, and examining the higher costs of goods, taxes, services that increase debt for African Americans, and limit the ability to achieve the "American Dream" of home ownership. I previously wrote about this, trying to give people an understanding of the difference in home values, education, and those government policies that have an underlying policy of discrimination toward African Americans.

It is difficult to evaluate or estimate the average economic cost of this discrimination. The government sends out figures on unemployment but always fails to include all African Americans in those figures? For African American households, racism has had an effect to the tune of over ten thousand dollars of yearly financial cost. Often the cost is even higher.

Often these businesses gain these cost in profits, through the services directly provided to African Americans. Usually by charging higher cost products or underpaying African American workers. Often it is laundered through some of the largest banks that provide money, and benefit from the lower level financial institutions that issue subprime loans, and hold thousands of potential African American home owners as a hostage to this kind of debt.

What White Americans fails to understand is that when economics fail for African Americans, the entire country will inevitably suffer the same loss. Young

African Americans today don't have the enthusiasm that their parents had in the past, and often lack creativity, because their lack of employment opportunities.

When you combine this with the number of African, who have graduated into the for-profit prison process, you can only conclude the obvious, that young African American youth are not reaching their potential, and achieving greatness.

More important than any other factor, White America continues to use both segregation and discrimination to maintain its power and control the economic policies of this country. These policies, which always keep African Americans and other minority groups in an economic box, where the political process will aide in this same down-keeping process.

Because of this shrouded process, we may never be able to come up with an accurate figure, for the amount of profit made buy the mainstream White American capitalist system, which is largely based on racism.

When we talk about both the law enforcement and the judicial system, we have to recognize the reality that there are currently one million African Americans are in the prison system in this country. This is more than the number of African Americans enslaved in 1850. Almost half of all African American men transition through some form of the judicial system before they are fifty years of age.

We have all seen the studies and statistics that tell the same story of young African Americans, especially males, being more likely to be arrested, convicted, and serve time, even when the illegal behavior is less in severity than their White American counterparts.

Of course the most obvious to these facts is witnessed in drug related arrests. The fact is that White Americans, and again, especially White American males are the usual likely users of illegal drugs, and far more likely to use them than African Americans, but this is not something that the mainstream media or White America in general chooses to recognized.

The expense of a family member imprisoned impacts African American families in a much greater way than White Americans. Losing an income because one adult in the household is in prison contributes to the downfall of the family, because of the loss income. In addition, it is virtually impossible to get a good paying job or career if you are a convicted felon, and you can receive no public services such as housing assistance or welfare.

Even is the person who is accused of the crime is found innocent, they still are strapped with the legal fees of attorneys and court cost. The legislative burdens of an ex-felon are extremely harsh, as they no longer have the privilege of casting votes in any election. This is however under reconsideration in many areas of the country, including my home city of St. Louis, Missouri.

The entire effect on the African American community is hard to add up, but once a member of an African American family goes to prison, it has got to end up being hundreds of thousands of dollar in loss.

I touched on this before, but from an insurance standpoint, African Americans who have the same cars as White Americans tend to pay more for car insurance and car taxes in many states, plus they often pay a higher percentage on the car loan itself. African Americans also pay a higher percentage on home mortgages.

Often African Americans do not have checking accounts at financial institutions, so they are forced to pay for check cashing services, and have fewer options than using financing institution such as TitleMax or other title loan places that charge outrageous interest on loans, sometimes as high as four hundred and fifty percent.

African Americans are also regular victims of these rent-to-own (Rent-A-Center) type businesses that coax people in with the idea of paying for furniture or electronics over time, but in the end are charge triple the cost of these goods.

White America tends to blame the inability of African Americans to gain wealth on the belief that "Niggers have no financial discipline." Sometimes this statement is accurate, but they never take into account that these same people must often hold at least two jobs to make ends meet.

This means there is no time to shop around and compare prices for services, and they are often taken advantage of because they have to have it, and many White Americans are fully aware of this fact.

But there is no getting around the fact that African Americans must pay a significantly higher price for goods and services, many of which are comparable, but are often of lower quality.

The idea of owning a home, the "American Dream," means that you have achieved something in life. It brings a feeling of security, and sets an example for other family members, especially if there are children in the home.

Percentages for Home ownership among African Americans is a little over half compared to White Americans, and the reality of this is regardless of income level, African Americans are more likely to acquire their first home loan through a subprime financial institution, than White Americans.

African Americans who are on a low income will pay a higher price when it comes to taxes and home owners insurance, and for the most part White American homeowners see the price of their home increase while they are living in it. White Americans follow the standard plan of retiring and downsizing their lifestyle.

They often purchase a smaller place to live, often in a neighborhood where housing is less expensive. This is plan put in place for their retirement process, because it helps the ultimate goal of being able to leave a nest egg of some type to grandchildren or some other heir. They know that when the worth of their home rises, it will be a factor in accumulating wealth.

Using this same process, and taking into account the economic discrimination that exist in the housing market in this country, African American home owners will likely not see the same appreciation in the value of their home. They will in fact see a moderate decline in their homes value.

President Ronald Reagan's era as leader of this country saw a disappearance in the fight against discrimination. When George Bush (I) was elected President, the EEOC began setting a precedent of disregard patterns, or what was referred to as "unintentional discrimination." That is unless there were complaints by specific individuals, it really didn't get much attention. Many cases that made it to the Supreme Court that involved Affirmative Action often made discrimination legal.

When George W. Bush's (II) was elected, this trend not only continued, but it also became a standard mode of operation. Judges that were placed on the Supreme Court under Bush (II) had less than appropriate rulings. Justice Roberts, who was leftover from the Reagan Administration fought hard to destroy all Civil Rights decisions, and in particular, kill Affirmative Action policies once and for all.

Because of the results of thirty years ago, racial discrimination is alive and well in big business, finance and in the real estate industry today, and nobody is ever called on the carpet to account for any of it.

Fortunately, President Obama's administration pushed ahead and made history with the Affordable Health Care Act. For the first time in history of this country, we have a universal health care plan. Many programs that are available are sometimes implemented in a racist way. This is still the country that we live in. They are intended to rid the country of minorities, and in particular, African Americans. This can be summed up in a single word.

Katrina.

CHAPTER 8

HOUSING DISCRIMINATION AND WHITE FLIGHT

In the twenty-first century, the visions of J.C. Nichols and Walt Disney have come full circle and joined. "Neighborhoods" are increasingly "developments," corporate theme parks. But corporations aren't interested in the messy ebb and flow of humanity. They want stability and predictable rates of return. And although racial discrimination is no longer a stated policy for real estate brokers and developers, racial and social homogeneity are still firmly embedded in America's collective idea of stability; that's what our new landlords are thinking even if they are not saying it.

—Tanner Colby

WHILE OUR NATIONAL story portrays racial

segregation as a closed chapter of an unenlightened past, in reality, segregation continues to characterize the present lives of many African Americans in the United States. Segregation is a key component of contemporary, on-going urban poverty. Housing segregation and economic inequality is an ongoing form of discrimination and continues to keep the country from moving toward true racial equality.

The areas of the country most overtly defined by the segregation, the legacy of slavery, sharecropping, Jim Crow laws, and restrictive housing covenants continue to experience the greatest diversity struggles today.

Racial segregation did not always characterize the cities of the United States in the way it does today. As African Americans began moving north following World War I and II, the local and federal governments began intentionally creating racial segregation, through various public housing projects such as urban renewal, public improvement, and various public housing programs. This caused the stereotypical picture of the urban ghetto to develop.

Local governments began adopting racial segregation policies. White Americans began exiting out of the urban areas and into suburbia in a widespread pattern. This was termed "White flight." Industry quickly followed and began leaving the urban areas in favor of cheap land and tax incentives. Various zoning ordinances, designed to facilitate segregation, separated blocks by race, and restrictive covenants allowed for legally backed racial discrimination and segregation. St. Louis, Missouri was a perfect example of this process. Urban decay and "ghettoization" are the clear result of deliberate and discriminatory housing policies of every level of governments.

Our government gave birth to policies and procedures to keep racial discrimination and segregation in place. Since the beginning of its existence, the Federal Housing Administration (FHA) has done nothing but keep discrimination in place, just like a wall around all White neighbourhoods.

They created a housing practice called "redlining", which was created to move mortgage funds and home financing away from African Americans in suburban neighborhoods. White Americans who lived "all-White" neighborhoods were the major beneficiaries of the redlining process.

Even today, The Department of Housing and Urban Development (HUD) has kept these racist programs and policies in place. This is the reason that there are so many visually segregated communities in the United States. But all is not lost.

The judicial system has in fact found many of the HUD policies discriminatory and overtly racist, especially in the area of low income or Section 8 housing procedures. Judicial legislation has passed to prevent such discrimination, but the fact is this legislation has not held the water that it was expected to, and has failed horribly.

Today, African American and White American inequality remains a lingering social problem in the United States. This is partly reflected in the housing policy arena. Several explanations for ongoing segregation have been ranging from persistent economic disparities, to race specific housing preferences and programs.

The most convincing evidence points to the prevalence of discrimination in selected housing markets. It's less overt and harder to identify, but housing discrimination by sellers, landlords and housing agents continues to still be deeply embedded in the United States.

Many reports find that in major cities across the country, African Americans still face greater struggles to find a place to live, compared to equally qualified White Americans. Home buyers, and those seeking adequate housing in this country are still dealing with unscrupulous housing agents, who will look for exceptions in the laws to keep neighborhoods segregated, even with the Fair Housing Act and the Housing and Community Development Act is in place.

The laws were created to stop unfair housing practices, but in reality all they did was force the same unscrupulous agents and sellers to create new ways to discriminate and segregate against certain races, ethnicities and cultures, by using processes like showing buyers fewer properties.

The various levels of discrimination that occur in this could be universal, but the methods of operational discrimination will differentiate between cities. A factor in this determination is the size of the individual city, and the African American ratio of the population in those respective cities.

There have been studies done on the cities of Atlanta, Chicago, Detroit, St. Louis and a number of other major cities that have found that African Americans, who wish to rent a home or apartment are often presented with month-to-month leases only, while their White American counterparts are offered long-term leases of up to two years or more.

African Americans are often not even supplied with the information to move in such as fee requirements or even the price of a deposit, where White Americans are always told what fees are required at move-in.

African Americans almost always have background checks done, while again, their White counterparts were likely to receive a positive remark, without the background check. This puts White Americans in a position to receive the follow-up phone call from the agent.

Although we've come a long way from the days of blatant, in-your-face housing injustice, discrimination still persists, and just because it has taken on a hidden form doesn't make it any less harmful.

How does one make sense of high and persistent segregation levels, even forty years after passage of the Fair Housing Act? The most compelling evidence, derived from historical case analyses of residential turnover and contemporary audit designs, points to discrimination.

Indeed, and historically speaking, organized resistance has often been shaped by homeowner's associations, tenants' councils, and parent-teacher groups, as well as city coder enforcement agencies, real estate companies, and public school officials.

I briefly spoke about "White Flight" earlier, but I wanted to dive into it again. This phenomenon of upper and middle class White Americans moving out of cities and into the suburbs is known as "White Flight. The opposite of White flight is "gentrification." This is a process in which wealthy White Americans move back into an urban area, displacing the current residents and rapidly drive up the cost of living, so that the previous residents are forced to move.

Both practices have been extensively documented by the education of demographics and urban development. White flight, in particular, has negative connotations, especially for those left behind in the suddenly impoverished neighborhood.

White flight began on a large scale after World War II, when African Americans began to try to establish homes in America's cities. Many of these men and women were starting to enter the middle class themselves, with good jobs, education, and community values. In many cases, however, racism led White Americans to attempt to force African Americans out.

When this proved unsuccessful, the White population moved to the suburbs, establishing new and primarily racially homogeneous communities. This practice was termed "White flight," and resulted in class and racial segregation in pretty much every American city.

A number of factors have contributed to White flight. The first is racism itself. This has affected African Americans, but is especially true with the growing numbers of immigrants from other countries, such as Latin American and Asian nations.

Some White Americans may have a perception that crime rates are higher in neighborhoods with a high concentration of African Americans, which may or may not be true, but many are simply racist. In either case, they move.

"Blockbusting" was another real estate practice that added to the epidemic of White Flight in areas.

This practice continues to be relevant in regions of the country. Blockbusting refers to just what it means. It is the sale of a property in a primarily White neighborhood, to an African American family, which is facilitated by a realtor or simply "breaking up the block."

White America has a strong tendency to react out of fear when it comes to dealing with African Americans. White Flight comes after the "Blockbusting" process is initiated. The process is pretty simple. When a White American community learns of the sale of a home in said community, they all begin to "freak out" and fall into the belief that their home property values are going to plummet.

With this in motion, White home owners begin to furiously sell their property and move to another suburban area, all while the real estate companies make out like unethical bastards because of the ridiculous profit they make on this process.

Many secret policies, including restrictive covenants that were created to keep neighborhoods racially segregated, have contaminated American society. Many of these covenants treaded on a thin line between discrimination and full board segregation are perfectly legal in action and continue to be put in process today.

These practices continue to be illegal in the United States. They are prosecuted only when proof that it is occurring is supplied.

My home city of St. Louis could not escape the virus of White flight that has infected nearly every major city in the country. Wealthy families who had unsubstantiated fear of African Americans chose to stop with the support that these communities needed to survive, and instead left them to fail with African Americans living there.

They didn't fail because of African Americans. The failed because in a racist society, you cannot ask one race to operate a community, and not provide them the tools to operate it adequately, which is what happens with White Flight.

When White Americans flew out of these areas and removed their support, they did nothing more that widen the canyon between the haves and the have-nots. In addition, it all but silenced the ability to have a healthy cultural exchange between the races.

Racism has always had a hand in the never-ending segregation of minority communities to the most undesirable corners of society. For instance, on the surface, Ferguson, Missouri, is like any other suburban township on the outskirts of a struggling major metropolis. It has its fair share of poverty, an educational system, of which I am a product, that on the verge of losing accreditation, a high level of unemployment and a law enforcement system that has transitioned from a war on poverty, to a war on poor people.

St. Louis has always appeared to be stuck in the past. It is a place that gives the impression of a cosmopolitan region, when truly its older residents would be very happy if life never changed.

The embedded discrimination of the "Gateway City" is not something that died after the Civil Rights movement simmered. It has in fact continued under a shroud of secrecy and has grown expeditiously over the past thirty years. Today, St. Louis continues to enlist the restrictive covenants that were customary of the mid-century. These covenants were put in place for one reason, to protect White Americans and their White American neighborhoods by preventing the real estate advancement of African American.

These roadblocks made it virtually unthinkable for African Americans to move into prestigious White American areas around St. Louis.

As African Americans have begun to escape these covenants, White families have made an exodus that can only be compared to Moses leading slaves out of Egypt. White families really didn't care where they went, just as long as they didn't have to see any people of color, especially African Americans, or as they regularly referred, "fucking Niggers."

The rate of White Flight increased dramatically, and as African American populations rose in communities like Ferguson, Berkeley and Normandy, the White population declined at an equal, and actually, a more accelerated rate.

They moved to the West, to a small area across the Blanchett Bridge called St. Charles County. They were able to re-establish their discriminatory "redlining" policies like requiring a large lot and putting bans on apartment type housing, except in the "Nigger area." It was clear that as much progress as the United States was making as a whole in transitioning away from the era of segregation, St. Louis not only didn't keep up, it seemingly increased its ways to continue its discriminatory methods.

When we talk about a demographic transition, nothing exemplifies the term like my home area of Ferguson, MO. In 1980, over three quarters of the population of Ferguson, Missouri was White American, while less than one quarter of the community was African American. But, over the course of the next three decades Ferguson silently witnessed an astronomical shift in the demographics of this small suburban township, when the population shifted to where one third of the population was now White American, while two thirds was African American.

As is popular in many cultures, the African American culture is a proud one. St. Louis, like many populated cities, has communities of various nationalities. Often these communities make a conscious choice to segregate themselves. St. Louis has this also, but in a different way. In St. Louis, this is not community segregation, but often not by choice. There has always been a shrouded undertone that forces cultures to live in certain areas of the city. I always joke that I live in South St. Louis now as an adult. I laugh because as I was growing up, it was not a place where African Americans were welcome after dark.

The old saying was "Nigger, don't let the sun set on your ass in South City." It was an area of Italian and German immigrants, who had no use for African Americans or any other culture of color.

Like most areas of the city, when the economic success became critical to success of any community, rather than accepting and embracing African Americans moving in to these communities, White American residents, out or fear and hatred made the decision to break camp, intentionally alienating and abandoning not only these selected communities, and the newly transitioned African American residents, and with their exodus followed slow disintegration in many communities, Ferguson only being one.

CHAPTER 9

EDUCATION: SEPARATE AND NOT CLOSE TO EQUAL

The function of education is to teach one to think intensively and to think critically. Intelligence plus character—that is the goal of true education.

—*Dr. Martin Luther King Jr.*

WHEN DISCUSSING PUBLIC education in America it is quite difficult to find a starting point from which to address the deepening valley of the racially based inequities in America. The United States has painstakingly embedded racism and White supremacy into the very fabric of the educational process, through the fictional teaching of the keys to our children's future.

The legacies of American institutional racism and White supremacy are embedded within the public educational system. Racism in the public school system is, at times both conspicuous and inconspicuous.

Why don't we just say this? Racism in the United States is "conspicuously inconspicuous." It is much like carbon monoxide. It is a silent killer that attacks you without knowing, and before you know it, you have been killed. Worse is institutional racism. This form kills people physically. You see this form in cases of police brutality or in the public education system. It should be compared to having your head cut off as it has been referred to as "cognitive decapitation."

Even with the "victory" of the Brown v. the Board of Education case of 1954, there has remained two sets of educational standards in the United States. Many are in belief that desegregation cleansed the African American community of the infestation of racism and White supremacy in this country, but that simply is not accurate. Integration only truly works when the person integrating is allowed the same rights, respect, and overall privileges as the integrator.

Now, more than fifty years after this epic Supreme Court decision, desegregation has come to simply mean that African American students must adopt to the White-centric values of White America. A half a century later, we are still looking at virtually the same racially and culturally segregated schools as we saw in the 1950s and 1960s.

Low and disparate educational standards are the rule in present day America. This is broken down in a way that most people can clearly understand, by ways of both race and income. The unequal concerns are more race-based than it is based on class. Even the African Americans, who are considered to have "made it" that reside in predominantly White communities, are strongly persuaded to be educated on White supremacists, slaveholders, and murderers like George Washington. Called the "Father of our Country," Washington owned over three hundred African slaves.

Likewise, Andrew Jackson was documented for the murder of countless of Seminoles Indians. Finally, Christopher Columbus, who every young student has been told discovered America, murdered tens of thousands of indigenous people of the Western Hemisphere.

The myth that Columbus discovered a country is one of the biggest lies in history, comparing it to the Warren Report's account of the killing of President Kennedy in 1963. It is a myth because, first, Columbus did not land in the Colonies. He landed in the West Indies, and second, you cannot be first to discover a land WHERE THERE ARE PEOPLE ALREADY LIVING.

African American students are repeatedly force-fed lies about White American historical figures that White American has chosen to put on pedestals, full well knowing that these figures committed some of the most heinous crimes known to man against enslaved Africans and indigenous people. This was nothing more than clear and unfettered White supremacy.

Even though it has been tried, even the upper echelon of the African American students, from more affluent families are educated to believe they need to "drink the cool-aid" from a White American system that has committed every moral crime against society, all for the purpose of control over that same society. A society that has a purpose of oppression that has been successful over millions of African Americans.

African American students at the University of Missouri-Columbia decided to take a stand against this oppression in the fall of 2014. Jonathan Butler, an African American graduate student at the University decided to go on a hunger strike in protest of what he referred to as an "oppressive atmosphere" on the campus. This led to an outpouring of support from a large number of students, both African American and White American, including 32 member of the football team. Ultimately, this led to both the President and the Chancellor of the system stepping down from their post.

Many in White American have also been in a mythical belief that there is no such thing as privilege. This has never been more obvious that in academic society. This privilege has created a double standard that requires African American students to work three times harder, in able to achieve half of the opportunities White American students simply get because of privilege.

White America would have African American students not believe this, but it is in fact a very true statement. African Americans students should realize that just because it is true does not mean it is something that African Americans should accept.

Imagine what it would be like if African Americans had the ability to control the societal conversation, and dictate to White America with regularity that you should have no consideration for real and factual events, either past and present, about society when you evaluate the overall performance of White America. That would never happen. But this same White America has the nerve to question the performance of the first African American President of the United States, as if he does not know the complexity of the country's racial problem.

I will however admit that President Obama often reverts back to his professor days and feels the need to lecture African Americans on what they can and cannot take issue with. In his book, he states that institutional racism is sometimes an "excuse" of the moment.

I, like the President, agree that we have got to say to our children that yes, there are serious issues. If you're African American in this country, the odds of growing up surrounded by crime and gangs is likely. If African American kids live in a poor neighborhood, they will face challenges that most kids in a wealthy suburb will never have to face, but that is not a reason to get bad grades and purposely underachieve. That is also not a reason to not go to school at all.

No one has a plan for the young people except God himself. Their destiny is in their own hands and that must be instilled in them. As the African American community continues to make progress, it must set its own standards. My mother stressed one thing with me. It was very simple; "No excuses. No excuses." African Americans must get an education, and become even more resilient, because all those hardships have made African Americans stronger and better able to compete.

Complaining and refusing to accept institutional racism in America's public school system is just an indicator of African American people making strides to improve the system as a whole. African American people from inner cities should always reject the lack of educational funding for their schools and get educated on the inadequacy of property taxes. African American parents should deny the streamlining of their children into shop classes, instead of advanced placement courses.

African American parents should buck the very real "school to prison pipeline" that has been created by White America for African American youth. It is a system so nefarious that several states base the building of juvenile detention centers and prisons on deficiencies in first grade reading scores.

This means that instead of using state and federal money to invest in programs that bring grade school kids up to proper levels in reading, they use the money to build prisons for them knowing that illiteracy is a major indicator of someone's future in "crime."

African American parents should be vocal, worry about, and fight against the fact that school administrators throughout this country are allowing their schools to be privatized.

I use to wonder what my mother meant when she said, "No excuses. No excuses." White Americans would never try to feed that kind of crap to the White community. Even President Obama knows his limits on both sides of the racial spectrum. On the one hand he knows not to upset White America by publicly pointing to America's legacy as a bastion of racism and White supremacy.

And on the other hand he knows there are virtually no restrictions on how often he can castigate, vilify, and reprimand the African American community, as if African Americans are a group of children that need to know and accept their proper place in society.

When President Obama said, "If you get that education, all those hardships will just make you better able to compete." He was pretty much telling the African American community that we need to sit down, shut the hell up, and accept the institutionally racist and White supremacist country we live in. When he proclaims that our "hardships make us stronger" he is demanding that we acclimate ourselves to occupying an unnatural position at the bottom of society.

African Americans have always overcome tremendous odds in America, but that does not mean that we should stop fighting, organizing, and protesting until we are given the same human rights that White Americans have in this country.

President Obama often placates and appeases White America each time he scolds African Americans for being the victims of the American nightmare. He often blames the victims and not the institution that inflict upon the African American community. He, like most Presidents, speaks in a masterful code.

He often ignores the fact that masses of African American youth are presently having their destinies shaped for them from one institutionally racist classroom to the next. For each African American child that works three times as hard as some privileged White American kid in the suburb in order to succeed, there are scores of African American youth who are eaten alive by an institutionally White supremacist system.

If there is one thing we know, it is that educational and institutional racism cannot be fought in a passive way. African American people must organize, show civil disobedience and they must protest. They must never ever remain silent. They must never stop until every institutionally racist fiber of this system is shredded.

Today, discipline in school is a major factor, not like when I was growing up. Corporal punishment was in full effect during my early education days, but somehow through the legislative process, it slowly dissipated from the systems of the United States. I am a firm believer that if we had real discipline in schools instead of the phenomenon of "time out," society as a whole would not be in the shape it is in.

You would not have young men walking around with pants sagging off of their ass, girls looking like five dollar prostitutes and the crippling of the English language where you expect the next word out of a young person's mouth to be "you know what I'm saying."

But even discipline in the educational system is discriminated, and the fact is African American students receive punishment more than their White American peers, and in fact fewer White American students are suspended annually, compared with African American students.

In 1954 separate but equal was ruled unconstitutional, yet it is shown that African American students are frequently strapped with teachers who have less than five years' experience, and many are restricted to institutions containing the most new teachers fresh out of college. Often African American students, because of economics are forced to attend schools where teachers fail to meet license requirements, or the school itself is facing state take over because of accreditation issues. That is happening in the St. Louis city schools and in the districts of Normandy and Riverview Gardens at the writing of this book.

If White America does not understand the dropout rate of African Americans, they should look no farther these facts. Research also shows that many of the efforts of trying to ensure equal educational opportunities through both legislative and political avenues has done nothing more than fall short on a regular basis. This is obvious in the educational canyons between the haves and the have-nots.

The United States has a long way to go in building a bridge between these canyons, and honestly provide equal opportunities for every student to succeed.

So let's sum this up. African American students get less than their fair share of real access to the in-school factors that matter for achievement. Students of color get less access to high level courses. African American students, in particular, get less instructional time because they're far more likely to receive out of school suspensions or expulsions. And African American students get less access to teachers who've had at least a year on the job, and who have at least a basic certification. Of course, it's not enough to just shine a light on the problem. We have to fix it.

Though a small percentage of America's public school students are African American, they represent more than one third of students referred by schools to law enforcement, and more than one third of students arrested for an offense committed in school.

Figures such as these should likely add pressure to destroy the school-to-prison pipeline, which has served up many troubled students to the hungry and White profitable judicial/prison system.

These disparities begin as early as preschool. African American students make up less than twenty percent of the total preschool enrollment, but somehow over half of these same children receive more than one suspension out of school. White American students, represent nearly half of preschool children, but mysteriously are only leveled with about a quarter of the out-of-school suspensions more than one time.

Despite a recent report calling for measures to remedy discrimination, little has been done. It is shameful that not a single recommendation has been put into motion by the federal government. If it walks like a duck and quacks like a duck, then it's probably a duck. We don't need any more information to help us realize we need action.

Public education in the United States has been in turmoil for the last fifty years, and it has never been any secret that White America often chooses to play the part of the ostrich, and stick their heads in the sand on this issue.

Racial discrimination against African Americans has been a long-standing issue in the United States. Interested educators, the mainstream media, and even President Obama's administration has been able to draw this conclusion. The educational system of the United States has long been plagued by declining test scores, graduates who can't read or cipher, high dropout rates, violence, cheating and teacher sex scandals, and little to nothing has been done to substantively address those issues.

Instead, attention has lately been focused on the scourge of bullying, which has existed for as long as there have been kids, and on the phenomenon of unruly and disruptive students being disciplined for being African American.

CHAPTER 10

LAW ENFORCEMENT, DWB'S AND RACIAL PROFILING

Violence and racism are bad. Whenever they occur they are to be condemned and we should not turn a blind eye to them.

—Cate Blanchett

AFRICAN AMERICANS HAVE been the victim of stereotypes more than any culture in society. Because of this, it has put law enforcement in the United States on high alert, and the results are an alarming and disproportionate number of African Americans, especially males, being unlawfully stopped, searched, harassed and unfortunately, murdered.

It is because of these same stereotypes, that White America makes the same assumptions thousands of law enforcement officials make every day. It is the assumption that African American males are probably engaged in some type of criminal activity, with the number one of these assumptions being the dealing and trafficking of drugs.

This assumption has been validated by and has gained the support of law enforcement officers across the United States. It gained steam in the 1990s when State Highway Troopers from coast to coast defended the discriminatory tactic of racial profiling. Their reasons were very simple. They made a public conviction of stating that mostly minorities, African Americans in particular, engaged in the trafficking of marijuana and cocaine.

Well, common sense, which is not all that common, would tell me that if all you were looking for were African Americans trafficking and dealing drugs, then that is exactly what you will find: African Americans trafficking and dealing drugs. In other words, if that is ALL you are looking for, then that's ALL you will find.

This thought process then becomes an epidemic, spreading from one town, city, county, and state to another because the information from one area is both passed, and relied upon by another area to give justification for the racial profiling of African American males. In other words, this type of discrimination is perpetuated.

The hip-hop culture has changed the way both African Americans and White Americans look at the world. It has changed the way the youth of this country appear, talk, walk, and dress. For African American men, this has only heightened the negative stereotypes that White America has placed on them. In addition to that fact, African American males are, to this day, still harassed when walking or driving through the predominantly White American neighborhoods of this country.

I myself, am a professional man in my fifties, and I have been pulled out of my car, and placed on the ground while wearing a suit and tie, with the only reason being that "we have had a series of break-ins in the area."

An African American man driving a nice luxury automobile or, better yet, an expensive sports car is a magnet for law enforcement to stop. This happens mainly because of the stereotype that "if an African American man is driving something that nice, he must be slingin' drugs for somebody." It does not take a rocket scientist to figure out that law enforcement officials assume that every African American male is a threat to them and to society.

Discrimination such as this is not new, but White America has refused to show real empathy toward real problems. Such was the case in Ferguson, Missouri, where the city government and the police department were targeting minorities for traffic stops, especially African Americans, to pad the coffers of the city's revenue fund.

The fines would build up between the various communities, because the legal characters (the judge and prosecuting attorney) were all interchangeable. That means that the judge in one community was also the prosecuting attorney in the neighboring community.

And if you don't believe that these fines that multiply expeditiously don't play a factor in the type of sentence they receive for some other crimes, you are sticking your head in the sand too, because those traffic violations are always considered in the penalty phase.

How the city of Ferguson, and a number of the surrounding municipalities of St. Louis avoided a RICO Act charge (organized racketeering), when this was brought to light by the Department of Justice is completely beyond me.

What's most unfortunate about these unlawful and unreasonable traffic stops is that if they didn't happen, then the number of African American males being killed, and yes, in some cases, murdered by law enforcement, would be significantly lowered because they do have an identifiable correlation.

Nearly half a century ago, the United States Supreme Court placed limitations on the ability of law enforcement officers to stop and search people for no reason. "Reasonable suspicion" must mean something more than a hunch. The Supreme Court also stated that the conduct of law enforcement could not be based on ridiculous stereotypes.

For instance, just because an African American kid is wearing a hoodie sweatshirt, it does not mean that he is a drug dealer. Such assumptions are discriminatory in nature, and are a violation of the Fourth Amendment of the Constitution.

Even though these rules and laws are part of the judicial process and have been upheld in courts across the land, law enforcement officers in the United States regularly invoke racial profiling methods, when determining whether to detain African Americans.

African Americans who are detained by law enforcement, for whatever reason the officer can conjure up, have on more than a number of occasions claimed that the police trample on the Fourth Amendment of the Constitution. When this happens, it means that any evidence that is acquired during this illegal stop must be thrown out.

The problem is that often the standard for illegal searches does not require that the investigating officers have probable cause. They are only required to have "reasonable suspicion." Because of this loophole, the judicial process often consists of the courts regularly denying the suppression of this evidence.

This type of racial profiling can also be a most humiliating—and because of the high-profile events of 2014, beginning with the killing of Michael Brown Jr., a frightening experience for African Americans, especially for African American men who believe that any of these encounters could result in death.

The Supreme Court has also stated that often there are innocent victims, that will be at times subjected to such stops by police officers, and suggested that at times African American are entitled to a good explanation and an apology, but they have also set a precedent by allowing these instances to happen without penalty to these law enforcement agencies.

The Supreme Court often fails to recognize that too often the innocent victims, who are being stopped and humiliated by law enforcement officers, are African American males.

The Supreme Court has acknowledged that in the United States, all people have a right to be free from the terrifying and humiliating experience of being pulled from their cars, often with a firearm pointed at them. African Americans are handcuffed under the pretence of safety for both the detainee and the officer. They are then forced to lie face down on the street. I personally have witnessed this, as I was a victim of this type of treatment, in a five-hundred-dollar suit no doubt.

African-American men are treated this way by many (not all) White police officers every day, and I can assure you the police officers, and the agencies they work for go through the motions every day of "trimming a little fat" off of the constitutional rights of African American citizens.

There have been enough shootings and killing of young African American men brought to national attention, that there should be an easy recognition of law enforcement agencies' practice of stopping African Americans, particularly African American males, without probably cause or reasonable suspicion that they are engaged in criminal activity.

A number of studies support the conclusion, that the race and color of the driver has been the basis for state law enforcement officers to stop and search cars, driven by African Americans, particularly African American males. One of the most comprehensive and widely circulated studies on racial profiling was conducted in 2013 to determine whether state police officers, nationwide, engaged in racial profiling.

The study concluded that minorities were disproportionately stopped and treated differently than White American motorists. Officials of the United

States Department of Justice ultimately signed a consent decree to prohibit and prevent racial profiling.

African Americans represented over 70 percent of the individuals stopped by the police, even though African Americans make up only about seventeen percent of motorists. A similar individual study of traffic stops in Missouri also revealed that African Americans were disproportionately stopped and searched.

Lastly, in parts of certain states like Oklahoma, African Americans are disproportionately stopped and convicted of traffic violations. Similar studies of city law enforcement officials, find that minorities are also disproportionately stopped. African Americans are twice as likely as White American drivers to receive a traffic ticket.

These incidents support the real feelings of African Americans that their encounters with law enforcement have not occurred by happenstance, but instead, they were targeted, because of their skin and their gender. Police officers may say they have a legitimate reason, but more often than not, it appears that those reasons are based on discrimination.

Here is an example. An officer can use a car seat belt law as a reason to stop African Americans, because there is a belief that African Americans do not use seat belts to the extent White American motorists do. Law Enforcement often also uses bullshit like this to justify very bad behavior. Incidents of racial profiling of African Americans have inundated the social fabric of the country.

Ironically, there is evidence that the use of racial profiling is also used by White police officers to stop African American male police officers who are off duty. There is also evidence that African American male officers, who refuse to engage in racial profiling may also face reprisal, including termination. Even more troubling is that there is evidence that the White officers pretend they don't know the African American male officer, even though they may have worked together as partners.

After reviewing a series of Fourth Amendment cases, the Supreme Court found these cases foreclosed any argument that the constitutional reasonableness of traffic stops depends on the actual motivations of the individual officers involved.

They agreed with petitioners that the Constitution prohibited selective enforcement of the law based on considerations such as race, but the constitutional basis for objecting to intentionally discriminatory application of laws is the Equal Protection Clause, not the Fourth Amendment. They made clear that "subjective intentions play no role in ordinary, probable-cause Fourth Amendment analysis."

The Supreme Court, in random cases, has made it legitimate for police and other law enforcement officers to pull over motorists, most of them African American, for minor traffic violations, and then place them under arrest, only to be charged with a major crime later in the process. This was allowed even though the motorist had never committed a crime, that would have allowed the officer to pull them over in the first place.

The Court often looks past the fact that the officer could have had an ulterior motivating factor, like race, when he or she made the stop in the first place. Most people realized this, but White America sticks their heads in the sand about the true reason, because it is usually based on a stereotype of African Americans, and in particular African American men, being involved in illegal drug activities.

African American drivers in the United States have all accepted the reality of being stopped by law enforcement, and getting their vehicles searched for drugs or firearms. It is as second nature as taking the drivers examination. In fact, it should be required reading prior to taking the test, that this is going to happen.

I realize this is wishful thinking or even my own delusion of grandeur, but my hope is that law enforcement agencies will eventually get past the belief, that if they see African Americans driving down the road, they must be carrying drugs, and then come to the conclusion that they must be pulled over and detained. This is humiliating at the least, and the behavior that follows is even worse.

African American males who are stopped based on reasonable suspicion of a traffic violation are often lined up along the highway, assaulted, humiliated, and searched without probable cause. Such actions should undoubtedly be considered a violation of their Fourth Amendment rights.

Furthermore, if the law enforcement officer detains the motorist longer than necessary to determine whether a traffic violation has occurred, or searches the car without consent or probable cause, the Fourth Amendment may be violated.

Unfortunately, the new Supreme Court decisions are compared with the Supreme Court's decision in the historical Dred Scott case, which was tried in St. Louis' Old Courthouse. The Dred Scott decision resulted in African Americans being denied their constitutional rights as citizens. Even though the cases of today are more than a hundred years apart, the impact of today's cases on African American men may be the same as Dred Scott. In the Scott case, the judge stated that an African American man had no rights which the White man was required to respect.

The United States Supreme Court decisions of today often raise questions of whether African American men have certain constitutional rights.

African American males continue to be victims of racial profiling, even with new safeguards developed by state and federal law enforcement organizations. This selective enforcement is based on stereotypical biases directed at African Americans by law enforcement officials. Further remedies are needed to prohibit and punish law enforcement officers engaging in such discriminatory conduct.

Unfortunately, African American people in general lack the political clout to force Congress, and other governmental officials to respond in a meaningful manner, to prohibit the racial profiling of African Americans and other minorities. Moreover, the courts have failed to safeguard their constitutional rights to travel without fear of being stopped, searched, and arrested by law enforcement officials on the basis of their race and gender.

George Zimmerman did not stalk Trayvon Martin because he looked "suspicious." He stalked, pursued and killed this innocent young man because George Zimmerman is a racist without any question. He laid in wait and found a young African American man wearing a hoodie, and made a conscious decision that this "Nigger Kid" had to be up to something. He had that feeling because that is the way that society portrays young African American men. George Zimmerman conducted what I call "vigilante justice" and without reasonable evidence that this young man had committed any crime whatsoever.

This is not a rare occurrence, but more of a daily, and in some areas, hourly repetition in the United States. Vigilante justice is a regular occurrence, and most people turn a blind eye to it, because the people who are carrying out this type of justice have guns and badges, and the public assumes that it is perfectly legal because of the uniform. These detainment policies give police officers full permission to follow the same mind-set as George Zimmerman, and target African American men.

It is clear that the judicial system that operates in the United States has serious ethical problems and victimizes African Americans at a far greater rate than White Americans. It begins with local law enforcement officers, targeting African Americans with undue traffic violations that lead to exorbitant fines. These fines escalate because of the inability to pay them, and they are automatically processed into a system, that has all the players of the judicial system, including prosecutors, judges, and politicians.

The evidence of the victimization of African Americans is so outlandish that people would assume some laws are being broken at some point. The fact is, this system is so deeply embedded that it would be more realistic to believe that it was a standard law practice, and never subject to question. White America and the judicial system that it controls have virtually created "The New Jim Crow."

Racism has become the very fabric that continues to move the United States economy forward, because it is a way of keeping one class of Americans subjugated to another. The new Civil Rights Movement that has arisen in the wake of Trayvon Martin's murder by George Zimmerman forces society to answer serious questions, about the true fabric of freedom White America is always flag-waving about.

George Zimmerman made the accusation that Trayvon Martin was physically assaulting him prior to him pulling his gun and shooting Martin. This was proven to be a blatant lie during the trial, and it still had no effect on the outcome. I have often asked many in White America, what would happen if an African American kid made the accusation that a subdivision security guard attacked him for no earthly reason, and the kid made the decision to defend himself. Florida has the "Stand Your Ground" law, which has been tested several times as of late. In this scenario, could the kid make the argument that he felt "threatened" as so many officers have, which would then legitimize his actions based on the law?

George Zimmerman acted not unlike law enforcement officers all over the United States. Law enforcement officers behave this way every single day, and then hide behind or, as we have seen, manipulate the law to fit the circumstances. There are hundreds of occurrences that will support this fact.

When an arrest transitions to the judicial process, African Americans are completely behind the eight ball of the system and are likely to be strapped with a felony charge. Their legal assistance is limited often, because they have no means of securing an experienced defense attorney, and are usually saddled with your basic public defender, whose only aim is to plead the case and get a lower sentence, as opposed to fighting for the truth and defending the client. This excludes African Americans from jury trials and true due process, which will undoubtedly lead to a longer sentence.

Often, the judicial system gets a full circumvent, and due process is fully denied. The killing of Michael Brown Jr. in Ferguson, Missouri, is a perfect example of this, where a police officer became judge, jury, and executioner.

When law enforcement officials, who have sworn to serve and protect the very citizens that they then harass, brutalize, and in some cases murder, can then dodge the judicial process of prosecution, because of that same judicial process, why would anyone be surprised that the Darren Wilsons and the George Zimmermans of the world would never be truly held accountable, for their brutal actions against two young African American men? This is the United States, which is almost funny, because this country is far from being "united."

I have been speaking of African Americans as if they are the only victims of racist laws. Because of the United States government's ridiculous "war on terror," Arabs and Muslims have also been affected by racial prejudice and discrimination at an alarming rate. Laws infringing on civil liberties, that once would have been considered unconstitutional by mainstream political opinions, are now supported by Democratic and Republican politicians alike.

When you look at this overall picture of the real United States, it is hard to hide the truth. "United States" is a major play on words. It is kind of like "military intelligence" as there really is no intelligence for going to war. The society of the country is embedded with a White American way of life, that is, at the very least, racist and discriminatory.

The power players in business and politics bank on the fact that society has a natural and embedded suspicion and distrust of each other. These same power players and institutions (financial, economic, educational, etc.) rely on the fact that racism will always continue, and they encourage it through the media (e.g., Fox News). This will take society's eyes off the real perpetrators of real crime in our country, those money managers (Bernie Maddoff types) that steal and mismanage finances of hardworking people.

And as conservative people in this country are screaming, "Buy American," they should realize that Mexico, Asia, or China are not putting them out of work, but even more so, corporate America is putting Americans on the unemployment line by busting unions, killing factory work, and shipping those jobs overseas for one reason, and one reason only: to be sure that extremely high profits, corporate bonuses, jets, and yachts are still on the menu for the CEO.

The worldwide cry, in reaction to the racially profiled murders of Trayvon Martin, Michael Brown Jr., or Eric Garner, and the huge demonstrations against racism that followed, have proven that there is another route that society can travel. Instead of being suspicious and scared of each other, we can try coming together.

The 1995 O.J. Simpson trial was heralded as the "trial of the century." A moniker that reflected the sensationalism and hype surrounding the legal drama. It is the story of an African American football star, accused of killing his White ex-wife and her companion. This legal spectacle included two high-profile legal teams, and an attentive worldwide viewing audience. Indeed, the Simpson trial elicited all the suspense of a Hollywood murder mystery.

When a nearly all African American jury acquitted Simpson, the drama of the story intensified as White Americans and African Americans, who were divided sharply along racial lines responded to the verdict. According to surveys of the times, almost eight out of ten African Americans interviewed said they agreed with the decision, including over two-thirds who expressed strong approval of the verdicts. But over half of all White Americans interviewed said they disapproved of the jury's decision, including almost half who said they strongly disapproved.

The disagreement of White Americans and African Americans over the Simpson verdict aggravated racial tensions and prompted the country, including President Bill Clinton to acknowledge the existence of America's longstanding racial divide.

On August 9, 2014, eighteen-year-old Michael Brown Jr. was shot six times and killed by a police officer in broad daylight in the town of Ferguson, Missouri. Details of what happened are mixed and murky, but the police chief claimed that Brown assaulted the officer who killed him and even reached for his gun.

Eyewitness Dorian Johnson, who was with Michael at the time of the shooting, claims that he and Michael were walking in the middle of the street and were told by Officer Darren Wilson to "get the fuck out of the street." Michael and Dorian didn't immediately comply, telling the officer that they were almost at their destination.

Then, Johnson claims the officer told Brown and Johnson to come over to the vehicle, where the officer then reached through his window and grabbed Michael by the throat.

The White public absurdly concluded that Brown reached inside the car for Wilson's weapon (which was on the officer's right hip) in order to take it away from him and use against Wilson. Another potential and more likely scenario is based on the antics and behavior of the Ferguson Police Department. Because of the close-quarter contact of the situation, Brown was attempting to keep Wilson from shooting him.

In any event, Brown was shot in the hand and ran away. He was again shot **at,** as he ran away before turning around, hands raised (according to Officer Darren Wilson's own grand jury testimony), only to get shot again and again, six times all in all, with the final two shots entering the forehead and the top of Brown's head. Brown's body was left outside to bake in the ninety-six-degree summer sun for over four hours.

The community was shocked and outraged, and thanks to social media, the story broke out of the small St. Louis Township, and spread across the nation and the world. Every day after Brown's death, there were both vigils and protests. Some erupted into looting and vandalism, but most were peaceful yet powerful.

Well, they were peaceful until law enforcement decided to use tear gas and rubber pellets on the peaceful crowd, in a particularly tense protest situation. Journalists and protesters alike were arrested in masses in a spectacle so absurd, that even seasoned television anchors were left speechless by the sight. Even President Obama called out law enforcement for its actions

At some point, White America has to stop being surprised that an unarmed African American person is killed by a police officer. What I'm always surprised about is people deluding themselves into thinking that race isn't a factor in these shootings. Race has played a part in pretty much every tragedy such as the Brown killing, every step of the way.

Police brutality and racial profiling against African American people is a well-documented phenomenon. It's not just something that African American men such as myself just make up. It's a real thing. In Ferguson alone, the police are more likely to pull over African American drivers than White American ones. They account for nearly 90 percent of all stops, and are twice as likely to be searched and arrested by police as White Americans, despite the fact that they were less likely to possess anything illegal.

As my mom use to say to me when I screwed up as a kid, "What kind of shit is that?"

Oh, by the way, how often do you hear about unarmed White American kids getting gunned down by policemen? You don't because it doesn't really happen, and certainly not at the rate in which it happens to African American people. Again, this goes back to racism and stereotypes.

White America has been socialized to see African American people as scary and threatening. They have been socialized to see African American people as violent and unpredictable. White Americans are socialized to see African American people as uncouth and disrespectful. All these factors lead to African American people on a whole being totally dehumanized.

They lead to awful comments in articles surrounding this most recent tragedy that say things like "Well, he looked dangerous." They lead to mainstream media deliberately displaying photos of Brown, that made him look tough, in order to invoke the idea that this kid asked for the bullets because he looked like a "thug". Just a reminder. That description is used because it is politically incorrect to use the word "Nigger" in modern times. They lead to yet another death of another African American person, who didn't step on the sidewalk fast enough.

I'm outraged that this keeps happening, but I'm happy that people are using social media to call out the madness. The Twitter hashtag #iftheygunnedmedown was started in response to the media's use of unflattering photos of African American shooting victims. I am talking about the ones in which they're throwing up gang signs, as opposed to photos of them graduating from high school, decked out in a cap and gown.

Living, driving, walking, and the various other activities you can do, and be arrested while just being African American, continues to be difficult for African American men and women in the United States. With regard to this fact, there have been a series of demonstrations of civil unrest all over this country, and in certain pockets throughout the world.

These demonstrations were given birth after a traumatic event that changed and woke up America, to the reality of the brutality of law enforcement in this country. People, from songwriters to comedians, have always made comments and statements about police brutalizing citizens in the United States, especially African American citizens. This all came to reality on August 9, 2014.

Although the original demonstration was a peaceful candlelight vigil, it soon turned violent after being provoked by law enforcement, wielding automatic weapons and traveling in armored vehicles. These demonstrations continued in solidarity, and occurred on a regular basis almost every day in this country for almost six months. When the grand jury findings were read publicly in November of 2014, a firestorm of demonstrations erupted in massive numbers around the country. Besides Ferguson, Missouri, there were demonstrations in almost every city in the country.

The people who took to the streets, along with thousands of other citizens of a broad range of races and ethnicities, have been affected by the shooting of unarmed citizens. Citizens, many of whom are African Americans, are being brutalized, harassed, and yes, murdered by the police. This has all happened and was legitimized under the guise of law enforcement.

We have watched thousands of citizens protesting around this country to the same slogan of "Hands Up, Don't Shoot" and "Black Lives Matter." This is a reality of the Michael Brown Jr. shooting that White America wants you to believe never happened, when in fact it did. It is a fact stated clearly by Officer Darren Wilson himself to his Watch Commander on the day of the shooting, but because of the fact that the media favors White America, you will never hear this fact. I would, however, encourage everybody to read Darren Wilson's testimony and the testimony of his Watch Commander in the Grand Jury's report.

We have also witnessed a broad range of demonstrations, from lying in the streets, to arrests for blocking entrances of public buildings. Lying in the street mimics the fact that Michael Brown's body was left in the street in ninety six degree heat for over four hours on that August day. Having been on the scene of the shooting that day, I witnessed an organization of civil rights and outrage not seen since the late sixties.

This was followed by employees walking out of the places of employment. High schools, not only in St. Louis, but also around the country, were faced with students realizing their social awareness and expressing their displeasure of both the shooting and the Grand Jury findings.

Not only African Americans, but many minorities and surprisingly, many social conscious White Americans have also reached a level of frustration, that was a long time coming, and as usual, when there is frustration, there is soon to be violence and destruction. This was seen in the setting of fires, and the destruction of property in Ferguson and in various cities across the country.

It is amazing that even though a White police officer killed an unarmed eighteen-year-old African American man, White Americans, enhanced by the White American media, enacted a campaign of hatred against Michael Brown Jr. and his family. This campaign was behind the burning of Michael Brown's father's church.

We have even witnessed more hatred, as we have watched anti-protestors run over protesters with their cars in Minneapolis. Mind you that none of these anti-protestors have been arrested for any type of vehicular assault charges. The greatest part of this, is that the people who are standing up for Brown, and other victims at the hands of law enforcement and the entire "Black Lives Matter" movement have not been deterred.

Unfortunately, the world has not changed that much socially, and fifty years later, African American citizens are continuing to march and protest for equality and justice. These people march because they have lost hope for equality for African Americans in our society.

Yep, racism is quite obviously alive and thriving in America. Not that such a fact is particularly surprising, but it still is, nevertheless, disheartening. While the Facebook comment sections are clearly not a scientific or wholly accurate portrayal of the average American, I wouldn't be shocked to see it being close.

Media outlets such as ABC News, NBC News, NPR, and other sources have all shared stories from all over the country, and almost every top comment has implied racism. And it was abhorrent. Situations like this seem to bring out the ugliness in us. Comments like implying that African American people don't work, that they're all animals and violent, and that White

Americans don't ever riot or loot (which we know is nonsense).

When all this is taken into consideration, I still hear a term that has become popular lately. That term is "*African American Rage.*" African American rage scares White America because it confirms their worst racist fears that African Americans are animals, "Niggers" or "thugs". African Americans need to know their place and be docile, right?

What some seem to misunderstand is that their African American rage is sometimes justified. It doesn't justify the looting, but neither should we let racists disguise the real issue here, which is that African American men are being killed, and it is being masked by the law, and that has nothing to do with the looting.

It is a far less of a task for White America, if they are able to place all their judgment on African Americans setting fires to buildings in their own community, and outsiders preying on the tragedy of the situation by looting businesses, rather than to address the real reason for the civil unrest, which was why was a young African American kid, who arguably had a future ahead of him, and the many other African American people that have been subject to the unlawful behavior of law enforcement. Maybe the civil unrest was the one single action that the African American citizens of Ferguson had any guidance over.

I don't want people or readers to ever believe that I am in favor of or condone the behavior of my fellow African Americans protestors fully, because I don't. I believe that there is a better way to react to the situation that does not warrant violence and destruction.

I do, however, have a deep respect for the rage that we feel. African American people have been asking and, in some cases, begging for White America to recognize the atrocities that have been perpetrated upon African Americans for centuries. The reaction of this generation of African Americans is past the time of holding hands and singing "We Shall Overcome." Another young African American man is dead. Dead because a grossly untrained and arguably racist White police officer did not see him as a human being, but more as a monster who did not have a right to life.

I talk about the embedded racism because we live in a country that lies about both discrimination, racism and its own true history. I believe absolutely that Americans, specifically the privileged White Americans, seem to encase themselves in this sort of innocence about both history and the present. The state of Texas has even taken to rewriting the history of slavery by calling slaves "indentured workers." There's rarely any real honest talk about racism in America, and about the racist extension of police power in the United States.

CHAPTER II

AFRICAN AMERICAN CRIMES VS. WHITE (MISUNDERSTANDINGS) MISDEMEANORS

No punishment has ever possessed enough power of deterrence to prevent the commission of crimes. On the contrary, whatever the punishment, once a specific crime has appeared for the first time, its reappearance is more likely than its initial emergence could ever have been.

—Hannah Arendt

IT IS A fact that a large number of the murder victims and perpetrators of homicide are African American men. But we fail drastically to recognize that "White on White violence" is a significant issue in the United States.

Just like many Americans, I believe there needs to be a reform of the gun laws in this country. In addition to this, I worked every day for twenty-four years as a college football coach, to try and give African American men an alternative outlet to violence. I worked to help develop opportunities for these young men, trying to impress upon them the fact that if they want to improve their lives, and the lives of the people around them, the first step was to value education.

So if statistics make it clear, while all of America must continue to show progress at reducing the Black on Black crime factor, America cannot disregard the fact that "White on White" crime is a factor in the United States. The majority of homicides happen when African Americans kill other African Americans and White Americans kill other White Americans, but if half of the African American victims of these deaths are White Americans, then the other half of these perpetrators are White Americans.

While my previous profession was focused on teaching young men to confront feelings of what it means to be a man, and to help them find an alternative outlet to violence, I would be remiss if I didn't discuss the availability of guns to all Americans.

Everybody in this country has access to guns. No, I don't think that Americans should be barred from owning guns, but I do believe that not everybody should have access to them. We have evidence to support this fact, such as the shootings at schools, and on random college campuses across this country. Too many people of all cultures die from gun violence in America, and everyone in this country has a moral responsibility to reduce gun violence in the United States.

After the nationwide response to the "No True Bill" finding in the killing of Michael Brown Jr., and the release of former Ferguson Police Officer Darren Wilson, White America responded with a standard counterpunch of why African Americans never discuss and protest "Black on Black crime" as if we want to overlook it. Fox News couldn't wait to jump on the bandwagon.

White America, accompanied by the White American owned media, does not pay attention, and never sees African American communities working in their neighborhoods on a daily basis in many cases, to reduce crime. This is not recognized because it does not warrant news. In other words, it's not "sexy" enough to talk about. African American communities are working for change through education, job training, and violence interruption efforts. Again, this type of effort is almost never reported by the media.

Violence in the United States is rampant, but White Americans continue to refuse to admit the fact that violence exists in all communities. White America doesn't just have a problem of African American violence in America. There is a problem of male violence all over the country, which encompasses both White and African American men.

White American men, as well as African American men, commit violent crimes. In order to get this under some kind of control, America needs to acknowledge and take personal responsibility and accountability of our state. There are factors that need to be held accountable. Violence is in every aspect of lives, from the entertainment industry to the fact that our own government rages war on people, in parts of this world, for profit, instead of focusing on the violent factors of our own society.

The fact is, White Americans almost never puts themselves under the same microscope that African Americans are routinely subjected to. The epidemic of White Americans involved in felony drunk-driving fatality accidents is deplorable. The National Highway Traffic Safety Administration's 2013 statistics have shown that White American male drivers between the ages of twenty-one to thirty-four constituted the largest percentage of drunk drivers in fatal crashes, and of the nearly ninety-two thousand alcohol-related driving fatalities, almost seventy thousand were committed by White Americans.

We should also take aim at the violence perpetrated by White Americans in school. White American school children killing other school children must stop. The senseless and barbaric school shootings in Pearl, Mississippi; Paducah, Kentucky; Jonesboro, Arkansas, Edinboro, Pennsylvania; Springfield, Oregon; and Littleton, Colorado serve as chilling reminders of what happens when there is a failure of leadership in the White American family. This is often overlooked in White American society.

White Americans can't hide behind the stereotypical image of the African American violent criminal anymore. Before there was "gangsta" rap, you had Martin Scorsese, Brian DePalma, and Francis Ford Coppola winning award after award, and Oscar after Oscar for their films filled with White Americans committing brutal acts of violence.

What type of message does that send if we reward movies that depict such brutality? *The Godfather, Casino, Goodfellas, Scarface, Kill Bill, Pulp Fiction.* These movies have all contributed to a culture of White American violence.

The majority of this country's past serial killers have been young White American men, and they usually kill other White Americans. White American men are also the typical child abductor, child murderer, or child sex offender. There is no way we can direct any of these crimes toward "Black on Black" crime.

Susan Smith, Andrea Yates and Deanna Laney showed a pattern of neglect and killed their own children, but instead of taking responsibility or accountability, they had the audacity to blame it on God or the first random African American man that they could find.

When it comes to the financial world, while White America is looking for the African American man, with the ski mask and gun ready to carjack them, the Bernie Madoffs of the money-managing world are the true masked bandits, who are running off with the financial fortunes of hardworking Americans. This is not new, as there are dozens of Enrons, WorldComs, Tycos, HealthSouths, and ImClones in the world, and White America makes a conscious choice to look the other way when it comes to these situations, but goes batshit crazy over African Americans carrying signs that read "Black Lives Matter."

The country's recent economic crisis can be traced to the epidemic of greed perpetrated by the predominantly White American male, old boys' network of which Madoff was clearly a member.

There is not much of a difference when it comes to young people. White American youth rank as 70 percent of drug users, compared to 30 percent of African Americans. Drug users tend to buy their drugs from people that look like them. That means that White Americans, who use drugs, are getting their fix from White American drug dealers, which should put a damper on the belief that African Americans are the only ones selling drugs like Ecstasy and crystal meth, which are most popular in suburban America. Both the dealers and users are usually White American middle class men.

White America never wants to think of White American kids involved in drugs. They can't fathom the fact that their fresh-faced, White All-American kids are selling drugs to other White All-American kids. That would force them to believe that the kid living in their house is probably involved in these dealings also. White Americans almost never put themselves under the same microscope that African Americans are routinely subjected to.

Let's think about it. When the tragedy at Columbine, Colorado, happened, there were literally hundreds of news stories asking the question, "Why are OUR kids becoming so violent?" not "Why are WHITE AMERICAN kids becoming so violent?" but "OUR" kids.

Now let's contrast that with what happens when an African American child is killed in a predominantly African American community. The newspaper accounts more often than not refer to "the problem of Black on Black crime" or "violence amongst the African American youth." Society has to come to grips with the fact that White American crime is no prettier than its African American counterpart.

The issue in the minds of White America is "our" children and violence. White America has to understand that it is no longer "our" kids when in fact "those Black kids" are our kids also.

In this country, White Americans choose to concoct a repetitive false speech like the ones you hear all the time when a White American commits a heinous crime to convey, in part, the extent of White American criminal behavior not being as bad as its counterparts. For too many in White America, the facts of actual White American misdeeds are unbearable truths, which will never be faced.

CHAPTER 12

JUSTICE IS NEVER BLIND BUT FULL OF DISPARITY

No matter how big a nation is, it is no stronger than its weakest people, and as long as you keep a person down, some part of you has to be down there to hold him down, so it means you cannot soar as you might otherwise.

—Marian Anderson

FEW JUDICIAL ISSUES are more troubling than the prevalence of racism and racial disparity within the judicial system itself. At all stages of the system, beginning with the arrest and proceedings, through imprisonment and parole, significant racial and ethnic disparities are found in virtually all jurisdictions in the United States.

While these disparities have persisted for years, in many respects, these have also been exacerbated recently, despite considerable social and economic gains in many areas of American society.

The causes and consequences of these disparities are complex and dynamic and have been the subject of much attention on the academic and public levels. Research and analysis has considered the many influences of crime rates, judicial processing, and the broader social policies, that are clear contributing factors to these outcomes.

We cannot operate a society for the privileged and allow another significant proportion of the population to be marginalized. It impacts the quality of life for all Americans if we have people, who we contend are simply expendable. A justice system, that tolerates injustice in any way, no matter how just it is in certain matters, is doomed to collapse.

The United States as a country is confused about what we are trying to achieve with our judicial system. The public needs to move away from the idea that the judicial system will provide the correct answer to a crime. Our responses to criminal issues often exacerbates the problem.

Judicial agencies and, in particular, local police departments must learn to collaborate to get the proper message to the public and collectively get the message out of "This is what we can do and this is what we cannot do." We must then concentrate on improving the system, particularly in the area of reducing racial disparities, which come from our collective decision making.

While the impact of incarceration on individuals can be quantified to a limit, the wide-range effects of the competition to incarcerate members of the African American community, is a phenomenon that is only beginning to be investigated.

What does it mean to a community to know that four out of ten young men growing up will spend time in prison? What does it do to the fabric of both the family and community to have such a substantial proportion of its young men, immersed in the judicial system? What mental images and personal values are communicated to young people, who see the prisoner as the most prominent perverted role model in the community?

The United States is the most racially diverse democracy in the world, but our gains in economic prosperity are not shared by all across the whole of society, as segments of American society, in particular African Americans, have become unfortunately marginalized.

One fundamental aspect of this is the discriminating treatment of African Americans, which occurs often in small doses, across the entire spectrum of the judicial system in this country. Racial disparities breed a mistrust in this country in reference to the judicial system, and this prevents our society from promoting a sense of public safety.

Individuals who work within the judicial system are aware of the issues surrounding racial disparity. The fact is, they really don't have any significant way to fight it. We commonly speak to the fact that racial disparity, is a problem that stems from the issues of our society. There are actions that can be taken to lower disparity, but to no surprise, the society of this country has never gotten around to putting those changes into motion.

Racial disparity, with regard to the judicial system exists when the proportion of a racial group, who are generally under the control of the system, comprises a bigger number than the groups in the general population. The causes of these disparities is complex. It often includes various levels of illegal activities (with an emphasis on particular communities such as African American communities) and the legislative policies that aid to this disparity. It also includes the decision making by judicial system members, who try to practice objectivity, and what is referred to as "wide-berth" discretion in the judicial process.

When we speak about racial disparity within the judicial system, it is entirely consistent with two factors. The first would be a commitment to public safety, and two, a fair system of justice. If racial disparities that are discriminatory in nature could be reduced, the credibility of the judicial system would significantly increase, and it would most likely serve a more important and productive role, in stopping crime and increasing our response to criminal activity.

Unwarranted racial disparity in our judicial system is a product of the people, many of whom have similarities, but receive radically different treatment, all because of one thing: race. In some instances, this involves discrimination that is very clear, while in other instances, it may show the influence of factors that are shrouded by cover and are not clearly, but possibly could be indirectly associated with racial content.

In addition, as it is in many cases, disparity results from both individual decisions and institution level decisions, many of which are significantly based on a strong racial ingredient. Structural racism comes from the differential treatment, which has gone on for decades. It involves the characteristics that are mostly associated with race, which is also a huge factor in racial disparity as well.

When we discuss the subject of how to address racial disparity in the judicial system, we must first acknowledge the total nature of racial disparities in this country. The problem of racial disparity is one which is created at each stage of the judicial system.

It starts from arrest and continues through parole, and the intricacies affect the results of the actions at any single stage. We must also encourage communication across all the players involved in the process, and through all decision points of the system. In order to combat unwarranted disparity, strategies must be put in place to address the problem at each level of the judicial process. It must also be addressed in a coordinated way.

Without an approach that addresses the individual problem at each level of the process, gains in one area can be nullified, if others are going to be reversed.

We must also realize that what works at one level may not work in others. Each decision or component of the judicial system necessitates the use of unique strategies. Much of this will depend upon the degree of disparity and the specific population, especially African Americans that are affected by the actions of that factor at that level.

Above all, we must work toward a systemic change that is needed system wide. This type of change is impossible without educated judicial system leaders, who are both informed, willing and able to commit their personal resources, and those of whatever their particular law enforcement agency they are affiliated with, to address the levels of racial disparity, and to measure every stage of the judicial system, which would in turn measure the system as a whole.

Community and national statistics have shown the full impact of racial disparity that has affected every level of the judicial system. Often the decisions that are put into effect at one level have a long-lasting effect, which contributes to increasing the number of racial disparities at another level.

For instance, if African Americans are being held on bail at a higher rate than White Americans, who have committed the same crime, they will find themselves at a significant disadvantage when they go to trial, because they would naturally have less time to confer with their trial attorneys. In addition, they often have less access to community resources, which could be used in their defense, and other psychological treatment options.

One phenomenon that many in White America have truly failed to believe or even understand is the African American reality of "Driving While Black." This is a clear abuse of discretion, by law enforcement agencies all over the country. A study of nearly thirteen thousand officers who initiated traffic stops in St. Louis, Missouri over a two-year period, told the story of African American motorists being pulled over, stopped, and searched for drugs and drug paraphernalia at a significantly higher rate than their White American counterparts.

The reality is these officers were no more likely to find drugs and drug paraphernalia on, or in the vehicles of African American motorists than White American motorists traveling on those same roads. Other statistics find that African Americans who are charged with felony crimes are more than likely to be detained than White Americans. African Americans make up only 10 percent of the number of detained felons in St. Louis, and about one third in the state of Missouri. They were likely to be released before arraignment, unlike White Americans who are generally released when situations are comparable.

Although African Americans make up a little over 10 percent of the total population, they represent over one third of all prison and jail inmates in the United States. An African American male born after the year 2001 has just over a 30 percent chance of spending time in prison at some point in their lives.

The juvenile system is also in play. African American youth represent just under 20 percent of the general population within their age category, and they represent just under half of all juvenile arrests, almost none of the referrals to juvenile court, and under half of waivers to adult court.

Racial disparity is in contrast to the foundational values that the judicial system has built a societal structure on. It stands for a public rejection of the principle of "equal justice for everybody." This type of racial disparity is a result of embedded racism, and now requires a commitment to the values of both justice and fairness, and has activated professionals to speak with a sense of urgency about discriminatory and disparate treatment, where it exists throughout the judicial system.

There is a mythical belief that the judicial system in the United States is equally essential to the make a democracy function. There is a fundamental belief that there must be an association between the values of society and the personal values of the individual. There has to be a conviction to due process. Both the individual, and society as a whole depend on this as an absolute factor. Without both conviction and commitment, confidence in our judicial system and our system of laws will ultimately erode the foundation.

Since local law enforcement is the first line of defense of the judicial system, mistrust and suspicion by the general public breaks down the association between law enforcement and society, at the primary level between the two parties.

Essentially, there must be a proactive process, when it comes to establishing an air of trust between law enforcement, and the communities they have sworn to protect and serve. The problem is that both law enforcement, and the judicial system, have failed in communicating their own responsibility and recognition of the system. They have also chosen to turn a blind eye to the fact that, a racially imbalanced system will nearly always have a negative impact on families, communities, and the individuals that make up society.

All communities in the United States should dedicate themselves to nothing less than a full commitment to law enforcement. This is necessary if the goal is good government for all. Likewise, law enforcement must put forth more productive efforts, to instill public trust in the individual law enforcement agencies. This is essential if we are to have a society built on mutual harmony.

There has to be a commitment of individual citizens to not only to understand, but also comprehend and respect the judicial process. This depends on the belief that the process is set up to support the values of all Americans, not just the ones with White faces, that live in the community.

In recent years, and as in the city of Ferguson, Missouri, the criminal judicial process has been the focus of controversy for the community, and it was a true indication of the racial problems that exist in the United States. This is why it is of the utmost importance that racial disparities, especially the ones labeled "unwarranted" should be addressed. They should be addressed long before people take to the streets in protest, and show civil unrest and disobedience.

I realize that I am focusing on African Americans while discussing racial disparities, which technically includes other ethnic minorities, who also experience differential treatment in the judicial system. Unfortunately, judicial system data almost never separates the exact race from the minority classification.

This lack of data issue has been a concern, and has been brought to issue. Overall, some of the experiences of African Americans in the judicial system are similar to those of various ethnic groups, but not necessarily all.

There are a number of specific ways in which racial disparities may result from decision making at different levels in the judicial process. There are a number of proactive measures that can be taken by judicial system practitioners, to fight against those disparities.

These points of focus provide an opportunity to reinforce the fact that African Americans, receive different treatment and legal disadvantages than White Americans. It is imperative to remember that the judicial system operates often from a political realm, that that has a huge effect on the process. Often the "politics" of a situation will control how African Americans are treated within that system.

Judicial professionals can attack racial disparity from a number of angles. Because they are citizens first, they have the ability to influence and ultimately change the political process. As they are established professionals within the judicial system, they can and should actively work toward progression of a wholesale systemic change. They should also, as players in the judicial game, make a better effort of exercising professional discretion to counteract the effects of racial disparity.

Thus, professionals in the judicial system should become more aware of the social makeup of our society. This can give them an advantage in creating a way to be sure that the decisions being made within the judicial system truly are moving toward reducing racial disparity.

Because many violations of the law go unrecognized by the public, and unreported to the police, there is difficulty in forming conclusions on who is factually committing crimes, and determining the race of the offender. Reported arrest rates show an indication that African Americans are more than not involved in particular crimes.

The general public needs to understand exactly the how's and why's of an arrest. The majority of arrests, and the rates they occur are real indicators of police activity in clearing reported crimes. They are also a report of the crimes that police also see. But even though these limitations exist, arrest rates are pretty much always connected in some way to the rates of offenses.

Race and economic class are a major factor in the likelihood of being connected to crime and treatment in the judicial system. Citizens who are in a lower economic class generally encompass every level of the judicial system, and African Americans generally fall into this category.

While some claim that African American overrepresentation in the judicial system is based on the belief that African Americans commit a larger number of crimes, the factual math does not add up to this conclusion. Many state-level studies on why people are incarcerated, and on the severity of sentencing found that there is overwhelming evidence that African Americans are more likely to be incarcerated than White Americans, and in many judicial systems, they will often receive longer sentences.

These dynamics are partially true with regard to drug offenses, where African Americans are particularly overrepresented in drug arrests. Evidence of racially disparate treatments of drug arrestees, is apparent by viewing the rate of reported drug use among African Americans.

Another aspect that has to be factored into the incarceration rate of African Americans is previous criminal history. The more serious a prior criminal record, the greater the likelihood of receiving a much harsher prison term for a new offense.

In addition, areas that experience more public reporting of crimes, and a greater police presence also have more arrests. In St. Louis, Missouri, this is now referred to as "Hot Spot" policing. These are generally areas that are predominantly African American neighborhoods, which experience higher rates of arrests and ultimately more incarceration.

Accusations of racial disparities existing in the judicial system, mirror the desperation that African Americans feel, knowing that society goes by crime statistics that are incomplete. If the resources of police departments are mainly positioned in low-income neighborhoods, as they are in "Hot Spot" policing, and if there are not enough economic, educational, and social service resources, these racial disparities in the judicial systems will continue to pop up consistently.

When we talk about race in conjunction with the judicial system, you are almost forced to discuss the subject of class. Disparities in race have a direct correlation to the amount of crime committed by different races, but it is also definitely connected to the differing forms of treatment that relate to the background and resources of the person committing the crime.

When these patterns of criminal offenses are looked at, it suggests that crime cuts beyond the borders of race and class. The way society reacts as a whole does influence the expected course of a career of crime.

As previously discussed, if you don't have equal access to primary resources, you will without a doubt have different outcomes between middle-class White American parents, and low-income African American parents. The fact that they have the same problems from a behavioral standpoint is of no consequence.

When a decision is made to put all of your faith in the judicial system as the only response to the problems, which affect us in society, African Americans in low-income communities will continue to suffer from the everyday actions of judicial professionals that are ingrained in the system.

What I am saying is that law enforcement agencies arrest more people in low-income African American neighborhoods or in the "hood", because these neighborhoods don't have the resources to fight the drug epidemic that plagues their community. Often this stems for the misallocation of funds and resources in the judicial system.

This does nothing more than add to the discrimination of African American defendants as they transition through the various stages of the judicial system. There are numerous ways that misallocation will negatively affect African Americans during this process.

The process of posting bond, such as requiring a cash bond and other pretrial release screening requirements, is something that will have a significant effect on the judicial process. Others problems that are relatively overlooked by White America are the release policies, many of which are overwhelmingly biased toward White American middle-class conservative values, and the everyday resources, many of which are not available in the African American community.

Basic resources, for example, a release system with an electronic monitor or "lojack" ankle brace. This often means that the person needs to have a telephone in his or her home, for checking in with the court official. For many in White America, there is little understanding of the fact that often African American families do not have phones in their homes or places of residence. Without the phone, there is no option for pretrial release.

It can be totally different in the judicial system when it comes to minors. The juvenile systems requires youth to only be released to a legal guardian. This becomes a problem in the African American community, because if the child is from a single-parent home, that parent is often at work supporting that household. Because of this issue, that African American youth will be held longer by the system, when their White American counterparts are being released. This keeps African American youth in the judicial system by lack of choice.

Law makers at every level of the system are the creators of the judicial system. They make the laws that both punish and encourage. The penalties for violating these same laws are ambiguous at best, and so is the process of both disposal and the sentencing.

Both county and city lawmakers make a point of passing local ordinances. These ordinances are enforced by the police and the judicial system. Therein lies much of the problem, and certainly for small suburban areas such as Ferguson, Missouri, in that many of these laws have been shown to be disproportionate on the African American community. If these lawmakers were in touch with their African American constituents, this would have been foreseen, long before the laws were passed. That is, if the cared.

When our government declared a "War on Drugs," it had a major impact on the type of people that went to jail, and for exactly what type of drug was involved. I have already said that African Americans are imprisoned for drug offenses at a much higher rate, than their proportion for using drugs as a whole.

This is because of police department practices, but it all has a correlation to sentences that are handed down for drug-related offences. Every state in the country now has some form of mandatory sentencing that often applies to drug offenses.

While the federal sentencing guidelines for crack cocaine offenses was amended by the United States Sentencing Commission in 2007, many legislators contend that the racial disparities resulting from this law should have been predicted in advance. Representatives of the African American community, who were most likely going to be affected have never had an opportunity to be actively engaged in creating a more thorough, comprehensive, and effective strategy that would be less destructive to the community, when it comes to addressing their drug problems. Clearly there should be a way to differentiate between a minor and a major drug offense.

The ability to accurately separate the low-level drug sellers and professionals in the drug trade should not be left to the judicial system, because the system never takes a true look at the actual circumstances of the offense, or takes into account the criminal history of the offenders.

In 1993, many states began passing laws that required mandatory sentences of life without parole, for three-time repeat felony offenders. By 2006, twenty-five states had passed some type of three strikes legislation, and in some states, a mandatory life sentence resulted after two felony offenses. In 2015, Missouri actually released a man who had been incarcerated for over twenty years for a simple possession charge of marijuana.

Laws put in place that are motivated by tragic incidents, often lead to emotional decision making, with heavy punitive results. In reality, the result of the "three strikes" law that every state in the country has faced is the excessive imprisonment of many drug offenders.

The cost that comes along with putting these people in jail, many of whom are near or at the end of their criminal life anyway, is astronomical. These consequences have fallen disproportionately on African Americans. The sad thing is that these laws, have really had little to no effect on lowering criminal drug offenses.

Politics has played a major factor, because it often drives lawmakers to pass heavy, punitive-based laws that have aided in the huge expansion of the privatized prison system of the United States, and a large increase in jail populations. By the beginning of 2013, one in twenty people, mostly males, were under some sort of judicial supervision. A large number of that population was African American. Privatized prisons have become an enormous moneymaker for corporate White America.

The increase in the use of jails and privatized prisons has taken place, but has never been proven as a way of controlling crime. There is no real rehabilitation, or any job training experience, which means that if and when people are released, they have no real skill except what they already know. Although you hear the feel-good stories of people obtaining their degrees while incarcerated, there is little to no education that occurs in prison. Therefore, when inmates are finally released, they face obstacles that are often too hard to overcome, while they are trying to re-enter society.

When the judicial system is considering a sentence, it should both consider what happens now, and what will occur in the long term, if they choose to send someone to prison, as opposed to choosing other alternatives. Some states have already passed this type of legislation, because of the concern of the effects on African Americans.

As long as there is racism in American society, it will exist in the judicial system. Racism is what powers the public bias. It is shown in the language, attitudes, conduct and policies of judicial system.

Over the last twenty years, much of this open and clear racism has become taboo in the judicial system. But even with safeguards to follow, racism has a way of coming out of the shadows. When, and wherever racism manifests itself, we as a society must do whatever is necessary to combat it through the legislative process, and reduce racial disparity.

Bias in the judicial system comes in a number of different forms. It can start with poor interactions with the community, between law enforcement and individuals, which manifests in a mutual lack of respect. Both African American defendants and their attorneys are often treated indignantly, and disrespectfully in the courtroom setting. This fosters the impression that African Americans have second-class status.

Judicial system professionals, just like any other professionals, tend to gravitate to their own. Judges and prosecutors are more open to alternative considerations, when discussing both pretrial and sentencing options, especially when the defendants are White Americans, like most judges and prosecutors.

If you can understand the dynamics involved in the judicial system, you can keep diversity as a foundation of the judicial system. This keeps the judicial system on a level playing field for African Americans and other minorities.

There should be no relaxation of training in human relations, in the orientation to the cultures of the people with whom judicial agents interact with daily. We can always find a way to achieve subjective decision making that will affect the racial composition, of those who enter the judicial system.

Discretion is an important component of the judicial system, and is necessary for efficient system flow. It is neither desirable nor possible to eliminate discretion throughout the judicial system. Professional judgment has to be the foundation of making routine operations manageable. Nevertheless, individual discretion can lead to racial injustices.

If this happens, our only concern should be if these decisions prove likely to have a disproportionate impact, on one or more racial groups. Can the objectives that we want be achieved by other means that might stop or lessen the disparity? And what will be the impact on African Americans, and other minority groups?

The police are the first agents of the judicial system. They are also the most visible, and they have a responsibility to respond to calls for service and protection for the citizens of the community. They issue citations or arrest violators of law, and gather evidence for the prosecution of those cases that lead to an arrest. In order to fulfill these responsibilities, police departments often put a high preference on high-crime areas, which in the stereotypical minds of White America, are often heavily populated by African Americans.

There are some that would speculate that when you put more police officers in African American neighborhoods, it is only to spy on more African Americans for the judicial system. Police have a freedom of discretion to arrest anyone they want to, and this becomes a problem if they have not only more officers, but no safeguards in place to protect those same neighborhoods from tendentious law enforcement. In my business of public relation and crisis communications, I have offered various suggestions, as ways to counter the impact that misguided discretion can have at this stage of the judicial system.

The public tends to believe that all strategic and tactical decision making is the sole responsibility of police department, and that no other parties have any input to these decision making processes. That is far from the truth. The truth of the matter is that tactical command comes down from superiors. That list is endless and starts with orders from the Watch Commander, who issues the direct orders to officers. The strategy of those orders has been developed by superiors, and members of the judicial system that include prosecutors and judges. It also have significant input from legislators from across a broad range of political interests.

The problem with this type of input is that when you include this much contribution to strategy, you also increase the possibility of discriminatory strategy being put in place. There is no way to legislate what is in a person's heart, and because of the society we live in, there is truly no vetting policy for the racial disparity levels that those strategies contain. The transparency of these strategies is of the utmost importance.

Public transparency, and independent oversight of police departments increases the trust factor that is apparently the problem in every city in the country, especially in the African American community.

One thing that the city of St. Louis has attempted is a Citizen Oversight Committee, but these are not uncommon in professional arenas outside of police departments in this country. Professions such as medicine, law, and education have put in place such committees, to provide public input as an aid to the governance of policies. These committees can be put in place to counteract the public assumption of the "Blue Law," which is the belief that police officers will always take care of their own.

These committees also foster better relations between police and the public. In some communities, groups of residents and area businesses work with the police in formulating these strategic, and tactical decisions and reviewing their effects. These committees are much needed in the African American community, where there is overwhelming animosity. Because of the public belief of the "Blue Law," there are more than one hundred citizen oversight committees around the United States.

Community relations, when it comes to law enforcement, is complicated at best. The factors include a lack of knowledge about the African American community, the various cultures inside the community, and the language or "slang" barrier, since more often than not, most of these police officers are White Americans, working in areas that are obviously culturally different from their own. The problem is that very few local law enforcement agencies offer any type of training or cultural awareness education in this country.

This has caused enormous issues, because if you do nothing but deal with the language issue alone, if law enforcement officers are not trained in the simple "slang" terms of the "hood," it can lead to major misunderstandings of the African American community, discontent, disrespectful attitudes, anger, and eventual mutual hatred between the community and law enforcement, which has happened in Ferguson.

Long-term cultural training for law enforcement will help improve the issues that these police officers face. Those language walls can be torn down by the use of multilingual personnel. This can at least eliminate the excuse of "we didn't understand what they were saying" when it comes to dealing with the African American community. But education alone will not put an end to all law enforcement violations that have a racially based foundation.

In all reality, and as most would assume, law enforcement's disrespect of African Americans is statistically higher, than law enforcement's disrespect of White Americans.

Law enforcement officers often stop African Americans drivers for both apparent and phantom traffic violations. They then use these occasions to search the driver's vehicle for drugs. As was shown by the 2015 Department of Justice report on Ferguson, Missouri's police department, these pretext stops are a major issue, because of the suspicion which is backed up by significant data, that there is a strong overrepresentation of African Americans that have been stopped, searched, and arrested for nonexistent violations.

Department of Justice studies of traffic stops involving African Americans find that the discovery of weapons and drugs or drug paraphernalia is no more likely to occur among African American drivers, than among White American ones. The other thing that has been found is that when African Americans are traveling through White American affluent neighborhoods, they are more likely to be stopped based on racial profiling.

It is not only a right, but also a responsibility of the public to question authority. Police departments need to have questions put to them about specific rules, laws, and guidelines that they operate under, for responding to calls for stopping and searching suspicious persons. There also needs to be questions about the formal guidelines for arresting a suspect. Have these rules, laws, or guidelines been examined for the possibility of racially motivated bias?

Race-based differences and individual treatment are some of the most difficult challenges in American society today, and these are particularly apparent in the arena of the judicial system. Racial disparity in the judicial system is widespread, and its perpetuation threatens to challenge the principle that our judicial system is fair, effective, and just.

If the judicial system is to be viewed as fair, it needs the support and cooperation of the public. The existence of racial bias or unwarranted racial disparities reduces public confidence in the system, which will in turn affect public safety outcomes.

Judicial system professionals cannot eliminate all disparities from the system alone. The high rates of African American involvement in the system reflect a complex set of social, economic, and community problems. In many respects, African American overrepresentation in the judicial system is the result of disparate treatment in other areas, such as equal access to education, jobs, sustainable income, and affordable housing.

Judicial professionals might view themselves as being in the unfortunate position of being responsible for repairing racial differences, over which they have little control.

There are individuals that advocate for a systematic, holistic approach, which considers the long-term impact of decisions, on the racial composition of the judicial system. This should involve the use of resources, professionally informed discretion, leadership, accountability, public involvement, and coordination among many participants in the system.

Policymakers should remain involved and informed about evolving best practices, to eliminate the practice of disparate treatment of persons of color within the judicial system. Moreover, policymakers can advocate for reform, through sponsoring legislation that remedies racial and ethnic disparity in the judicial system.

Practitioners, policymakers, academics, and advocates in the judicial field have a duty to challenge themselves, to lead a national conversation on the role of race in crime and punishment. If jurisdictions can accomplish this successfully, we can expect to see other fields follow suit. This would be an important step toward addressing the racial disparity that permeates our society.

CHAPTER 13

AFRICAN AMERICAN ATROCITIES

Only when we have become nonviolent towards all life will we have learned to live well with others.

—Cesar Chavez

RIGHT AFTER THE Second World War, America began its new testing procedures for biological and chemical weapons. Scientists from countries, which we defeated were used in the development of these programs because our government admitted, that Germany and Japan were leaders in the field at the time.

What is more of a concern though is that these tests of biological weapons were conducted in the United States on African Americans, often with permission, but without clear knowledge of what the testing would consist of. I must stress this part again, **often without their knowledge**. There are confirmed and documented links between diseases such as cancer that have infected African Americans, who were involved in these biological testing programs.

There are even substantial links to death from these tests also. Originally the biological and chemical weapons programs were classified as defensive, but offensive weapons were later developed.

African Americans have long been the victims of chemical testing atrocities inflicted upon them by White America. These have ranged from the times of slavery, and continued well into the mid twentieth century. One such atrocity was the Tuskegee Syphilis Study.

This was a medical study that took place on the campus of Tuskegee University in Tuskegee, Alabama. The basis of the study was to monitor African-American men, who had been injected with the syphilis disease.

The ultimate factor of this testing was to determine, by examination, the effects of the disease when it reached the second stages. They would then be randomly, and without any notice, selected for examinations its effects.

The tests were held under a shroud of dishonesty toward these African American men. They even made up a name for this. They were told they were receiving treatment for a fake diagnosis, for a made-up disease called "bad blood." The reality is that these men never received any type of real treatment, after being used by the United States military as guinea pigs. The never received any antibiotics such as penicillin, or any other type of drugs. This was a deadly disease, which has killed some great Americans, like the famous African American composer Scott Joplin for one.

This experiment ruined the lives of African Americans, and continued for over four decades. The fact is that this experiment was criminally discriminatory, and it was clearly "race-based," because it only tested African American men. It was also clearly focused on older men of little education.

These men were completely naïve about what was happening, and about what was being performed on them. When this tragic story was exposed to a national audience, these men were finally told of the experiment, and that they had received absolutely no treatment for this experiment.

As is the practice of our military, and the government of the United States, these men were told too late. Many of the men in this disgusting test have long passed away. There was a small group of men, who were test subjects, who put together a lawsuit aimed at the doctors who performed these illegal tests. A man named Charles Pollard headed up this group of survivors, and included the federal government in the lawsuit, because they backed this testing by funding it.

Eventually, in 1973, this lawsuit came to a victorious conclusion for both the living participants of the testing, and the families of the ones who have passed away. The families were awarded a total of ten million dollars that was divided evenly among them. Later, during the Clinton administration, these families were issued a formal apology from President Clinton himself.

This ranks without a doubt as one of the most terrible, racially discriminatory and federally funded acts against African Americans in the history of this country. To date, there are only four men from the test who are alive and can bear witness to this act.

Our own government, that we supposedly "trust" for the well-being of our life, liberty, and freedom made a conscious choice, under the disguise of "government doctors" to destroy the lives of a number older, uneducated African American men. They were lied to by our government with the myth of "free exams" that would help them with their medical issues.

The government even gave a formal order that these ignorant men were to have absolutely no treatment during this testing. Their names were given to local doctors and hospitals. Those medical centers were told explicitly that they were told not to treat any of the testing subjects for any reason.

The incredible part of this is that the study continued, even after its exposure and did not stop until the summer of 1972. It was only after the story went public that it was immediately stopped. Our own government blatantly killed these men, and continued in an arrogant nature to keep doing it.

When these doctors did treat these men, they told them it was penicillin pills they were taking, but in all reality they gave these men aspirin. When these men did finally die, autopsies were performed on their bodies, without any notification to the families of the deceased patients.

Another major piece of history that White America refuses to acknowledge is something called the destruction of "Black Wall Street."

In the suburban area of Tulsa, Oklahoma is the historical town of Greenwood. At one time, it was a paradise for the African American community. When African Americans set out to construct communities, or dream of the type of life they wanted, Greenwood, Oklahoma was the model that they use.

Tulsa, like much of the rest of the country, was segregated, with African Americans settling just north of the city. Greenwood however, had the best of everything, and because it was operated by African Americans, it created a firestorm of jealousy in the neighboring city of Tulsa, and its rural White American citizens.

African Americans became entrepreneurs, and built solid communities that consisted of banks, hotels, cafes, movie theaters, and outstanding neighborhoods with wonderful homes. Greenwood residents enjoyed a lifestyle that their White American counterparts could only dream of. That included an education system that taught only African American children, who would matriculate to advanced degrees.

Greenwood was everything any American could desire. It was oddly modern, highly sophisticated and run by African Americans. It also happens to be a place and time that White America wants to block out of their destructive history, because next to slavery itself, it was one of the most deadly atrocities and acts of domestic terrorism ever perpetrated upon African American citizens, in the history of this country.

It has been nearly one hundred years since what has become known as "Black Wall Street." This country does a great service in memorializing tragic events. We have events recognizing the Battle of Pearl Harbor, where men were lost, after the surprise attack by the empire of Japan on December 7, 1941. President Franklin Roosevelt called it "A day that will live in infamy."

We recognize 9/11/01. Everyone remembers where they were on that Monday morning, when terrorist used jet airliners as weapons, and murdered over three thousand American citizens. But, those epic incidents in history are remembered as tragic because they personally affected the lives of White America. In the "Black Wall Street" destruction, just as many lives were destroyed, but there is one significant difference. The lives were African American.

It all began when a young White American woman accused a young African American man accosting her. Not much different than today, this was a taboo subject, as White America had no interest and despised the idea of any White American woman being touched buy the hands of a "dirty Nigger." This would eventually give way to vigilante mobs taking to the street, which is exactly what happen. Their target? The rich, affluent and African American town of Greenwood.

The town never saw the attack coming. Over three hundred African Americans were killed in the attack, and more than nine thousand more were beaten, brutalized and left homeless. Greenwood was burned to the ground in 1921and there was no limit to what was lost in its destruction.

The White Americans of Tulsa were envious, and as most of the United States felt, they committed to putting African Americans in their place, and keeping them down at all cost.

When you hear the term "race riot," that would imply that White Americans and African Americans, having an actual physical confrontation in large numbers. That is not what happened in Greenwood. What happened was the murder and destruction of African American lives and their property.

The White Americans of Tulsa burned over 40 square blocks. That included over a thousand homes. It did not stop there. They burned every hospital, every school, every church, and over 150 of the African American owned businesses.

To add insult to injury, members of the Oklahoma White American deputies and members of the National Guard arrested nearly 6,000 African American. They were not released from jail unless a White American citizen from Tulsa would vouch for them. In the end, over nine thousand African Americans of Tulsa were left homeless, and were forced to live in tents during the winter of 1921."

When President Lincoln emancipated the slaves, he promised by law, that each slave would receive forty acres and a mule, as a reparation. It was a law, but what most Americans, both White and African American don't realize is that Lincolns successor, President Andrew Johnson immediately vetoed that law, and freed slaves received absolutely nothing.

Even after slavery was abolished, any advancements towards the American dream that African Americans had paid most dearly to establish, was met with revulsion and terror, often from those whose legal obligation was to serve and protect. For that a debt is surely owed. This could not be more accurate than in the case of Greenwood, Oklahoma.

We see these examples in the society of the United States, that proves how wealth inequities and disparities are a part of the substance of this country. White American atrocities must be considered before we go blaming African Americans for the downfalls, this nation has experiences.

White America is quick to scream about the terrorism of Muslims, and other religious factions in the world. They consider this the "new face" of terror. They are also quick to forget terroristic event committed by White America upon Native Americans, African Americans and a number of other minority groups on a daily basis. Greenwood was destroyed by White America because of jealousy, and there is no getting around that fact.

In my home city of St. Louis, it has been proven that the Air Force and Army conducted secret chemical testing, in the impoverished neighborhoods at the height of the Cold War. These test have been the cause of an unusually high number of cancer cases. Between the mid-50s, and again a decade later in the mid 60's, the Army used motorized blowers atop the low-income housing high-rise complex known as Pruitt-Igoe.

Radioactive particles were blown into the air, at schools in the neighborhood, and from the backs of station wagons just driving through the area, to send a potentially dangerous compound into the already-hazy air. These neighborhoods were predominantly African American areas of St. Louis.

At the time, local officials were told that the government was testing a type of smoke screen, that could potentially shield St. Louis from aerial observation "in case the Russians attacked," but in 1994, the federal government reported that the testing was a part of a biological weapons program. For some reason, the city of St. Louis was chosen because it apparently resembled many Russian cities that the United States might attack.

The material being sprayed was something called zinc cadmium sulfide, which is a fine fluorescent powder. Later, research caused greater concern about the implications of those tests, and it raised the possibility that the Army performed radiation testing by mixing radioactive particles with the zinc cadmium sulfide.

As these reports became public, they stated that the area of the secret testing was described by the Army in these reports as "a densely populated slum district, where about ninety percent of the residents were "black." None of the families living in the Pruitt-Igoe Project knew that on the roof, the Army was intentionally spraying hundreds of pounds of radioactive zinc cadmium sulfide into the air. Later, the Army admitted to using blowers to spread the chemical.

There has never been any payouts, or even an apology from the federal government or the military to the families that were affected. This secret testing was exposed to Congress in 1994, which prompted a demand for a study on the health effects. A committee determined that the testing did not expose residents to harmful levels of the chemical, but the committee also stated research was inconclusive, and the findings relied on limited data.

However, it was noted that high doses of cadmium, over a long period of time could and would cause bone and kidney problems and lung cancer. It was recommended that the Army conduct follow-up studies to determine whether inhaled zinc cadmium sulfide turns into toxic cadmium compounds, which can show up in the blood, to produce toxicity in the lungs and other organs, but no follow-up studies were ever performed.

The idea that thousands of American citizens would be unwillingly exposed to harmful materials, in order to determine their health effects is absolutely unforgivable, and given the nature of these experiments, it's not surprising that African American citizens would still have concerns about what exactly did occur, if there may have been any negative health effects and if cancer was to be expected.

The United States has always had a brutal history of domestic violence against African Americans in this country. This history is quite ugly, long been neglected and African Americans have regularly been told to "get over it." African Americans, since the Reconstruction Era began have been victims of the horrific atrocity of lynchings, and the major race riots of this period, which have again recently resurrected in this country.

At the end of Reconstruction, the United States basically reinstituted the White supremacist control to the South and adopted a "we really don't care" policy in regard to African Americans. African Americans were and have in fact today been betrayed by this country. This underlying and unwritten policy resulted in African American disfranchisement and social, educational and employment discrimination.

Systematically deprived of their civil and human rights, African Americans were reduced to a status of second-class citizenship. What followed was a tense atmosphere of racial hatred and fear, based lawless violence, murders and the. lynching of African Americans.

Despite the belief of White America that the so-called founding fathers believed "all men are created equal" and even that the Fourteenth Amendment to the U.S. Constitution guarantees "equal protection," race-based oppression in the United States shows that our society has rarely measured up to these principles.

Why has deep-embedded racial conflict in America continued for so long, in what many have called a "post racial society?" That is the basis of this book. To examine this topic and explore the evidence and consequences of what appears to be the equivalent of an "addiction" by White America to racism in the United States.

The atrocities inflicted upon African Americans have had no limit. This was made no clearer that with the shooting of nine black worshippers at the historic Emanuel African American Episcopal Church in Charleston, South Carolina. Add this to the list of horrific incidents.

The murder, committed by a lone White American gunman will without question remain as one of the most polarizing atrocities in American history. The severity of this crime, that came without warrant or warning is beyond comprehension for anyone. The senseless murder of six women and three men, including a pastor and South Carolina state Senator will forever revel in the minds of all.

The pain from this event was felt far beyond the walls of that house of worship, and resonated far past the city limits of Charleston. But we must realize that this is not the first of these events.

Charleston has been added to an infamous list of atrocities upon African Americans, such as:

1. The 1955 kidnapping, beating and shooting of 14-year-old black Chicagoan named Emmett Till, whose broken body was dumped in the Tallahatchie River in Mississippi for allegedly whistling at a White woman.

2. The 1963 murders of four little black girls, ages 11-14, who died in a KKK-led church bombing in Birmingham, Alabama.

3. The 1963 assassination of NAACP Mississippi field secretary Medgar Evers outside his home in Jackson, Mississippi.

4. The 1964 murders of civil rights workers James Chaney, Andrew Goodman and Michael Schwerner in Neshoba County, Mississippi.

5. The 1968 assassination of the Rev. Martin Luther King in Memphis, Tennessee.

Add these to the list of recent police killings of unarmed African-Americans like Michael Brown, Eric Garner and Walter Scott, and you have a major list of atrocities against African Americans that is not soon to diminish. There are hundreds more, and I apologize for not acknowledging them, but I have to cut this off at some point. May they all rest in peace, and may we all not let their lives be in vain.

CHAPTER 14

DIRECT AND INDIRECT RACISM

In this country American means White. Everybody else has to hyphenate.

—*Toni Morrison*

THE BELIEF THAT any one race is above all other races can have many faces. Direct racism occurs when racist acts, or statements hit you right in the face. The indirect style of racism is much more sinister, and occurs subtle in nature. It is usually covered in the shroud of laws, rules or covenants. This makes indirect racism very hard to challenge in a court of law. The indirect style is also in the form of "benign ignorance," jokes, banter, imitations and mockery.

These behaviors are often well thought out, and are used to purposely make people feel that they are not included. When African Americans challenge this behavior they automatically alienate themselves by refusing to be associated with these types of conversations, or by bringing attention to the fact that these attitudes are discriminating at the very least.

I personally have been in situations where my White American counterparts choose to engage in jokes or conversations, which in their ignorance, they believe to be non-offensive, but in fact is extremely inappropriate and insulting. I, like many African Americans often choose the path of blowing off the comments, but deep down feel uncomfortable and hurt by such rhetoric. If these tactics do not help, then ignoring the behaviors and joining another group for small talk might be an easier way to get through the moment.

White Americans have the luxury of claiming "benign ignorance" in their racist behavior. They truly believe they are trying to be helpful or complimentary, in enlisting discriminatory comments or racial jokes. They truly don't comprehend that these comments are actually degrading.

Everybody has heard the statement made toward African Americans like "he/she speaks so well," or "he/she is so articulate," as if the fact that because they are African American, they must speak as though they has marbles in his mouth.

Although these comments have the best intentions, and many White Americans truly believe that they are paying African Americans a compliment, they truly don't understand that the "compliments" they are intending are based on the history of this country, and the prejudice and stereotypes that African Americans have been subjected to for over three centuries.

African Americans risk putting themselves even farther on the outs, when they challenge White Americas benign ignorance. I have never been afraid to let White America understand why these assumptions put African Americans in an uncomfortable position.

African Americans should force the conversation, and always reinforce the fact that the abilities of African American people come from education, talents and a lifelong wrath of having to do things five times better, just to have an opportunity, to be judged half as good as their White American counterparts. African Americans usually find a polite way to confront the issue, but keep the conversation as cordial as possible at the same time, as to not get labeled "angry and confrontational."

White Americas indirect racism is often excused by stating "but I was just joking!" or the infamous "no offense," as if you didn't have any idea that your statement was going to be offensive in the first place. The truth is that White America really knows why African Americans don't find these "jokes" funny, but they continue to make these statements on a regular basis anyway. It is thoughtless and cruel.

What is worse is when African Americans make the choice to join in on the jokes. This does nothing more that give White America a green light to continue this type of behavior. As difficult as it is to deal with a world that discriminates against you at every turn, this is absolutely the worst solution possible.

White Americans must come to realize that if African Americans are not joining in on the racist banter, it may be that White America needs to understand the actual meaning of a joke. We must as a society begin to strive toward total avoidance of all racist banter.

Regardless of how amusing White America finds this type of dialog, it must be conveyed that conversations, jokes and banter along these lines should be avoided. It is racist, insulting and discriminatory.

Making racial fun in the form of imitations and outright mockery is along those same insulting and discriminatory lines. We have all been around someone, or even imitated an accent or a cultural mannerism. This is always an issue when talking about African American stereotypical characteristics. Rap music, styles of dress, family lifestyle and anything from what African Americans drive, to what type of home they live in, is imitated on television, movies and in every form of the media.

White America will defend themselves by using the same excuse they always do, that gets them excused within society. They say "no offense because I didn't mean anything by it" or even worse, calling out the person who feels offended as just being "too sensitive."

Excuses such as these are often deflected by African Americans. They allow White Americans to believe that even if the person who made the statement didn't mean anything by it, or believe African Americans are too sensitive or not, you really don't care. It is fundamentally wrong for African Americans to have to take responsibility for White American opinion.

Indirect racism is virtually impossible to challenge within White America, because of a lack of sensitivity, most White American don't even know that they are engaging in this behavior.

Very basically, racism is the unfair treatment or hatred or individuals of a certain race and it can be found almost anywhere, including in sports and athletic arenas. Some recognized sports institutions, unfortunately, have a long history with racism though any profession, even something as sedate as teaching, can become embroiled in racism if those associated with it, whether students or faculty, show racist attitudes or actions. Racism has become less visible, but it can still be present, and it is up to everyone to help make it go away for good.

Racism is disgusting in all forms, but unfortunately it does still exist, and is deeply embedded in the fabric of American society. Individuals who encounter racism should be prepared to deal with it. If the institution itself does not respond to racism, then it might be wise to seek professional, legal advice about the situation.

Although we spoke of it earlier, it must be emphasized that racial stereotypes, more specifically, anti-African American color phobia, is still very much alive and well. Researchers found that preteen White American kids had an overwhelming penchant for associating White skin, namely theirs, with anything positive. The darker the skin, the more likely they were to associate it with anything negative.

In multiple studies, African American and White American children were asked to select White American or African American dolls as their play preference. Though these studies were not a controlled scientific study, there's no reason to doubt its painful validity.

Variations of these studies have been conducted over several years. They've all found the same thing. African American children given the choice of playing with White and African American dolls choose White dolls, and the Whiter and blonder the doll, the more likely they'll choose them.

The NAACP attorneys have always used these studies as the cornerstone of many court fights, to dump legal school segregation. These attorneys have chalked up a litany of social and psychic ills in young

African Americans, including low self-esteem, self-hate, and a profound sense of inferiority, to anti-African American color phobia.

Although the Supreme Court, under Earl Warren agreed, and unanimously outlawed school desegregation in its 1954 decision, the study, and its many clones have proved to be relics of past racial thinking.

Polls and surveys have pretty much found that many White Americans still cling to the same anti-African American stereotypes. Penn State University researchers conducted a widely noted study on the tie between crime, and public perceptions of who is most likely to commit crime.

The study found that many White Americans are likely to associate pictures of African Americans with violent crime. There was, however, a mild surprise in this study. It found that even when African Americans didn't commit a specific crime, White Americans still misidentified the perpetrator as an African American. Further studies have found that much of the public still perceives that those most likely to commit crimes were poor, jobless and African American. The surprise was that the negative racial stereotypes also applied to anyone, no matter their color, who was poor and jobless. If a White person committed a crime, the odds were that the respondents would reclassify that person as African American.

The psychological anguish that White America puts themselves through, trying to figure out when they see an African American, and then deciding if he/she has established themselves financially, or if they have been a visitor of the state prison system never ends. Even the election of the country's first African American President could not alter that.

President Obama's re-election in 2012 was a huge moment for African Americans, and the country as a whole. It also should have been a clear indication that the stereotypes associated with African American men could and should be put to rest. That presidential victory did not alter how some White Americans viewed African Americans. That's been painfully clear in the years since, but it did leave a significant mark on history

The cartoon drawings, public ridicule and typecasting of the President and his wife, which have been visible in conservative republications, and at your typical run-of-the-mill White Supremest tea party rallies is a clear indication that stereotyping, based on race is alive, well and living in the hearts and minds of a significant faction of White America.

This is hardly the revelation of the ages on racial stereotypes. Yet, it still has value in again reminding White Americans and African Americans both that racial stereotyping is anything but dead in America.

White American privilege is constructed on the basis of White Americans having a "Teflon" immunity, where they reap the benefits of this immunity every day. Most White American are completely clueless to the fact that they have this immunity in more ways than you can count. This privilege exist in the United States for the sole purpose of maintaining a racial hierarchy in this country.

The largest issue in dealing with the reality of White American privilege, is the public shroud, and invisibility factor that always continues it exacerbates White American supremacy in the United States. Like recognizing the destruction of a bad aroma of broken wind because it came from you, White America has never had the ability to recognize the privileged advantages that they have over African Americans and other minorities, because they are clueless to the fact that it exist.

White American privilege means never having to be concerned about things most African Americans know as normal, in American society, like being followed in a department store while shopping. It's about thinking that your clothes, manner of speech, and behavior in general, are racially neutral, when, in fact, they are White.

It's seeing your image on television daily and knowing that you're being represented. It's people assuming that you lead a constructive life that is free from crime, and off welfare. It's about not having to assume your daily interactions with people have racial overtones. White American privilege is having the freedom and luxury to fight racism one day and ignore it the next. White American privilege exists on an individual, cultural, and institutional level

White American privilege is not a purposeful act by White Americans. It is not blatant, but more transparent in the behavior of society. White American privilege provides White Americans with "perks" that are embedded in the behavior of society, most of which have been inherited, but none of which have been earned.

African Americans cannot possibly, and will probably never enjoy these perks and privileges, as they have always been treated as a second class citizen. These privileges create advantages for White America, and construct the foundation of the society that we live in.

White America receives all kinds of perks as a function of their skin privilege. When White Americans get cuts, they get a flesh toned band-aid. When White Americans stay in a hotel, the complimentary shampoo generally works with the texture of their hair. When White Americans purchase hair care products, those products are in the aisle labeled "hair care." African Americans are forced to look is a small section labeled "ethnic products."

White American privilege is a simple understanding of supply and demand economics. White Americans still constitute the numerical majority in this country, so it makes sense to manufacture the products that will be in demand by the majority of Americans. That majority happens to be White Americans.

Even if I agreed with the supply and demand argument, that would mean totally ignoring the purchasing capability of the African American community, and it won't alter the belief in the perks, implications and potential dangers that White American privilege has on American society. I understand supply and demand. This is how White America experiences society.

If White America all of a sudden did not receive the perks that they have embedded in society, there would be a ripple effect of galactic proportion and they would lose their god-loving minds. White America expects these perks. Even more so, most White Americans, think they are entitled to them.

White American privilege is not limited to perks, as it also creates real advantages for White America. White Americans, generally do not have to deal with or even recognize many of the issues that African Americans have to deal with.

Skin color does not work against White America. White America is not forced to justify a perception of financial responsibility. They never have to explain how or why they dress the way that they do. They don't have people judging them on their public speaking abilities, nor are they scrutinized on a regular basis on their ability to how steady employment.

Society does not judge them on their upward mobility in life, because of benefiting from an affirmative action loop-hole, and rarely are they followed around a department store, because of a shoplifting suspicion. Lastly they are rarely detained, harassed, brutalized or murdered by law enforcement, because of having brown skin.

White American is rarely forced to deal with these issues, and when their skin pigment is shown to them as a liability, they absolutely lose their minds and are uncontrollably offended.

The over sixty municipality police departments in St. Louis County, like so many other law enforcement agencies throughout this country, use policing tactics that target African Americans.

In 2013, I was driving down Wild Horse Creek Rd, a street that runs through a predominantly all-White and very upscale area of Chesterfield, MO at night. I was looking for a house that I had never been to before, so I was driving slowly, stopping and moving as I searched for numbers on residences.

Out of nowhere, three police cars pulled me over, blue lights flashing and sirens blaring, and a handful of well-armed police officers jumped out of their cars and surrounded my vehicle. I did as what I was told, and got out of my car ("Hands above your head; moving slowly!"). I then succumbed to a quick assault to the ground, including being handcuffed, a physical pat-down, as well as a search of my car.

The officers had pulled me over as they say, because of my erratic driving, but also, because, in the words of one officer, I was "an African American man driving down Wild Horse Creek Rd after dark." They thought I was looking to break in a home, since there had been a "series of break-ins."

When I went to my office the next day, I told my story to several White colleagues. They shared my sense of violation, of anger, of rage. These co-workers encouraged me to report the incident. I later told the story to another colleague who is White, and who lives on Wild Horse Creek Rd. I said to him "You just never have to worry about those things, do you?" He just looked at me and then walked off. Without even saying too much, I validated his sense of White American privilege.

White American privilege sets the tone for how the world views White Americans as a whole. White Americans get educated on history in a significantly different way than the rest of the world. They are shown that White America made the United States what it is, which everyone knows is inaccurate, but perception is reality.

The schools that I attended used textbooks, which paraded White Americans as the leading constructors of the "free world." White America is celebrated on our national currency, although there has been some serious consideration of putting Harriet Tubman on the ten dollar bill. Why have African Americans been excluded from the foundational construction of this country, when their contributions have been significant to say the very least. African Americans have a right to the same representation in this country as White Americans.

More accurate is the fact that African Americans have been the backbone of virtually every essence the United States is, but because White Americans have been in control for so long, they have been able to manipulate how history has been written. The cannibalization of history by White America is a perk of White American privilege. The world rarely questions or ask White America to validate their history. White America will never come to the reality that African American history is really United States history.

And as is the case in the state of Texas, when White Americans discuss changing the way their kids are educated, and what information will be taught, they change history because they are not willing to educate accurately for the sake of truthful African American representation. African American history is regulated, or if you may, restricted to the month of February, and that has been a since of discomfort for me since the first grade. As if we didn't do anything else the rest of the year. We were on only creative or heroic in the shortest month of the year.

The problem and fear White America has in my opinion is that if the truth of African American history is truthfully and objectively revealed, it would shake the education system in the United States to it's core. It would then be revealed, for example, that there were two riders on the night that Paul Revere made is ride, to warn citizens that "the British are coming." The other man was African American.

The University of Missouri-Columbia, you know, good ol' MIZZOU, had a group of African American students lobby the faculty of the university to add additional literature to a freshman English Literature course. One of the White professors raised a real stink, and questioned if they should substitute Chaucer writings for Alice Walker, author of "The Color Purple?" Why does White America place a higher value on White literary pieces, and the writings of African Americans are reduced to the second tier? And you wonder why students protested on that campus?

The fact is, White American privilege is a hidden, and tough to talk about because much of White America does not believe that it exist. You have to really pay attention to the entitlement benefits that promote the status of White America. These advantages place White Americans in significant, and advantageous positions in society.

In addition, we must not down-play the way the White-owned media world plays to the perception of White America. Media companies make their living, by broadcasting on crime, murder and drug use in the African American community, but rarely ever cover the criminal activity that is being perpetrated in White American society. This distorted coverage was even more prominent in August of 2014 as the entire world was suddenly knowledgeable about a small town, in the suburbs of St. Louis, MO.

African Americans have been in a battle with oppression and discrimination, from the White American society that has reigned over them for four hundred years. The White American media have been a huge catalyst in heightening the reasons and effects of this behavior, and in contributing to African Americans' continuing their status as second-class citizens.

White America really has no idea of the history and culture of African Americans and, in a sense, has no true understanding of who we are as a people. White America truly has no realization that African American people are what America really is, because they are so fixated on the stereotypes that are perpetuated by the mass media. But, where do these negative stereotypes originate from?

I believe that this problem started a long time ago, and is still strongly upheld by White Americans. In the eyes of many African Americans, the White American owned media produced in the United States, is a reflection of White American views regarding the African American communities.

The most underrepresented and misrepresented group in the media, both in the past as well as today, are African Americans, and the media perpetuates that misrepresentation by continually reporting the downfalls of the African American community. This does nothing more than legitimize the inequalities in class and race relations.

Newspapers and the entertainment industry have never been allies of African Americans. Both of those industries have continuously practice discrimination, to a point where it has almost become their form of art. Since White America has had total control of those industries since their birth, there is no wonder why it has been set up to maintain the status quo of the ruling culture. Because of this factor, it will always show African Americans in as much negative light as possible.

The White controlled media in the United States has made a conscious effort to drive a wedge in the working class, and stereotyped African American men as gangsters, drug dealers and the new term of endearment, "thugs." As a result of such treatment, the media has crushed African Americans youths' prospects for future employment and advancement. The media has focused on the negative aspects of the African American community, while maintaining the cycle of poverty that White America would prefer.

There are no universally accepted rules or standards that journalist are required to operate by. The media spends a great deal of time and space, as I say, oppressing the oppressed, and too little time talking about the real issues that are faced African Americans.

They tend to make an incident in the African American community a crisis of epic proportion, and add a visual of the same incident to be sure that the White American viewing public has support for the negative reporting. This was never so true as when the Ferguson police released the video tape of still footage, of a "strong armed" robbery to them, when at the same time, they refused to release Officer Darren Wilsons name to the public, under the guise of "protecting the welfare of the involved officer." The motive was clearly to project Michael Brown Jr. as the "thug" that White America needed to see.

As a fifteen year member of the St. Louis media, I had never seen the release of "strong armed" robbery footage (robbery without a weapon), which in all reality, show Brown pushing a store owner. Furthermore, it had ABSOLUTELY nothing to do with the shooting, as even the officer was unaware of the incident at the convenience store.

The media thrives on the controversies of racial stories. They are "sexy" stories, meant to give White America a "wow" factor. Again they cater to the White American viewer because that's whose paying the bills, and in the meantime, they focus little to no attention to the real issues, that fester underneath the sensationalism, until it explodes into their next crisis situation, where they can "go live" on the scene.

Today's media suffers from an ailment called "a lack of journalistic integrity." They completely ignore the African American community in today's society. The reporting of gentrification, poor educational opportunities and poverty in the community are not as popular or sell as many tickets to the show as murder, assault and drug trafficking. The St. Louis media tried to associate these issues in Ferguson, Missouri in 2014 because it would play well with their "downfall of American society" narrative.

Race is the pipeline that associates the issues of today's society, but contrary to the popular belief of White America, it is not the deciding factor. The White American media wants you to believe that race is the ultimate reason for the season of violence we have in today's society. Their agenda is about selling papers, selling advertising, and getting more clicks on a website, which ultimately acquires more advertising, and with that comes more revenue.

The media would have you believe the events surrounding the killing of Michael Brown Jr. manifested the entire perception that the citizens of the African American community were the only ones responsible for what happen in the aftermath of the shooting.

These reports stated that those who were taken under arrest for vandalism and looting were mostly African American, were part time employees and were not associated with any political party. The rest were White Americans. Yes! There were actually White Americans involved in the looting also, believe it or not.

But because the media is controlled by White America, and used to make White America feel safe, this fact was never reported to the public. Moreover, the media gave the impression of the events in Ferguson, as the fault of the African Americans that live in that small suburb of St. Louis. Just as in Los Angeles in 1992, the media found a way to inflict a negative image, and immediately damage African American awareness in the United States.

In addition to inflicted a negative image, the media made a conscious choice to follow standard protocol, and show more of the violence and pictures of

African American destroying communities and looting businesses. If they were actually covering the story, they would have chosen to dive into and research the real question; why did this happen? And, what are the underlying issues surrounding the African American community that led to this tragic event.

CHAPTER 15

PSYCHOLOGICAL ASPECTS OF RACISM AND THE WORD "NIGGER"

We have made enormous progress in teaching everyone that racism is bad. Where we seem to have dropped the ball . . . is in teaching people what racism actually IS.

—Jon Stewart

TWO OF THE most polarizing words in the English language are "racist" and "racism." They are offensive to some, and unfortunately they bring a sense of security to others. These two words are a part of American society, and that will never be questioned by anyone. When you are African American, you are force to deal with the reality of these two words every single day of your life.

White America has had it engrained into the fiber of their being, that race is the end all determining factor of adequacy in society. Often White Americans act as if their race makes them superior in this adequacy level to African Americans. Society even responds differently to African Americans than they do their White American counterparts. This behavior hurts all of society, and in particular, African Americans.

Instead of focusing on the deep rooted reason for racist feelings, White Americans over last four decades have had a centralized aim on how individual people behave in our society. Institutional racism is a much larger issue because of the behavior is hidden and unclear. They have underlying discriminatory policies that give them the ability to exclude minorities without drawing public attention, giving them the racist comfort of excluding anyone they really want to. This gives the option to treat White Americans and African Americans by separate guidelines.

White America has never understood both the long-term physical and psychological implications, on the African American community. This is a major concern in the issue of racism. To understand this aspect is to understand why African Americans often react the way we do, when we feel we have been discriminated against.

If White America would consider taking time and breaking down the behavior aspects, and the individual discrimination experiences of African Americans, and pay particular attention to the psychological effects of those individual situations, White America would get a truer understanding of why African Americans react in certain manners. Triggers could even be pinpointed and thresholds understood. This would undoubtedly be helpful in situations that involve law enforcement.

African Americans feel racial stress based on a random of encounters. They could be on an individual basis, or come from an institutional standpoint like dealing with an employer or a service industry encounter. The belief that racism can affect someone psychologically in not recognized from a medical diagnosis, and therefore not truly recognized in society.

Some of the smartest education minds in the world have analyzed racial associations, and the sensitive nature of such associations. These minds have had little success in connecting racism to the effects of mental health. The stress of racism can create traumatic events, as we witnessed in Ferguson, Missouri.

These traumatic events can translate into psychological depression, and carry a number of physical symptoms among African Americans. This type of psychological distress, expressed in the form of physical pain and anxiety, is just a small number of the mental health effects African Americans report from these traumatic events.

Perceived racism can prove to carry even more than discriminatory action. This type of racism occurs when White America shows a negative attitude through either behavior or action toward African Americans, because they are perceived as being a lower social status.

African Americans are affected by racism, and that should not be ignored by medical professionals. Medical Institutions need to devote real time and effort in researching the mental health aspects that surround racism. In addition, there should be additional research done on the relationship between racism, and social interactions of various cultures

What we learn is not always what will never change, although we learn it from people who have the most power in our society. Our minds train us to validate the most powerful, but we must never close our minds to the fact there is another way, another thought and another outlook. We must recognize that one issue that affects a culture, can be detrimental to another, and have compassion for the difference. This has never been so accurate then as to the usage of the word "Nigger."

Back in 2005, a White American man named Nicholas Minucci, assaulted and robbed an African American man named Glenn Moore. While Mr. Minucci was committing this attack he repeatedly called Mr. Moore a "Nigger." It was because of this, that the judicial system made a determination to prosecute the attack on the basis of a hate crime. The testimony at the time of the trial by two other African American men were of great substance, as they testified about Mr. Minucci's repeated use of the word "Nigger."

It was made clear that the word "Nigger" was not only used in terms of a racial insult. It was explained that the word has now become a regularity in the youth culture of American society. Mr. Minucci's legal representative also argued that the jury should not fall into the assumption that Mr. Munucci had not insulted Mr. Moore racially, but that his client was only speaking to Mr. Moore in street terms that were more understandable.

This argument did bring to light a reality of pop culture. The reality is that we cannot jump to the conclusion that every time a White American uses the word "Nigger," it is being used to express a racial insult. Can a White American person actually use the word "Nigger" in a non-prejudicial way?

The testimonial twist did not save Mr. Minucci from being found guilty however, and African Americans will always continue to argue that it can never be justified. The usage of the word "Nigger" by White Americans will never be acceptable by African Americans. There is no way to justify that the usage of the word, especially while committing a violent crime, should be and will always be viewed as the major factor of a hate crime.

Hate crimes are unique, but not of a rare occurrence. Most crimes such as murder involve one prime ingredient, when it falls in the hands of the judicial system. They must be proven beyond a reasonable doubt. But in the case of hate crimes, it must also be proven that the person on trial actually sought out the victim, because he was of a different race, plain and simple.

That means that there must be psychological evaluations of the defendant's mindset, to determine their true reason and motivation. In fact you almost need to get the defendant to admit their true racial feelings, which is difficult at best, because most racist are very good at keeping the true reason close to the vest, much like a good poker player.

Even when the defendant purposely chose the victim because he was African American, a confession to support this very important fact is not likely to be forthcoming.

In order to substantiate the racist claim, both law enforcement and judicial officials have to find evidence that addresses the claim directly. Often, the motivation is covered up deeply, and like most secrets, uncovering them is often traumatic and dangerous. When you find out the real reason, it often takes a strong person to handle the evidence.

The only evidence that matters in the perpetration of a hate crime, is the kind that is physical. The kind that is visible to the eye, or the kind that you heard first hand. You can no longer go with the assumption that, just because it was a White American involved. When there are symbols associated with the crime, such as a cross a fire or Nazi Germany symbols like swastikas, then you would be safe to assume that hate played some motivation in the crime.

The fact is that when someone is committing a crime of violence, the type of language that is spoken can give a true picture of the real meaning, especially when it is a White American criminal who attacks an African American. If the White American attacker refers to the African American victim as a "Nigger," it can only be viewed as a hate crime.

The word "Nigger" has a way of igniting a series of feelings in this country like no other word in the English language. The funny thing about this fact is that it is visibly used more among members of the African American community, than in any other segment of society.

A variation of the word has become ingrained in pop culture, in the form of "Nigga." It is mainly used in certain segments of rap music world, but is often used in the routines of popular African American comedians. Because of this normal use of the word in these arenas, there is a belief among White Americans that the word "Nigger" has been reduced to standard speech and no longer hold the racial power or the negative connotation that it once had.

White America has joined in the norm of society, but under a false impression that because of the use of the word "Nigga" in pop culture or because of the people in their relationship circle, they mistakenly believe they can use the term "Nigger" or "Nigga" in the same way or connotation as their African American counterparts.

But there has been a transition in the racially charged English language. White America along with the media, which is controlled by White America has now become accustomed to the universal usage of a new label for African Americans. "Thug" has become the new "Nigger."

There is a clear rule that has been laid down by African Americans in past and present society. It is that the word "Nigger" is never to be used by White Americans, even when there is no negative intentions associated. The only time where is might be possible for a White American to use the word "Nigger" is when they are around their African American friends, who have found it acceptable.

I personally have many White American friends, whom I am very close to, and even with the relationship that we have, there is no possible way that they would say it, or that I would ever allow it to happen without a very professional confrontation.

The only faction of White America that has been given a pass on the usage of the word "Nigger" as a form of expression, would arguably be White American rap music artists. These White American artist, such as Eminem, have ingrained themselves into the hip-hop culture. But, even these White American artist rarely use the term "Nigger."

The fact is that there is really no situation that is clearly identified, where White Americans have Cart Blanche on the usage of the word "Nigger." Nor is there ever a time when the word can be taken in a manner other that prejudicial meaning. White America uses the word "Nigger" and it can only be taken as uneducated and ignorant, even when it is spoken among relationships of like-minded people.

In late years, there has been a significant reduction in discrimination based on raced, but there is still some deep rooted hatred felt by White Americans and directed toward African Americans, and those feelings continue to run deep in the hearts of racist White Americans.

The phenomenon of this is that White America has a practice of not putting their private feelings on front-street, for all the world to see. White America will never openly discuss their racist feelings, and in many cases they don't even know they have these attitudes. One of the reason for not putting it out there is because the world we live in is more socially acceptable of cultures, which makes it less acceptable to harbor those biases.

In the eyes of a large portion of the citizens of this country, Barack Obama being elected to the Office of the President of the United States should have put the history of discrimination and racial inequality in this country at a conclusion, but, it did not.

This was evident when within three to four weeks, both before and after the 2008 election of the first African American president being elected, there was a spike in hate crimes perpetrated against African Americans, other minorities and immigrants. This made it clear that the ugly head of racism was far from dead in this country.

Violence committed against individuals because of their race is still, to this day, a serious problem in America. It has been over twenty five years since the Hate Crime Statistics Act was put in place. Since that time it has been reported that a hate crime occurs in the United States, to the tune of one every hour on every single day.

Furthermore, these assaults intimidate both the individual, and all members of the cultural community, and the residential community where the victim lives.

It even intimidates members of other communities that have been historically victimized by hate.

These hate factions have an ultimate plan to divide, conquer and destroy these communities creating an air of fear and suspicion of other cultural communities. They even magnify a sense of anger toward law enforcement. In this way, they destroy an established feeling of community.

Anti-immigration extremist are set on creating a mindless concern, of illegal immigration in the United States. This has stirred the immigration debate by focusing on racist stereotypes and bigotry of hate groups. Why do you think there people are speaking out, in the anti-immigration conversation? They are treating immigrants as devils that have brought a plague upon our communities bringing disease and crime.

Hate crimes require a stringent approach by law enforcement agencies in this country. There needs to be, because of the economic downfalls of recent society, a re-education period, to change the psychological thought process of how violent bigotry is viewed in this country. When you do not deal with bigotry, especially the violent type, you end up creating a powder keg situation in communities that if unaddressed will eventually explode.

A perfect example is the oppression by law enforcement, upon the African American community in

Ferguson, MO. The bigotry imposed by the local police, and the municipal court system was a catalyst that lead up to the incidents during the summer of 2014

If we are going to remove prejudice in the United States, we must first begin to evolve to a society that respects the difference of each individual. One of the problems with evolution is conversation or lack thereof. Society has to open the lines of communication, regardless of the racial or cultural lines that separate us. We must become culturally aware and more accepting of the differences of individuals. We must look for solutions that can be establish to reduce racist behavior in this country

Effective legislation, and responses that actually have real ramification by law enforcement and the judicial system will be a key ingredient in putting an end to hate crimes, and creating a healthier and stronger society for all Americans.

One of the issues facing national hate crime legislation is each state has a different definition, for what makes up a hate crime. Right now, only about half the states in the union even have hate crime laws on the books. Based on these laws, if the prosecution can prove the victim of the crime was designated because of their race, culture, religion and or sexual preference, the perpetrator can actually receive addition to their sentence.

CHAPTER 16

CHILDREN, RACE, AND RACISM: HOW RACE AWARENESS DEVELOPS

Hating people because of their color is wrong. And it doesn't matter which color does the hating. It's just plain wrong.

—*Muhammad Ali*

OFTEN CHILDREN ARE not aware of race or racism. Adults don't give kids enough credit, or they teach kids the art of being color-blind, which never works. Kids are not stupid when it comes to race.

They can clearly recognize differences between their peers, and society should take a lesson from the children, because very rarely do children evoke racism or racist behavior in any interaction with each other. Even though they are aware of the physical differences, they are not afraid of their unknown and unrealized fears.

When children are indoctrinated into the ideology of being color-blind, it perpetuates the issue of not having a dialog, when it comes to the topic of race. It also perpetuates the idea of "out of sight, out of mind." As has been the practice of society, if the dialog can be avoided, then we will never be put in the uncomfortable position of having to address the effects, and repercussions of racism.

The first step in addressing any problem, especially the problem of embedded racism in American society, is first admitting that there is a problem of embedded racism in American society. Denying the fact that it exists does not make it go away, nor does sticking your head in the sand as if it doesn't exist.

What much of society fails to realize is that as much as African American children are scared by the effects of embedded racism, White American children are also mentally affected by racism. Racism affects the overall culture, so it gives culture a warped sense of entitlement, and other cultures a feeling of less deserving, of the same respect. White American children are never corrected to realize the reality of a White American child's world.

Our racist society keeps them under the illusion that they are the center of all that is. This falseness keeps White American children from dealing with the false truth of American society, especially when the status quo is challenged by African Americans.

All children learn hypocritical behavior when it comes to cultural difference, and they acquire this knowledge during their developmental years. When a child learns this behavior, they are basically being cheated out of opportunities to learn about other cultures. When children fail to learn about other cultures, they fail to experience an opportunity for learning about themselves as individuals. Thus they fail to learn about acceptance within humanity as a whole.

This should not be the case in dealing with children. Children regardless race or culture have a natural acceptance of people. Children love all kinds of animals. How often have we heard the story of some child bringing home a stray cat or dog. Children are the same way when it comes to other children. They truly are not affected by race, until adults somehow integrate them into the evils of society in this country.

It is important we give all children an opportunity, to develop their own sense of judgment and knowledge, when it comes to both racial and cultural awareness. It is also the responsibility of the adults in our society to allow, without influence, children to grow outside of the racism boundaries that we have created.

African American as well as White American families face this task, but it is inoculated in the children of these races in different ways, and often White American families fail to point out to their children that they have a racial identity at all.

White America has never been faced with the idea of having to come to the realization, that there is a White American privilege factor in the United States. Let's just be honest. White America has never had to view themselves as a separate racial culture, or the feeling of discrimination that goes along with it.

The feeling that "White is Right" has enveloped society, and has provided White America with a self-centered identity, because the liberal, free thinking, and moral compass of society that was challenged by the events of August of 2014.

White America has never taken responsibility for perpetuating the racist system that exists in the United States. White America has viewed themselves as individuals, and because of this, White America has been able to deny ownership of the racist systems that exist in the country.

Because they have never taken ownership of their own culpability in the system, White Americans have developed a negative attitude toward African Americans. Often this attitude if very visible, but sometimes it is hidden deep at a subconscious level.

For African Americans, we are forced to deal with racism every single day. African American children learn this in the same way they learn reading, writing, and arithmetic. This is key to basic existence in the world they are facing. On the other hand, if this is key for African American children, then White American children should be obligated to learn anti-racist behavior, which is never the case. Instead they are recommended or taught to be color-blind, which never works.

The concept of "color-blind" is wrong because adults use it as a way not to discuss racism and the real reasons for it. While they avoid the subject, they forget the fact that children are smart, and understand significantly more than they get credit for. Children realize that the child across from them that might have darker skin, is different.

What they don't understand is why that child or why that child's father is being pulled out of a vehicle, put on the ground, and the police are standing on the side of his head, calling him "Nigger." Children are trying to make sense of their experiences.

White America believes that racism is caused by publicly discussing the differences in society between the races, instead of the social class system which exists in this country, and places African Americans in a position of show-dog for financial profit. This allows

White America to walk away from the consequences of a structural systems that perpetuate racism.

If parents choose to go against the color-blind theory, they could begin a new position of building a new attitude, for the children in this country. By training a child at home, where there is the opportunity to present attitudes of positivity, you give children a more stable environment for learning, and dealing with racism. Children could grow up with different attitudes, and maybe create, or at the least contribute to the creation of a non-racist society.

Regardless of this happening or not, the adults of the United States, both White American and their African American counterparts, are obligated to navigate all children toward developing a non-racist attitude toward society. This must include telling an accurate history of the United States' transgressions and atrocities toward African Americans, native Americans, and other minorities. The problem is that if you tell the accurate history, it will rock the very foundation of White America. A light will be shined on all of the misinformation being taught in the education system, and White America is simply never going to let that happen.

There must also be a sincere appreciation of the various cultures, racism that affects these cultures, and an understanding of how it works in the United

States. More importantly, they must be educated on what it takes to fight racism on every level.

Children are not the problem, as much as it is the attitude of the adults. Most adults in the United States have all witnessed, or were raised in an atmosphere of some type of racist attitude, even if it was the theory of being color-blind. It is impossible to separate the influence of racist attitudes, heard or seen by young children in their contacts with adults.

We must not forget that children are also influenced by other children, children's books, and the entertainment industry. Often, it is possible that what starts out as an inappropriate, and unassuming comment can very quickly turn into a racist situation.

Regardless of where they receive their information, inappropriate stereotypical conversations, or images based on race, can be damaging to the psychological development of any child. Children, not to be funny, have very small minds, and cannot fully process what is real and what is unreal, or even humorous.

Often what is a catalyst in this equation is the fact that adults don't listen or totally respect the opinion of children, even though they have the same or even more interaction with people of color on a regular basis.

Children take things personally, and they tend to connect and relate things they learn to their individual lives. They don't understand the concept of "that group of African American kids" or "that group of Hispanic kids." They truly look at kids as kids, regardless of what race or culture they are. In some cases, it only matters if you have the latest Xbox game. If so then they will get along.

The easiest concept for children to understand is that they got their looks and characteristics from their family, and in particular, their mother and father. The culture they come from is nothing more than an expansion of this concept.

Adults can help children by teaching them that this larger cultural concept relationship never goes away. It would also be helpful if adults would acknowledge what a child sees, regarding cultural awareness and identity, and correct children when they spout misinformation, or generalize other cultures of people. Make children understand that these expressions are socially unacceptable and prejudicial in nature at the least.

In some cases, children need both understanding and support when they discover that racism is affecting their world. This is very much the case with African American children. African American children are acceptable to White America as long as "they don't grow up." While they are small and have no effect on the economy or society as a whole, but once adult status is achieved, White Americans, in their minds, would be forced to deal with their beginning awareness of the phenomenon of racism.

When it comes to affecting change with children, there are numerous ways to address the topic of racism. By increasing education on the subject, we give them the tools to fight racism at the grassroots level. We also have an opportunity to make children and young adults both more socially aware, through community projects directed toward fighting institutional discrimination and racism within the community.

This is a time when racist attitudes are manifested, but also a time when attitudes can also be consolidated. It is a time when minds can truly be molded for better, or for worse.

Adults have the opportunity to both encourage and discourage racist attitudes in the hearts of young people? Adults must recognize the opportunity to demonstrate model attitudes and behavior, verbally and nonverbally, even if we are not conscious of it. Children are extremely observant and will mimic adult behavior and mannerisms at every turn.

Education, by commission and by omission, occurs with the children of the United States every single day. As adults we have an obligation to be aware of our behavior, as it will have a lasting effect on the children.

We must also be aware of the background of the people who work with children. Often we are unaware of the personal feelings, of the people who are educating and influencing our children. Many adults are not adequately prepared to deal with racism, or its emotional effects on young people, and are subsequently unprepared to deal with questions associated with it. They will either give bad information or worse, not answer the questions at all. Rather, as noted earlier, they will burrow their heads in the sand.

Racism is an uncomfortable subject at the very least, and discussions with children tend to heighten that level of discomfort. Children have a natural level of embarrassment and anxiety about how to address issues in general. I have always believed that you never lie to children, especially when it comes to issues that affect their daily lives.

Adults often choose this route under the disguise or excuse of "protecting children." What I have found is that the protection factor is mostly for the adults. In dropping the idea of protection, adults are forced to come to a junction of their own feelings, and are truly faced with understanding their own behavior. Only then can we influence the behavior of the children that we have a responsibility to guide in the right direction.

As I have stated, you can never address a problem until you first acknowledge that there actually is a problem. As adults, we have an obligation to share the things we have experienced with children. Then and only then can we truly craft a true and honest future for the children of the United States, the same children who will undoubtedly lead this country someday.

CHAPTER 17

MOVING FROM BEING COLOR-BLIND TO BEING CULTURALLY AWARE

Racism is cruel and unjust. It cuts deep and lingers long in individual and community memories. And it is not a thing of the past . . . We all have a duty to do what we can to turn this around.

—William Deane

THE ISSUES OF race make people uncomfortable. That is undeniable in our society, but we have made significant progress, in coming to grips with the uncomfortable feelings associated with the topic of race. The controversy that the issue of race creates is without question, and it screws with the mental state of this country as a whole.

If you choose to give it value, on the surface, colorblindness seems to be a thought process that would work because society would be judging each other on character instead of on skin color, because it is aimed at finding things that people have in common.

In a perfect world that is focused on mutual humanity, colorblindness would work. But colorblindness can't work in today's society, because it does not address the history of race and the deep-seeded, embedded racism that exists currently in the United States.

A colorblind society frankly gives White Americans the ability to ignore any and all racial issues. This would do nothing but keep their mindset at the status quo. Their comfort level would never be challenged, White American privilege would continue, and the social order that White America has become accustomed to would carry on.

This is exactly what happens when African Americans are forced to deal with the idea of a color-blind society. We are all force to deny our heritage and put our culture to the back burner, for the so called "good" of society.

Colorblindness gives White America society an opportunity to excuse themselves of the accountability, from the atrocities they have committed in the past against other cultures.

They massacred Native Americans, and stole their land under the guise of "westward expansion." They captured, kidnapped, and enslaved hundreds of thousands of African Americans, where they received free labor for their own personal gain.

Being color-blind actually means looking at people, and only seeing what you want or need to see, in order to keep your life comfortable. I am an African American, and that should be of significant meaning to the rest of the world. There is nothing in society that should be put in place that would force a particular race, or culture to be invisible or vacant to the rest of the world.

This kind of thinking sets a precedent that cultures, need to be ashamed about who they are. We teach children every day to be proud of who they are as individuals, and the culture that they come from. The process of being color-blind does little more than reverse those teachings.

Race should not be an uncomfortable subject in our society, yet in our society, and in particular White American society, the topic of race is similar to walking across a live mine field. You can walk very lightly, and one wrong step will cause you more destruction that you could imagine. On the other hand, not walking at all gets you absolutely nowhere. The first step in fixing a problem is recognizing that there is one.

White Americans are under the belief that being color-blind makes society better for African Americans, because it gives all of society the comfort in knowing that race is not an issue. African Americans are not incompetent, just as most Americans are not. An intelligent objective person will tell you that race does matter, because it affects every aspect of society, from perceptions to social respectability. There is virtually nothing that it doesn't touch.

When the civil unrest began in Ferguson, White Americans looked at the situation as separate, individualized moments. First there was the convenience store "strong arm" robbery. Then there was the actual shooting of Michael Brown Jr. It then moved on to the civil uprising of the citizens, then the police confrontations and the counter protest. Finally, there was the reading of the Grand Jury finding.

White America paid attention to the conflicts (which I call the vegetables) instead of getting their eyes on the big picture (which is the meat of the meal). They would much rather discuss the burning of a building or buildings, than to seriously delve into the deeper reason why these things are happening. They don't want to discuss the differences in culture, racial privilege, racist stereotypes that are placed upon members of the African American community, or simply the value of an African American life.

White American society continues to ride the fence about racism mainly because:

1. They don't believe it affects their life.

2. They really don't care about African Americans, or for that matter, America society as a whole.

Color-blind implies not being able to differentiate between colors. When you are driving a car, not being able to tell the difference between the colors red and green could pose a serious, and potentially dangerous problem. African American people don't want this kind of problem, and don't want the danger of associating with people that can't see either.

Being able to see society clearly can make White America uncomfortable. I have a number of White Americans friends, who live by the colorblind motive of operation. They act as though race does not matter. Unfortunately, African Americans can't afford the luxury of being blind to anything in society.

Colorblindness will not educate people on the different cultures of the world. It does not make our society more aware of the fact that there are different people in the world, and in fact it shows a great deal of disrespect. As I stated previously, it gives White Americans the ability to ignore any or all racial issues.

As in the case of Ferguson, Missouri, given how that situation played out, we can no longer afford to be blind to the realities of the world. It's time for change and growth. It's time for White America to open their eyes and see society as a whole, and for what it truly is.

The alternative to colorblindness is cultural awareness, where we actually respect, and in some cases celebrate other cultures. It validates the belief that other cultures have value, and should be respected. It shows in society that there are other cultures of the world that have faced strife based on race. There is something to be said for a multicultural society, so how do we become multicultural?

Transitioning from an act of colorblindness, to a feeling of multiculturalism is a process. The definition of insanity is doing the same thing over and over, while expecting a different outcome. We need to change how we do things in society. We need to transition from not validating culture, to a true recognition of all cultures as valuable to our society.

Cultural awareness should be the foundation of communication in our society. It is the ability to get away from ourselves and our personal beliefs, long enough to open up our hearts and minds, and explore what other cultures have to offer. It will, however, require interacting with people that don't look like us.

White America confuses the world because they invoke their societal definitions and make light of issues that are real problem for other cultures, in particular African Americans. Other cultures see White Americans as people who are always on the go. Does this mean that they are hyperactive?

As we become more aware of our cultural differences, we open up our minds to tolerance. We learn things, both by looking and not looking, but because of the difference in cultures, there is a difference in how we learn things. We must step outside the walls that keep us separated, in order to truly see the world. Only then will we know how it affects us, and our own individual impression upon society.

CHAPTER 18

REDUCING THE EMBEDDED DISEASE

> *What is it you most dislike? Stupidity, especially in its nastiest forms of racism and superstition.*
>
> —*Christopher Hitchens*

RACIAL PREJUDICE AND racism feed on each other. If racial prejudice is not reduced, it could lead to racism, and if racism is not addressed, it could lead to more prejudice. This is why strategies to address discrimination on the basis of race should be thorough and multifaceted, so that both individual attitudes and institutionalized practices are affected.

There are several reasons why racial prejudice and racism need to be reduced. Often, they impede or prevent the object of racism, from achieving his or her full potential as a human being. They prevent the object of racism from making his or her fullest contribution to society, or they impede or prevent the person or group engaging in racist actions from benefiting from the potential contributions of their victim, and as a result, weaken the community as a whole.

In addition, they will increase the present or eventual likelihood of retaliation by the object of racist actions, and go against many of the democratic ideals upon which the United States and other democracies were founded. Racism is illegal, in many cases.

In addition, there are numerous reasons why racial prejudice and racism should be addressed in the community. There can be a true effort building, if more than one racial or ethnic group is involved. Every participant in the effort has their own understanding of the world and how it works.

The White American residents in the neighborhood don't understand why African Americans and Hispanic Americans have to stand at the street corner to get work. They think it is because they are too lazy to find full-time jobs. Part of the problem is that the residents have not had the opportunity to debunk these stereotypes, through direct interaction and contact with the day laborers, and to hear their stories.

Every participant in the effort needs to be polite, respectful, and empathetic toward each other, and understand that in order to address a common concern, they all have to work together. Yet they have not been able to engage a representative from the African American group in their community. It helps to understand why African Americans have traditionally been "left out," and how important it is to keep finding ways to engage them.

The city council of a local community center needs to get together, to discuss ways to improve the center, so that it is more welcoming to people from diverse racial and ethnic backgrounds. They come up with ideas, such as hiring more culturally diverse staff, posting notices in different languages, hosting food festivals, and celebrating various cultural events.

It helps the participants to understand that even though they are taking the first steps to becoming culturally sensitive, their institutional policies may still be racist, because they have not included anyone from the various racial and ethnic groups to participate in the strategic planning process, thereby not sharing their power.

Addressing racial prejudice and racism also means dealing with racial exclusion and injustice. Ultimately, this means that your community-building effort is promoting democracy, a value of the United States and our Constitution.

In other words, there are both moral and sometimes legal reasons to act against racism. There are strong pragmatic reasons as well. Racial prejudice and racism can harm not only the victims, but also the larger society, and indirectly, the very people who are engaging in the acts.

Racism is embedded and pervasive in American society and remains a silent code that systematically closes the doors of opportunity to young and old alike.

Visibly identifiable members of racial and ethnic oppressed groups, continue to struggle for equal access and opportunity, particularly during times of stringent economics, strident calls for tax revolt, dwindling natural resources, inflation, widespread unemployment and underemployment, and conservative judicial opinions that are precursors to greater deprivation. Unless curbed, these conditions invariably lead to greater ethnic and racial rivalry, and to greater political, social, and economic oppression.

The United States has had notoriously unequal accessibility, when it comes to the educational system. Minorities, in particular African Americans, have been kept from the rights of equal access, regardless of what the Constitution says. The country has rarely paid attention to the African American community and the circumstances that affect said community. Systematic racism, educational and corporate discrimination, and the lack of educational opportunities are just a few of the issues faced.

Many African Americans have discussed the need for an educational curriculum that fully encompasses everyone's heritage, instead of the overwhelmingly White American curricula that stresses the steady historical untruths that have been ingrained into the heads of children, since the dawn of modern education.

One of the reasons for this is the lack of sufficient representation at both the secondary and higher educational levels in the United States, is because White America is comfortable the way it is, and always claims there is no funding for change. Once we stop using a lack of funding as an excuse, because African Americans have been told that lie for decades, we can begin to educate society as a whole.

Employment situations have always been a breeding ground for racism and discrimination. In the case of African Americans, these have nearly always been affected by the down-turns in economic prosperity. We are the low hanging fruit when it comes to companies, and corporations that are faced with the typical cycles of budget cuts or downsizing, because the days of factory employment and assembly line employment have all but been phased out of American society, in favor of cheap overseas labor, African Americans are more affected by the employment factor.

White American society has not taken kindly to Affirmative Action programs. I personally have never been a fan, but I understand why we have to have it. Affirmative Action is in place because human beings will never inherently do the right thing.

Affirmative Action is not enforced in business hiring practices, and in fact, human resource departments have developed screening practices of their own in order to target the "look" of employee they are searching for. Employers, especially state and federal organizations receive more federal funding if they have the adequate amount of minority employees. Once again, there becomes a financial benefit to having African Americans on the payroll.

The housing industry is where African Americans have faced significant racism and discrimination. Price gouging has been a regular practice, as is the illegal practice of redlining mortgages. As recently as 2013, an $11-million dollar settlement regarding redlining mortgages in minority neighborhoods, was agreed to in the Washington D.C. metropolitan area. It is the twenty-first century, and these practices, such as steering and discouraging certain racial and cultural groups from moving into a certain neighborhood or area, continue even today.

Studies conducted, have found that discrimination against African Americans is still a regular practice by financial institutions in the United States. These illegal practices aggravate and intensify the inequality, and are part of the reason that African Americans are so disproportionately affected by being homeless, and never truly able to achieve the White American dream.

White America never wants to discuss it, but there are double health care standards in the United States. While most White Americans have access to adequate health insurance, African Americans are often forced into the fees-for-service and public care route. This system is highly inadequate, and will never satisfy the health care needs of any community, especially the needs of African Americans, who are often faced with a higher probability of heart disease, diabetes, cancer, and the like.

In addition, many health care facilities, mental health services, and health care providers are located in areas of metropolitan cities that are inaccessible to African Americans. Furthermore, as health care costs continue to rise, the ability to adequately service the needs of the underserved will continue to decline.

Even with the passing of the Affordable Healthcare Act, there are still fifty million Americans who do not have health care. This is particularly troubling to African Americans, because they face a stiffer economic crisis, which makes it even more difficult to get private health care, or any type of mental health assistance, because they do not have the funds and access to medical insurance coverage.

This is important because in the United States, life expectancy for African Americans is significantly less than that for White Americans. In my city of St. Louis, there is a difference of eighteen years in life expectancy between the city of St. Louis, and the city of Clayton, located in St. Louis County. To bring that into understandable terms, it is the difference in zip codes of 63105 (St. Louis City) and 63106 (St. Louis County).

White America makes the negative assumption, based on stereotypes that nearly all African Americans are on the simple handout of public welfare. Well, obviously that would be inaccurate, as there are nearly three times as many White Americans on some type of public assistance than there are African Americans. In addition, the public welfare system in the United States is at the least, a complex and chaotic system.

It is not a handout system, as many White Americans want to believe. What it is, is a true example of employers, because of our free markets and capitalism, not being held accountable for not giving a job and adequate income in order have a decent way of life, to anybody and everybody who is capable and willing to work. The welfare system has been used to keep wages low, and to maintain a pool of people, mainly African Americans, who are available and limited to work at menial, unskilled jobs.

As I have stated, the days of the unskilled laborer have gone away. It is standard practice of major companies, to ship those positions out of the United States, in exchange for cheap labor. If public welfare really intended it to be a productive service, in addition to the funds received, it would include budgeting services, job training, educational assistance, child care, and unemployment insurance services, to take the place of the significantly expensive system known as COBRA.

When you are forced into public welfare, or other social services, minorities, and in particular African Americans are forced again to deal with a system that was set up by White Americans, and serviced by White Americans. This automatically sets up a discriminative situation, and never addresses the real problems of racism, unemployment, illiteracy, and poverty that affect the African American community. This White American system does nothing more than hold control over a culture, by encouraging said culture to use entitlements.

In the United States, White American society blames African Americans for the lifestyle they live, and directs its efforts to adjusting African Americans to live by a standard that White America approves, while showing a total disregard for changing the environment wherein this is all happening.

African Americans have little to no representation in legislation. Therefore, in all reality, laws that affect everybody, are being created without full representation in the legislative bodies. Studies have found a standard mode of operation, in the harassment of African American elected officials in the United States. African American lawmakers are forced to deal with IRS investigations and audits. They are also fall victim to unauthorized surveillance, such as phone wire taps.

The statistics, which are the clearest tools for determining and measuring the quality of life in American society, show that African Americans continue to lag behind White America in every possible category. Not only does this point to the depth of racial inequality in this society, but it clearly undermines the idea that racism is simply a matter of prejudice, existing only on an ideological level.

As the economy of the '90s drew to a close, African American poverty rates dropped to a record low. African American unemployment fell to a record low also, but this did little to close the gap of economic inequality that continues to separate African Americans from White Americans.

Even with these historic lows, African American unemployment still was twice the unemployment level for White Americans. These numbers did not take into account the nearly one million African American men who are incarcerated, which by some estimates would increase the overall unemployment level by 2 percent.

African Americans still tend to be the last to be hired, when the economy is booming. That means that they also tend to be the first to lose their jobs, when a downturn hits. Job losses have been deep in manufacturing and construction, and these losses have also hit retailers. Jobs in those industries tend to be disproportionately held by African Americans.

Currently, unemployment among African Americans is rising at a faster pace than in any similar period since the mid-1970s. Nearly all of those jobs are in manufacturing, with African American workers hit disproportionately harder than White ones.

The disproportionate impact of layoffs on African Americans, in the recession of early 2008, further illustrates how racism compounds an already bad situation, when the economy begins to contract. It was reported during this recession that a significant number of major corporations cut African Americans' jobs, at a much higher rate than for White American workers.

From an employment application standpoint, studies show the racist obstacles African American applicants face. It has been found that job applicants, with African American sounding names such as LaKeisha or Jamal, were twice as likely not to be called back for an interview, as applicants with White American sounding names.

Ironically, even White American applicants with prison records, were called back more frequently about jobs than African Americans with no prison record at all.

Unemployment today for young African American men (16-21) tops out at more than 30 percent, double that of young White American men in the same age category. In spite of that appalling statistics, Republicans are frequently looking for ways to cut funds for urban job training programs.

In addition, by age twenty-eight, the African American population will have reached the cumulative level of lifetime poverty that the White American population arrives at by age seventy-five.

As stated, access to health care is a major problem for African Americans. Twenty-three percent of African Americans have no health coverage at all. Poverty, and a lack of health insurance mean that African Americans die on an average six years younger than the rest of the population. It means that African American infant mortality rates are more than twice that for White American babies. The same deadly mix, has helped to produce an AIDS epidemic among African Americans.

Today, African American women are only slightly more than half of the population, but they make up over two-thirds of all new AIDS cases for women, and over two-thirds of all new pediatric AIDS cases are of African American children.

We have discussed the toll that the judicial system has had, on the lives of African Americans, and has been well documented in journals all over the United States. African American youth are dealt with no more sympathetically. They are treated much more harshly in the juvenile justice system than their White American peers.

Among first-time youth offenders, African Americans are six times more likely than their White American counterparts to be sentenced to prison by juvenile courts. For drug offenses, African American youth are twice more likely than White American youth to be sent to prison.

Currently, there are over 1,600,000 African Americans enrolled in institutions of higher education, but there are nearly another million, who are locked up in federal and state prisons. Moreover, it is estimated that after an African American man turns twelve years old, they will have a 40 percent chance of spending time in jail in their lifetime.

Furthermore, although racism has been a problem historically in the South, It has been identified that the five most segregated cities in the United States today are in the North. Those cities have been identified as Detroit, Milwaukee, New York City, Chicago, and I am so sad to say this, but my city of St. Louis has made this infamous list.

The day before the national Martin Luther King Jr. holiday in January 2009, there was a study released, showing that American schools are beginning to "re-segregate." According to researchers, the South surprisingly went from being the most segregated region in the country, to being the most integrated.

Now the reverse is happening. But these studies have gone on to point out that although re-segregation in the South is happening most rapidly, institutions in the Northeast, and on the West Coast are still more segregated. In fact, in today's society, the country's most segregated institutions are in New York City. This trend in institutions was precipitated by court decisions weakening desegregation orders from the '60s.

All of these terrible statistics, are underscored by the fact that when it comes to making the laws that have an impact on the lives of African Americans, there is a woeful lack of representation. In the history of the United States Senate, one of the most powerful decision-making bodies in the country, there have only been a few African American senators.

There have been four African American governors in the history of the United States. As of the printing of this book, there are none. There is just one African

American in the Supreme Court; right-winger Clarence Thomas.

This picture of racial injustice in the United States points to the systemic embedded nature of racism. The degree of racial disparity and inequality, are not just the result of ignorance, or a lack of tolerance. The greatest proof of this is not just the conditions that exist today, but the deterioration of conditions for African Americans, in the aftermath of the social justice struggles of the '60s Civil Rights Movement, which pointed to the institutionalization of racism.

The social movements of the '60s pressured the United States government to devote more resources into fighting poverty, and creating opportunities for African Americans' access to higher education, and as a result, African American poverty decreased.

Before President Johnson administration's "War on Poverty," there were nearly forty million people living in poverty in the country. During the mid-1960s, President Johnson and Congress adopted a series of programs, directly geared to helping those caught in the poverty circle. Those programs, paired with a strong economy, succeeded in reducing the poverty by over 15 million. As a result, the poverty rate dropped to just under 12 percent.

If racism was caused only by ignorance and prejudice, then economic disparity between races, should have ended in the '60s. The Civil Rights Movement, and the African American power struggles of the times exposed racist injustice. When the administration of Lyndon Johnson reacted, and implemented his "War on Poverty," that should have been the end of the story. Instead, the disparity never disappeared, and instead, it has grown expeditiously again in a very short time.

The result has been a widening earnings gap between the best and the brightest African Americans and White American workers. This is a fact of economic life that stands in raving contradiction, to the many popular assumptions about African American success.

By the end of the twenty-first century, the economic gap, as measured by median income, would have returned to the same level, as at the end of the 60s. The economic advances of the Civil Rights Movement, and African American power movements have been virtually erased.

It would be wrong, nevertheless, to conclude that things are just as bad as they were before the Civil Rights Movement. Many of the legislative gains from that period, from affirmative action to ending segregation, are once again under attack. But the impact of the movement has been longstanding, and fundamentally changing the attitudes and perceptions of millions of White Americans about African Americans.

On many of the issues, White Americans are more sympathetic to the realities of African Americans in society, and they also have closer contact and relationships with African Americans than they did fifty years ago.

Nearly two-thirds of White America believes the federal government should be responsible, for ensuring that African Americans have access to education that is equal in quality, to that of White America. It is also a fact that over half of White America feels the federal government, is responsible for ensuring that American Africans receive equal access to health care.

Over two-thirds of White America feels it is the government's responsibility to make sure American Africans receive fair treatment by the courts, and police equal to White Americans. Nearly two-thirds of White America believes that there are still major problems facing American Africans in this country.

On social issues, findings have been equally telling. When asked if it were better to marry someone of their own race or a different race, over half believe it doesn't matter. Over three-quarters of White Americans believe race should not be a factor when it comes to adopting children. When asked if you live in a racially integrated neighborhood, over two-thirds of African Americans responded yes, with about one-third of White Americans saying the same.

These all should be contrasted to the dominant ideas prior to, or at the beginning of the Civil Rights Movement.

The list goes on and on, but all the changes tend to be large and all are in the same direction. They are all moving toward more tolerance and less racism. Moreover, where available, data indicates that the White American working class moved even more heavily in this direction, than did other White Americans. These are impressive changes.

Indeed, comprehensive analyses establish that racial attitudes are the area of public opinion, where the largest and most consistently liberal attitude changes have taken place.

None of this is offered as evidence that racism ceases to exist. It merely suggests that ideas within the population at large, although not significantly, have changed, thanks to the struggles fought by the Civil Rights and African American power movements.

In contrast, the previous statistics, outlining the conditions of African Americans point to the depths of institutional racism in the United States. While racism still manifests itself in many ideas, its most significant expression is systemic. That is how it affects the ability of African Americans to obtain and keep jobs.

This would lead to decreasing poverty levels, accessing quality education and health care, and avoiding the disproportionately harsh impact of the American judicial system.

While statistics may show that attitudes, of the majority of White America have shifted over the last fifty years, there remains the common perception, particularly among Democrats, that all of White America benefits from the racial oppression of African Americans.

There is little argument that White American executives, who run the boardrooms in corporate America, control the courtrooms in the judicial system, and exert the most influence in the government benefit, not only from the oppression of African Americans, but also from the oppression of all workers.

White America has this important asset that allows them to escape the greatest liabilities and disadvantages of poverty. It is simply their "Whiteness." White Americans who are homeless, unemployed or uneducated for the most part, still believe in the great American narrative of opportunity and upward mobility.

If they scrape together enough money to buy a new suit, they will find it relatively easy to obtain employment. They know with the same set of skills and level of educational attainment, as the African

American householders across the street, they stand a superior chance of being hired.

Whiteness creates a comfortable social and psychological safety net for the White American poor. Every day may not be a lucky one, but White America really never has to sing the blues for long.

There is the issue of consciousness. Whether or not White Americans think that they have an advantage because of their race, is really no great revelation because of the idea that many White Americans, already buy into and can accept racist ideas. But this doesn't explain why many African Americans do the same.

Moreover, there is a crucial difference between ideas and reality. Just because many White American workers may think they have it better, the reality that White American workers, and the White American poor face, is something entirely different. The real economic picture for millions of White workers is also not great.

In numbers never seen in history, and just like African Americans, millions of White Americans are confronting unemployment, poverty, and hunger. Studies have documented the growing crisis of White America. The fact is that of half the Americans living in poverty, nearly 18 million of them are White.

This is not a statement on the great financial gains, or future of the vast majority of African Americans. Rather, it speaks to the declining economic situation of millions of White American, working class people in the United States over the last three decades. This situation is exacerbated by the growing concentration of wealth, in the uppermost echelons of American society.

"Reaganism" and "Reaganomics" was a practice of both Republicans and Democrats, aimed to deepen the wedge between White American workers and African Americans in particular. At that time in history, the degree of racism emanating from the White House, was frequently staggering. Nearly every social spending cutback was justified with a racist stereotype. "Welfare," "drugs," and "crime" have been the racist code words, scapegoating African Americans for over the past fifty years.

Surprisingly, Democratic President Bill Clinton, who I described as "America's first African American President," not only completed, but made more acceptable the attacks that Reagan and George Bush (I) got started.

Abandoning any notion of government action to correct racial injustice, has been central to Democrat politics from the start. In fact, the conservative Democrats who launched the Democratic Leadership Council, the faction that catapulted Clinton and Gore to the top of the Democratic Party, saw it largely as a vehicle to compete with the Rev. Jesse Jackson's Rainbow Coalition.

At best, the Clinton-Gore administration promoted a "race-neutral" approach to social policy that simply tried to avoid issues of racial discrimination. At worst, it pandered to racism, by scapegoating African American welfare recipients. On several occasions, this administration took actions it knew to be discriminatory.

While perfecting the symbolism of inclusion, by promoting a national dialogue on race and appointing a cabinet that "looked" like America, the Clinton administration also ordered the end to dozens of affirmative action set-aside programs. It maintained, and actually defended against critics, of the racist criminal sentencing guidelines. These are the same guidelines that overwhelmingly discriminate against African American crack cocaine users.

It pressed the Congressional Black Caucus to drop provisions from the 1994 Crime Bill, aimed to safeguard against discriminatory application, of the vastly expanded federal death penalty. The Clinton administration's greatest social policy innovation was called "welfare reform." It supported the elimination of a sixty-year-old guarantee, of a minimum standard of assistance for poor people.

While a great number of White American workers throughout this time bought into the racist scapegoating of African Americans, this didn't actually make their lives any better materially, socially, or psychologically. Instead, it allowed the complete looting of the wages and income of all workers, both African American and White American.

The fact of the matter is, both African Americans and White Americans have been exploited by "the man." The real deal is this. These company leaders were making out like bandits, all the way to the bank, with the money they were expropriating from the labor of both African American and White American workers. The point is that this wedge was driven and widened. Racism was, is, and will always be a strategy of dividing and exploiting all working people.

These business leaders in the beginning, start out as basically idealist and not materialists. They claimed that the fundamental force that drives the motor of African American oppression, is race alone. They argued that all White Americans benefit materially, and ideologically from racism, which in my view, looking at the data and looking at the facts and experiences of White Americans, is a disastrous misinterpretation of White American and African American social history.

Former African American slave and abolitionist, Frederick Douglass, made the point most clear when he wrote in the late nineteenth century, under conditions far more violent and racially polarized than today. He said, "The hostility between White America and the Negros of the South is easily explained. Both are plundered by the same plunderers, and the hostility was incited on both sides by the poor White Americans and Negros by putting enmity between them. They divided both to conquer each."

The ongoing debate over the true beneficiaries of racism, is important for both leftists and liberals. If White American workers benefit from racism, then what hope is there to ever build a majority to fight back against racism? It is doubtful that an entire group of the population would ever fight against something that put more food on the table, more money in the paycheck and provided more health care.

Also, given the growing concentration of wealth in the hands of an elite few, and the austerity it means for the majority on the bottom, the question for both African American and White American workers becomes this. How can we fight back, and take what is rightfully ours? Can White American and African American workers unite on a class basis?

The issue is not whether White American workers buy into racist ideas. That is a question of consciousness. The issue is whether backward ideas can be broken down and ultimately changed. The evidence shows overwhelmingly that through the course of struggle, racism and other backward ideas can shift.

The statistics outlined earlier, detailing the change in attitudes and perceptions of most of White America since the '60s, and the height of the Civil Rights era, is a case in point. Whether or not those changes remain intact is a political question, tied to the level of struggle and resistance to racism in the American society.

All truly African American politics, must begin with the real truth. The American system does not work for the masses of society, and it cannot be made to work without both radical, fundamental changes. The challenge is thrown to communities all over America, like the City of St. Louis. It is the challenge to consolidate, and organize the African American role, as the vanguard in the struggle for a new society.

To accept the challenge, is to move to independent African American politics. There can be no equivocation on that issue. History leaves us no other choice. It has never been shown that White politics will bring the changes African Americans need.

Current society, unfortunately is a long way from where African American politics are, at the beginning of the twenty-first century. Today, one African American holds the most powerful position in the administration of a White American, right-wing, Republican administration.

This powerful African American tries, but struggles to improve the lives or lessen discrimination against the vast majority of African Americans in the United States, and often he is forced, because of partisan politics, to uphold the policies of an administration that has increased the level of racism.

There is a huge political gap between the militancy of the debates, the realities of African Americans and the politics offered today. This is the result of two main factors. The first is the opportunities, both economically and socially, that opened up for the African American middle class, after the Civil Rights era and African American power movements of the '60s and '70s. The second is the result of the absorption, of African American political operatives and organizations, within the folds of the Democratic Party.

Before the Civil Rights Movement, there were few African American politicians, business owners, and college graduates who could make the most from their opportunities, due to racism and segregation. The movement helped to break the legal fetters that limited African American's upward mobility.

The changes among African Americans are not just financial. They are political as well. As African American commentator Henry Louis Gates said, "We don't have to pretend any longer that 35 million people can ever possibly be members of the same economic class. Nor do they speak with one single voice, united behind one single leader. As each of us knows, we have never been members of one social or economic class and never will be."

Although middle-class African Americans experience racism in their daily lives, as a group they have chosen to make a deal with the system, rather than fight against it. So while the African American middle class has been the main beneficiary of the Civil Rights Movement, it has moved far to the right since then.

This has even included veterans of the movement. Reason being, the growing conservatism of the African American middle class simply mirrors the trend of the entire middle class as a whole, regardless of race during the '80s and '90s.

This is also a reflection of the changes that have taken place since the days of the Civil Rights Movement. Prior to the '60s, the miniscule African American middle class that did exist, had an interest in joining the fight for Civil Rights. So while the vast majority of participants in the Civil Rights Movement and African American power movements were African American workers, its leadership was middle class, and the desire of the movement reflected this.

The African American middle class joined with African American workers to demand the right to vote, and an end to legal segregation in the '60s, but they sought to remove the barriers to their advance within the system, not to transform it.

This dynamic was even clearer when it came to the transformation of electoral African American politics. The number of African American elected officials has increased from fewer than 200 in 1964 to over 8,000 today. Today, there have been more than forty seven African American mayors in cities of 50,000 or more, including Houston, Dallas, Detroit, Philadelphia, and San Francisco.

The permanence of the African American political establishment, within the Democratic Party today is a given. This was not always the case. The absorption of key activists, within the Democrats in some cases, was part of a conscious effort to draw activists into the party.

In 1972, Democratic presidential candidate George McGovern adopted something called an "African American Bill of Rights" into his platform. But more often than not, African Americans had to kick in the door to the Democratic Party, often waging campaigns against racist party machines in cities such as Philadelphia and Chicago.

In reality, African American activists had to fight to even get into the party, not just in challenging the bigoted "Dixiecrats" in the South, but the hugely racist big-city machines in the North. The huge shift of the

African American population to the Northern cities during and after World War II wasn't reflected in the local officeholders.

Electing African American officials could appear to be a radical step, especially in the face of White American racist opposition. African American power could be used to justify African American elected officials.

As the movements began to recede, so did the pressure African American elected officials may have initially felt to produce real change. Instead, African American political figures settled into their governing positions, managing austerity on a city, state, and federal level.

Throughout the '90's, African American m yours were in control of some of the largest cities in the U.S., yet did little or nothing to alleviate the hardship of African American workers living in those cities.

African American Mayor David Dinkins, who was elected mayor of New York in 1989, oversaw both backbreaking austerity, and a racist police force that made its reputation terrorizing, and then extorting the African American population in the city. In his attempt to hold onto office when challenged by Rudolph Giuliani in 1993, Dinkins led a crackdown on the city's homeless population.

African American Mayor Tom Bradley was steering the ship, when his racist police force, lead by Police Chief Darrell Gates, became the focal point of the riots that swept Los Angeles in 1992.

The list of betrayals by African American mayors goes on and on. Washington, D.C. Mayor Sharon Pratt Dixon, in 1993 stupidly suggested the National Guard take over patrolling the city streets, in order to stop drug dealing. Wilson Goode, the former mayor of Philadelphia, once conjured up an idea, and ordered the bombing of a street, in an African American neighborhood that housed the radical MOVE organization.

The Congressional Black Caucus, with thirteen African American congressmen when it formed in 1969, has referred to itself ever since as the "conscience of the Congress." But it has dramatically moved away from its grassroots thought process and movement influenced origins.

If the Congressional Black Caucus says that it has been "the conscience of the Congress since 1969," why then is the caucus not taking a leadership role on major progressive issues of the day? Because like the vast majority of members of Congress, the caucus has been bought off in droves by White commercial corporate interests.

In the '80s and '90s, it was the African American mayors and the African American middle classes that opposed the aspirations of African American workers. But because of the relatively weak position of this class of African Americans, they attempted to increase their influence within the system.

The integration of the African American middle class within the Democratic Party, and capitalism itself is unlikely to be reversed, despite of the racism within the American society at large. This however does not represent a victory for the mass of African Americans, but a retreat from the politics of the '60s and the Civil Rights Movement.

Any strategy for confronting racism today has to start from an understanding of the nature of racism, and the role it plays in society. Equally, it is important to understand the crucial institutions that help to shape the political environment, in which challenges to racism unfold.

Contrary to the assertions of Republican conservatives, racism continues to exist, blunting the life chances of African Americans. This reality coincides with the undeniable and positive liberalization, of attitudes on racial issues that has taken root throughout American society, since the heyday of the Civil Rights Movement.

Although many African Americans gained from the triumphs of '70s and '80s, the disproportionate beneficiaries have been a section of the African American middle class, who have become well integrated into the economic and political system and its principle institutions, especially the Democratic Party.

Because a large and significant segment of the African American population has a stake in the existing arrangements of society, struggles against racism characteristic of the '60s and '70s have receded. For this reason, the Clinton and George Bush (II) administrations' attacks on the gains of the '60s and '70s met with little organized resistance.

The most significant gains for African Americans have come from mass struggles that affected society as a whole, including large sections of the White population. Understanding the nature of racism in the twenty-first century is the first step to devising a strategy, for confronting, and building a movement that not only stops racist attacks, but that begins to win real gains for the future.

Clearly, there is a need to further discuss the conditions of Latinos in the United States, and given the ongoing "war on terror" and its impact on Arab and Muslims in this country, the scope of the discussion as it relates to racism can and should be broader.

However, the historical fetter on the struggle of workers in this country has been anti-African American racism, which began with slavery and continues to this day. In the United States, racism is manifested at the individual, group, and institutional levels.

It has been institutionalized, maintained and hidden in educational, economic, political, religious, social, and cultural policies and activities. It is observable in the prejudiced attitudes, values, myths, beliefs, and practices expressed by many people, including those in positions of power.

Racism is functional, meaning it serves a purpose. In the United States, racism functions to maintain structural inequities that are to the disadvantage of African Americans.

Organized racism, against members of visibly identifiable racial and ethnic groups, has permeated every aspect of our lives, including contacts with the legal system, religion, and social relationships. It has become deeply embedded and institutionalized through folklore, legal restrictions, values, myths, and social media that is openly supported by a substantial number of people, including those who maintain control of the major institutions of American society.

Racism has negatively impacted both the oppressed and the oppressor. Institutional racism has historical roots and in injustices perpetrated by our ancestors, on Native Americans in conquering and populating this country, and recognition of historical injustices is the beginning step in combating racism.

One has to acknowledge the fact that the sons and daughters are not responsible for the sins of their parents, but the sons and daughters must analyze the present reality to ascertain if, as a result of the historical injustices perpetrated by our parents, results of one group in society being in a more advantageous, and favorable position over and at the expense of the others.

It is incumbent in solidarity with those groups, who are subordinate to join forces together with the profession of social work, to bring about a more just and equitable society in which power, status, wealth, services, and opportunities are enjoyed by all. Even those who are not consciously racist tend to accept White American privilege, and the benefits of discrimination against others. Racism limits and minimizes the contributions many citizens can make to society.

The existence of racism in American society is age old, and has become embedded in the very fabric of our everyday lives. There is a faction of White America who believes that racism has had a reduction, but as an African American who faces it every day, I can say that it is alive and well and shows absolutely no signs of decreasing.

If White America would consider looking at racism at its true meaning, they would probably have a clearer understanding. Racism is institutionalized and an embedded factor of society, and it is far more than just a few redneck idiots in white sheets, running around terrorizing people of color.

It runs much deeper that just one race hating another race. Racism is a virus that is incubated in the laboratories, of the government of the United States. It is a sickness that is virtually impossible to cure, because it is maintained by the corporate entities, and legislative power that determine the rules. The people involved in these corporate entities and legislative hierarchies couldn't eliminate this virus if they wanted, because the infection is way too deep.

If you are going to put a simple understanding on what racism truly is in today's United States of America, it can be summed up as, White American society having an embedded belief, because of some overzealous understanding in DNA make up, that they are superior to other cultures, who do not share their biological association.

This means that White America, because of this illusion of superiority has been able to acquire enormous economic power and dominance over all of society, because they feel they are better. This has done nothing but continue a false dominance, and kill any progress that has been made in this country, to fight the racism and discrimination that comes with this feeling of superiority.

From the Bus Boycotts in the South and African Americans just trying to get a meal at a lunch counter, to a historic demonstration on a famous bridge, in a little Alabama town called Selma, and the same hands that picked cotton moving toward picking Presidents, it had been assumed that relations at that time were on the verge of improving. But with every step toward progress, the United States has still dragged their heels in truly bringing the various cultures of this country together.

From an outside perspective, racism in the United States has generally been the battle between White American and African Americans. That scenario has changed because of immigration. In the United States today, society is a mix of multicolored and multicultural. Racism in this country has touched cultures today that were not a factor sixty years ago. Hatred of Muslims in the United States is on the rise, and there is a high increase of animosity toward other diverse populations, entering and living in communities in this country.

The turn of the century delivered a broad range of changes in the world we live in. Many of those changes have come in the form of formal political legislation, against discrimination in its many forms. Affirmative Action laws are being enforced at a higher rate, to be sure that all people are given equal access to opportunities. But we need to realize that this is not enough and will never be enough.

White American society continues, whether by hook or by crook, to separate themselves because of a false racial superiority that they feel. The historic wall, even if it is shrouded, is still surrounding us, and making us realize that you will never be able to pass a law, or legislate the hearts and minds of a society. There will always be those who will fight for change, while others resist, seeking to maintain the status quo.

White American society has controlled the economy, the government, and the media since its existence, and that kind of control is not easily relinquished. With racism as the foundation for this control, it will never change unless White America resolves its feelings of superiority and works toward bringing cultures together. This will be a difficult task at best, because the whole belief has been one of separation, segregation, and discrimination.

Over the past half century plus, there has been a racial foundation in this country that is the basis of every one of society's institutions. When Barack Obama was elected President, the virus of racism moved out of the dark seedy place that White American society doesn't want to talk about. It was put under the public spotlight again, almost as if we were right back in Birmingham 1955. We needed the first African American President to prove to the world that our society could be one of acceptance and true tranquility.

The struggle of African American communities across the nation for rights has given birth to a brand new Civil Rights Movement. This is a younger, more power movement that never sleeps and never runs out of energy. Their mission is to put an end to racism in African American communities in the United States.

They refuse to sit back and cave in to the conservative, Republican, and Tea Party attacks, with racism as their weapon, tearing down the lifelong progress that has been made by the founding sisters and brothers of the original Movement. These same factions are attempting to destroy accomplishments and ending programs like Affirmative Action.

White America will only take notice and begin respecting African Americans, when as a people we stop turning the cheek that has been battered and bruised for over a four-hundred-year period. African Americans must step out on faith and speak out, demanding to be treated in a dignified manner and given the same respect as that of White American society. This is the focus of the new Civil Rights Movement.

The new Civil Rights Movement believes that this can only be achieved by attacking from the grassroots, and by developing the youth of the community. The youth of this movement think outside the conventional box and have already achieved a great deal. The most reactionary provisions of the Federal Anti-Immigrant Bill has already been eliminated and the preposterously racist proposal, that 2016 Presidential candidate Donald Trump discussed, of sending eleven million illegal immigrants back to Mexico, and turning twelve million others, without papers, into felons is now eliminated.

What is amazing is that both the Democratic and Republican Party now has legislation that would help undocumented workers, and some illegal aliens become citizens of the United States, but once again there is so much more that needs to be achieved. To win full rights for all minorities, and especially African Americans, this new Civil Rights Movement needs to strengthen their drive. This Movement has the opportunity, and because of the world of social media, the means to end the discriminatory ways that African Americans are treated every day.

The prejudice, discrimination, and the more than often physical attack African Americans face in schools, on jobs, and by law enforcement can become a thing of the past. The promise of equality can be made real, but only if we build a leadership for this new movement that will not stop fighting until victory and equality is available to everybody.

Youth leadership is the real key. By developing a politically conscious group of young leaders, the future of the United States can be bright. The potential of a new movement, how broadly it is built, and what is achieved, will be completely determined by who is in leadership of the movement.

Few issues in American life have been as intransigent as race. In every century of the United States, race has presented the nation both its greatest challenges, and it greatest opportunities. This has called into question the mythological principle of equality on which this country was supposedly founded.

During the '50s and '60s, the Civil Rights Movement awakened the nation's collective consciousness around issues of racial equity. But the victories of the movement, however decisive they seemed at the time, did not bring the long-term equality that activists and policymakers hoped for.

The things the new Civil Right Movement are fighting for are significantly different that they were sixty years ago. The battle to sit at a lunch counter or to cast a simple vote in an election have been surpassed by unemployment, substandard housing, crime and drugs. These new problems make the playbook of the old movement obsolete, because often they fall outside the jurisdiction of political legislation.

The contributions that the old Movement made will live on with a legacy of immortal importance. It was essential in stopping the basic segregation that had enveloped this country since its creation, and started a lasting belief that African Americans could truly follow a legislative path that would lead to righting the racial wrongs in the United States. It led to other protected groups like women, homosexuals, and environmentalists standing up for the rights of affected parties, and to be a critical of the decisions affecting their interests.

Unfortunately, because these other group began fighting for their rights, the issues of African Americans were forced to compete for the eyes of the court. And, as new issues, such as assumptions by both White Americans about African Americans, began to come out in what has been referred to as a "post-Civil Rights America," the old Movement was ill equip to handle these new issues.

White America still believes that the unfinished Civil Rights agenda is about racial issues, and the government reforms should have no involvement in addressing these long-term problems. White Americans believe that compelling evidence of African American progress can be found in the middle class, because a miniscule amount of us have achieved some type of status.

This helps explain why many in White America, who are opponents of any agenda that is based on race or culture, harbor the feelings that they do. Meanwhile poverty in a large and intractable African

American underclass continues to expand deeper into inner cities and rural communities across this country, and decisively restricts the life chances for African Americans, particularly, African American children.

Racial disparity has never been and will never be removed from the agenda of the movement, only now it needs to be reassessed to include the multiracial and multicultural members of the United States' ever-changing society.

African American and White American inequality and disparity is a factor in personal income, education, health care, and housing. The national media reports on law enforcements practice of racial profiling (driving while black), and in law enforcement arrests, sentencing and in the criminal court system when it comes to African Americans, but often passes on discrimination in the housing industry, and the still highly used practice of redlining.

Republicans argue that the responsibility for solving these problems should fall in the laps of African Americans. The old argument of "pulling yourself up by your bootstraps," but we don't understand that you have to start out wearing boots in order for that to happen. African American cultures didn't even start with shoes in this country.

There is an additional issue on the new Civil Rights agenda, which involves the rapid growth in the immigrant population. Individuals of Hispanic origin nearly outnumber African Americans, and by 2050, they will be the majority-minority population in the United States, which could make the issues facing African Americans, a secondary thought on the agenda of society.

As a nation, we have already moved away from the sole White American and African American model of race relations, to one that reflects the United States broad diversity of race, ethnicity, gender, and lifestyle. The nationwide increase in interracial and interethnic marriages is already changing the historical thought processes of what it is to be a member of both the White American and African American race.

High-profile individuals and athletes like Tiger Woods (although his golf game has gotten worse after his cheating scandal) represent a generation of Americans who are redefining race by choosing to embrace their ethnic diversity and its broader implications on society. It is conceivable that at midcentury, the United States will view race as fluid, rather than fixed and precise terms.

One of the shortcomings of the Civil Rights Movement of the '50s and '60s was its failure to see the need for this fluid model, to address new Civil Rights issues in the coming decades, and still the search goes on. One of the issues today is how does society develop various flexible remedies to combat racial disparity and the nation's changing racial and ethnic diversity.

The Reverend Jesse Jackson's Rainbow Coalition was a step in the direction of setting up shop, under whose shelter young and old African Americans could find common issues and agendas. A new generation of Civil Rights leaders now focus its work on eliminating social and economic disparities, particularly for the indigent.

Using some of the '60s strategies for community organizing around community advocacy and service delivery, these leaders are bringing technical proficiency to such problems as economic development, improvement of education systems and the organization of community development co-opts, whose missions range from building housing to creating small industries.

Most of the successful leaders in the post-Civil Rights Movement operate in the nonprofit sector, primarily in community-based groups. They know how to reinvent themselves and their strategies by developing alliances and partnerships between various cultural groups, based on technical competence as much as on common goals.

This creates an opportunity to build public and private resource bases, and navigate the bureaucratic governmental maze for funding. They are actively training a new generation of young leaders to succeed them.

The skills they bring to these positions include expertise in planning, finance, technology, and government. They know how to design programs that are appropriate for the complex issues associated to their work, and how to find the resources to rebuild the decaying infrastructures. These skills prepare them to overhaul human services in order to make them more efficient and less costly, even while pushing constituents to practice self-sufficiency.

The leaders of today's Civil Rights Movement are different. Many of them experience issues that their older counterparts would never have imagined. Most have attended integrated schools and have grown up watching integration on television. These twenty-first century leaders are in many cases, at the helm of traditionally African American organizations, as well as corporate, government and nonprofit entities.

Sure, all African Americans have their own race story about the first time they were called "Nigger" or treated poorly in a store or other public place. But we also have the images of Rev. Martin Luther King and Malcolm X along with the historical expectation that we would carry on for the four little girls from Alabama, whose dreams were cut short, and in all places, a church.

Some would refer to the reality of powerful African American leaders in the twenty-first century as a privilege, because they did not face the true potential of losing their lives during the struggle, while others would call it a dream fulfilled because of the torched being passed.

Transitions in leadership are difficult in the best of circumstances. We live in what I describe as the best and worst of times for African Americans. Our elder influencers worked, struggled, and in some cases, died for the opportunities that we currently enjoy. It is understandable that our elders would have some level of concern about the future of the African American culture.

Sometimes I hear young people using words to address each other that would have brought tears to my eyes when I was a kid, if they were uttered by a White person. Nevertheless, the torch must be passed, but in a way that always appreciates those who brought us to where we are, by ensuring the stories and struggles are never forgotten.

None of these young leaders have traveled to their respective positions on any form of the Underground Railroad, but I do believe that they have all heard Harriet Tubman's drums, lowly and slowly beating in their heads. It is this younger generation's time to mark their steps in history by the steady drum beat for racial and social justice.

CHAPTER 19

ST. LOUIS, THE "GATEWAY CITY"... GATEWAY TO WHAT?

As you grow older, you'll see White men cheat black men every day of your life, but let me tell you something and don't you forget it— whenever a White man does that to a black man, no matter who he is, how rich he is, or how fine a family he comes from, he is trash."—**Harper Lee**

—Harper Lee

I WOULD BE completely remiss if I did not address my hometown. Even with all of it problems, St. Louis is my home. There are days when I dislike this place with every fiber of my being. Then there are moments when I am sitting at the corner of Euclid and Maryland Avenue, having a cocktail at Culpeppers, watching the hustle and bustle of people enjoying the Central West End, that I say, "There is no place I would rather be."

When it comes to racism, St. Louis has shown a tortured inability to make decisions, when it comes to the issue of race relations. Two hundred years ago, Missouri was a slave state, but it still had no unified answer to the question about slavery.

Many were dead set on maintaining it, while others carried the torch of abolishment. And, like Ferguson, there were opponents on both sides of the question, who voiced their concerns in public protest that were often violent at times. The state called slavery acceptable by the standards of the day, and legitimized it in every way of life, including by legislation.

Luckily for history's standpoint, there were people in this state who were unwilling to sit back and accept the times of the era.

The City of St. Louis fell into a proverbial hailstorm of controversy, because of their involvement in the Dred Scott case in the years previous to the beginning of the Civil War. The Supreme Court of Dred Scott contributed to the Civil War, but it also made public the involvement of the White Americans of St. Louis, as proponents in the case of Dred and Harriet Scott and their two children, and the abolition of slavery.

In fact, the 13th, 14th, and 15th Amendments to the Constitution were designed to do just that, except that it truly didn't work out that way. Instead, the reconstruction of the country began, which was followed by the heightened segregation, exacerbated by Jim Crow laws, which although camouflaged, still exist in the modern era.

Another faction began to take aim at the society of St. Louis. This group was known as the "Colored Aristocracy." They were African Americans who owned their own businesses, large portions of land and held their own prestigious events in the St. Louis area that were attended by dignitaries of the city.

St. Louis in the mid-1800, was made up of White Americans who were born in America, along with German and Italian immigrants who settled in the south side of the city. It also had its share of both slaves and free African Americans. Around this same period (1846), Dred Scott and his wife were suing for their freedom.

The Old Courthouse in downtown St. Louis was the historic scene of this epic battle, and the ramifications and outcomes of this trial would serve as a precedent for any challenges, on the subject of slavery. The Scotts, and their case went through this not once, but again in 1857, when the United States Supreme Court denied them their freedom.

In a small suburb northwest of the city of St. Louis, a famer named William Ferguson sold a portion of his farm to the North Missouri Railroad (aka the Wabash Railroad) around the mid-1800s. It contained a requirement that the railroad build a train depot on the property, in order for it to become a regular stop on the line.

Mr. Ferguson sold off other lots, built a community and by the early 1900s, Ferguson, Missouri, was booming with a population of over a thousand citizens. The community that had started with a farm was incorporated in 1894 as a fourth-class city. Among those who contributed to its growth were former slaves.

St. Louis has a great deal of positive history also, and has been a haven for musicians. The 20th century saw a large migration of both ragtime and blues musicians, and composers like the Scott Joplin who both lived and performed in St. Louis.

But as the population increased, the positive characteristics of the city were traded for deep-seeded racism and segregated housing laws. Areas outside of St. Louis were thrown into the mix of an already complex history of racial tension in the area.

Those segregated housing laws, which began around 1915, in layman's terms simply stated that no one was allowed to move to a block that had more than 75 percent of another race. So African Americans could not move into White neighborhoods. There were a number of institutions, including real estate agencies and financial services that were at the foundation of the housing laws.

The NAACP decided to throw their hat into the ring of this very public and constitutional fight, and was successful. But because of this success, these same White communities were forced to embed their racist laws and creed even deeper, and created associations that cloaked and could enforce segregated housing, through the use of restrictive covenants that outlined to whom properties could (and could not) be sold.

Based on the covenants, the African American population was expected to live in the northern part of St. Louis, St. Louis County and near the waterfront, while the White Americans of the city reigned in the southern area.

Because of the increase in the population of the city in the 1950s, the city powers decided to try an experiment that was becoming all the rage in large cities similar to St. Louis.

Large, high-rise public housing projects were constructed, and one of the most famous in the country was on the Northside of St. Louis. It was called Pruitt-Igoe. It was designed by the same architects who would later go on to design the World Trade Center's twin towers.

Pruitt-Igoe was made up of over thirty buildings, with nearly three thousand small apartments. For some reason it was equipped with elevators that would skip two floors, and stopped on every third one. This was to encourage physical exercise of tenants, for some reason.

This experiment went into effect in 1956, with the original plan of keeping the buildings segregated for both African American and White tenants. The problem with this experiment, is that the White Americans who were expected to move into the project, instead moved to the suburbs, and turned Pruitt-Igoe into an all-African American housing project that housed the lowest of low-income families.

Pruitt-Igoe soon turned into sea of high crime, horrible living conditions, and as with nearly all publicly managed projects, follows a mismanagement of public/federal funds. After twenty years of the experiment, in 1976 the project was demolished. Although African Americans were able to sprinkle themselves in a few communities before this time, about this same time African Americans began an exodus and started leaving the city of St. Louis.

Ferguson was one of the suburbs that attracted African Americans, because it gave them the best opportunity to achieve the American Dream. But no one could have imagined that from 1980 to 2010, the White population would have such a drastic drop from 85 percent to 29 percent.

In contrast, the African American population increased from 12 percent to nearly 70 percent. The protests in 2014 go far beyond the shooting of Michael Brown Jr. Ferguson is not unlike other suburbs of St. Louis that have had decades of watching the racial makeup transition, and the cultural issues build to dangerous levels.

This same tension in St. Louis continues today, as it does all across the country. For White Americans in St. Louis, there is a great deal to be proud of, but there is also just as much to be ashamed of when it comes to the history of race relations in the city. Likewise, for African Americans, there is much to be proud of, but because much has not changed in the Gateway City, there is much that brings an embittered feeling.

Racism in St. Louis, much like the United States, is usually thought of in terms of White Americans having negative attitude toward African Americans. In many cases, these negative thoughts of White America include all minorities. While racism is a national issue among all races and cultures, the most popular contrasting cultures are White America against African Americans.

This is no more factual than in St. Louis, which has been sometimes called "one of the most racially polarized cities in America." The question should be "how do White Americans in St. Louis view racism today?" The problem with asking this question is that you can never get an honest answer, but one that is glossed over in the mask of political correctness.

The August 2014 tragedy in Ferguson, Missouri, where I grew up playing football, running around January-Wabash Park, and having more than the occasional White American person call me "Nigger," I was truly awakened. This is the same place, with its militarized law enforcement equipment and a predominantly White police force confronting, harassing, and declaring war on angry and hopeless African-Americans history was made. Except this is not a story unique to Ferguson, St. Louis, or this moment in history.

Many major cities and small towns in the United States are confronted with the very same problems of my "Gateway City." They also are faced with embedded racism, a lack of employment opportunities, inequality and various law enforcement agencies using its African American citizens as human ATMs, in order finance the livelihood of city governments.

This is what has been happening in the city of St. Louis, and has absolutely been happening in the more than ninety municipalities, surrounding the metropolitan area of the city. Believe it or not, there are cities in the country that are even worse.

Underneath the story that everyone has heard about St. Louis, there lies a significantly more sinister history that tells of an agenda of hatred regarding race relations. This is the poison that White Americans in the city want to believe does not exist, or regularly turn a blind eye to. Because of this, St. Louis will never be fully cleansed from the poison of racism and prejudice that is keeping all citizens of the Gateway City, from achieving the complete American mainstream.

For over eighty years, the State of Missouri has either been the birth place, or has been a magnet to a large number of this country's most racists organization. This has included a large number of Arian Nation Clubs, neo-Nazis, and of course segmented Klaverns of the Ku Klux Klan. Most of these have always been associated with some form of violent crime, and use some lunatic form of Christianity to justify their extremism.

These groups have never had much influence in the post-civil rights era, and have been the subject of humor by both African Americans and White Americans in the St. Louis area at times. But beyond these segmented groups lies another powerful White supremacist group, hiding before our eyes in plain sight.

The leadership of this group has received its power and finance from a large group of conservative Republican politicians, who long for "the good ol' days" when African Americans both knew, and were kept in their place. The days when African Americans were "Niggers on the back of the bus." This group is known as the Council of Conservative Citizens.

The CCC had their headquarters St. Louis. They were the perfect representation, and legacy to the old Southern ways. They focused on "White resistance" in the form of racial progress like desegregation, and it mirrored such Southern organizations like the White Citizens Council that was prevalent in almost every city and town south of the Mason–Dixon Line, during the 1950s, and as an alternative to the Klan, the CCC attempted to gain an air of "respectability."

This is not some organization that fizzled out after the Civil Rights era. It is an active, but a fairly secret national organization with strong ties in the St. Louis area. Their website currently stresses the fact that the CCC is "the only serious nationwide activist group that sticks up for the rights of White Americans!"

But, what that really means is that they hate African Americans, Hispanics, Gay people, and any other minority or protected classes of American citizen. The group promotes the old Southern way of life and old Southern based values. In essence, the CCC is the foundation for the modern day "Tea Party," whose national meetings feature well known elected officials, authors, popular talk-show personalities, clergy members and other prestigious people as speakers.

Just like the feelings of the CCC, the protests leading up to the Grand Jury's decision, in St. Louis County in the fall of 2014, not to indict Officer Darren Wilson, a White police officer, for the fatal shooting of an unarmed African-American teenager in Ferguson, Missouri, also gave a clear indication of the complicated, and continuous history of the racial strife that has enveloped the St. Louis metropolitan area for decades. Although the names and faces have changed over the years, the underlying foundation has not, and does not show any signs that it will.

The reality is that there are about a dozen neighborhoods in the St. Louis area that have fallen victim to the majority of violent crimes in the last fifteen years. I refer to these neighborhoods of the city as the "areas that time forgot," and these are also the areas that always receive grandioso plans of improvement that usually last about three to four weeks, when what they truly need is a long-term law enforcement plan that will improve the quality of life for the entire community, and that includes procedures for reducing crime.

But another clear indication of the double standard of policing in the St. Louis metropolitan, is that when crime happens in other neighborhoods, mainly White neighborhoods, it gets different attention.

When African Americans get killed in North St. Louis or in the North County area of the metropolitan area, it is less common because in the eyes of White American citizens, it happens all the time. You can turn on the local news every morning and get a detailed report of heinous crimes in those areas, and although law enforcement is aware of this situation, it is a general consensus that it gets the attention due.

In contrast, if one young White American woman is killed in the Central West End, which has been the case, law enforcement puts together a comprehensive plan, a "Task Force" if you may, and drops a preverbal "net" on the city to find the culprits of these crimes.

Likewise, if a minority person is killed in an affluent area, it will get little attention, but if a White person is ever killed in a predominantly African American area, you can believe that law enforcement will destroy the area, looking for the person who did it, and they will without a doubt find an African American that will fit the description.

City government, and law enforcement officials are always talking about having a better relationship with the African American community, as if the African American community is that different, and has a different agenda than any other community. That is the problem.

There is this belief that we are different. Truthfully, the Africa American community is not different. They want quality housing, quality education for their kids, employment opportunities, and to be treated fairly, and with dignity by law enforcement.

As someone who was significantly involved in the events in Ferguson, Missouri, I actually made the suggestion to Mayor James Knowles that both he and former Chief of Police Tom Jackson make a public gesture during the protest, by handing out water to the protestors. It would have shown some simple empathy for the situation that involved one of their officers.

It would have been a small gesture to make up for not doing what they should have done, on the day of the Michael Brown Jr. shooting. If they had chosen to meet with Brown's family on that day and simply said, "Today is a tragedy and we are sorry for your loss," because at that time only two people knew what exactly happened. One of them was dead, and the other had already lawyered up.

There quite possibly would have been a different response. By not doing this, they perpetuated the "Us vs. Them" relationship, which is something that

African Americans in the St. Louis area experience on a regular basis, every single day.

Subsequently, when the decision by the Grand Jury came down in November of 2014, it enlarged the wall between White Americans and African Americans, and further perpetuated the oppression of the African American citizens of Ferguson, a city that is over 80 percent African America.

St. Louis County Prosecutor, Robert (Bob) P. McCulloch, a man whose father, a former police officer, was killed by an African American armed gunman, made the decision to present, and as many like myself feel, flood the nine White Americans and three African Americans with every single piece of evidence, instead of just the evidence needed to get the indictment, which according to the duties of the job, he is supposed to.

The killing, and some say execution, of Michael Brown Jr. started fires of civil unrest all over the country, and in various parts of the world. This debate was energized by protestors, mostly young, but of all races and cultures. It also set fire to a national debate on racial discrimination and police brutality, inflicted upon African Americans, many of whom are male, in this country.

The world was able to see and better understand, because the national media put the city of Ferguson, with police officers in riot gear, dogs, and militarized vehicles, with armed cannons on top corralling African Americans, even limiting their demonstration area to a space directly across the street from the racist police department.

I took the opportunity to stand in line with the protestors a few times during day. I saw the largest group of eclectic people that I had ever seen. If anybody had opened their eyes, and looked passed the looting by outside agitators, you would have seen a true, and very possible picture of a real United States. You would have seen, African Americans, White Americans, Hispanics, Jews, women, and every faction under the sun. I even saw six Tibetan Monks, in full robes standing hand in hand with every faction named. It made me very proud to be a member of the United States of America.

At 5:00 p.m., hours prior to the Grand Jury reading in November of 2014, Governor Jay Nixon of Missouri stood up publicly and announced that the National Guard had been put on "high alert." It is amazing how much of a blatant lie (and I don't mind being blunt) this turned out to be.

Moments after the announcement of "No True Bill" by the Prosecuting Attorney, a St. Louis County police car exploded ten feet in front of me. From that moment until early the next morning, the city of Ferguson lost twenty two businesses to arson.

The mayor attempted to contact both the Governor and the Attorney General, to no avail, meaning they would not answer the calls. Furthermore, the National Guard, who were stationed in a parking garage in the business district of Clayton, never came to the rescue and control the demonstrators. That duty fell to the St. Louis County Police and the Missouri State Highway Patrol.

Jay Nixon, the lying Governor of Missouri left local law enforcement outgunned, outmanned, overwhelmed, and feeling screwed with their pants on. Come to find out later by investigation, the Pinocchio of the Missouri state government never intended to protect the lives and property of the citizens of Ferguson.

How else are African Americans supposed to feel? It was summed up in a sign I saw an African American woman holding the next day. It read "the system failed us again."

In order for things to change in St. Louis, the powers that be must first recognize the injustices that have been committed by the majority ruling force of the city; Outrageous behavior that most White American citizens don't know about.

For instance, on Interstate 70 in the North County area between Berkeley and Woodson Terrace sits the oldest, historically African American cemetery west of the Mississippi. The Washington Park Cemetery is the final resting place to a number of influential African Americans in history. The remains of Dred Scott and his wife were laid to rest there and later moved to another location.

The cemetery was created in 1920 and was the first "for profit" cemetery for African Americans in the St. Louis area, and it was built by two White American men. It was built adjacent to an African American community called Kinloch. Kinloch was considered the "Harlem" of St. Louis. African Americans were unable to do much publicly because of the segregation of the times. Kinloch was the place for African Americans to live, play and eventually settle down. When these people died, they went to Washington Park. Imagine two White American men coming up with a plan to capitalize on, at the expense of African Americans. That never happens, huh?

In 1955, during the expansion of the intercontinental highway, Interstate 70 was constructed, and although some of the remains of African Americans were moved to other locations, many more including the remains of my great-grandparents were paved over in the construction of the highway.

The cemetery was subsequently divided, with a portion on the Southside and a larger portion on the Northside, just east of Lambert Field Airport.

Is this something that would even be comprehensible, not to mention acceptable, to the White American citizens of St. Louis? I would think not, but because it does not affect the White American community of St. Louis, there is no general knowledge or discussion of this. The White American community of St. Louis, needs to come out of this mythical land they refer to as "Cardinal Nation," where everything in downtown revolves around one of the most racist organizations in all of baseball.

If you would like to verify that statement, just go to the front office of the Cardinal organization and start looking for people of color. In fact, other than a sprinkling of African Americans in the crowd, the only real time you see African Americans at a St. Louis Cardinals baseball game, are the people who are dressed in lime green. These are the vendors who are selling food, drinks, and souvenirs.

What has been so frustrating is that the African American community is truly not being included in the popular vision of St. Louis. I had a conversation with the editor of *St. Louis Magazine* once and told her that she should rename the magazine "St. Louis *White* Magazine," because of its lack of any African Americans in the magazine.

How can you speak of St. Louis without including African American culture in the conversation? I told her that the entire magazine is racist, and projects an image that only White Americans live here. She stated that "we have had African Americans such as Chuck Berry and Steven Jackson on our cover." I almost laughed, and I asked her if the only impression of African Americans she has is "an eighty-five-year-old convicted felon or a professional football player, neither of which live here?" She quickly deflected the conversation and hung up the phone.

If you have a conversation about St. Louis, it's impossible to have an honest conversation without talking about the African American culture, and depending on what section of town you live in, that experience can vary.

Unemployment among African Americans is high, accompanied by disenfranchisement, depression, a lack of educational opportunities, and of course violence is the common norm in the African American community, and is our unfortunate way of life in some neighborhoods.

One would like to believe that since the events of August 9, 2014, there have been great changes in the Gateway City. Yes, there have been some, but unfortunately not enough. The media and many of the White American communities have manipulated the actual story, and have lost focus on the real problems.

This often happens when you try to repair major situations, by starting at the top. Michael Brown

Jr. didn't die because of the traffic fine racket that was happening in Ferguson, and so many other municipalities in St. Louis. He was killed because of a poisonous culture that exists not only in St. Louis, but in the United States as a whole.

We saw it in Ferguson, New York (Eric Garner), Florida (Trayvon Martin), Texas (both at the pool party incident, and the suspicious hanging of Sandra Bland outside of Houston), and the list of cities goes on and on. We continue to see it in Presidential candidates like Donald Trump, who by running for President of the United States, give everyone in this country a clear indication of how many complete "nut-jobs" there are in the republic. Unfortunately, until this poison is irradiated, the list will continue to grow.

There has got to be a systemic change. Someone has to accept the blame for the way things are, and nobody wants to accept any amount of blame. Therefore White Americans will get defensive when discussing the racist circumstances that exist, mainly because White Americans have been running this game since the dawn of time. When people get defensive, then you can count on any and all progress coming to a screeching halt.

Race and racism are at the forefront of almost every conversation, when the subject is St. Louis, Missouri. The disparity in the simple economics of the city are visible in every aspect. This, accompanied by the clear inconsistencies in the law enforcement and justice system, and the obvious inequality of educational opportunities, are not some rare occurrence.

However, we can change things by continuing the conversation about every one of these situations. We must decide as individuals to step out on different roads; roads that as people of different cultures we have not traveled down before.

Often those roads will not be easy to travel, but if we are to change as a city and achieve the true greatness that the city of St. Louis is destined for, it must be willing to travel down that difficult road, and if necessary build some bridges between communities.

Although much of the Gateway City is an embedded version of the 1950s, there are many citizens of St. Louis who work very hard, and would prefer to leave the past in the past. The segregation of the communities is St. Louis is not something that just goes away, because it is so prominent and truly stood the test of time.

But by opening the minds of the younger set of citizens in the city, we finally began to tear away the invisible barriers that have separated the various cultures of the city. Maybe then we can embrace each other in the true spirit of the city.

We cannot speak about St. Louis without talking about the "Black Lives Matter" movement and its importance.

The "Black Lives Matter" movement has been countered by White America stating their belief that all lives matter, and the lives of law enforcement officers also matter. The fact is that nobody is disputing the belief that every life matters. You can also use that as the foundation for the entire Black Lives Matter movement.

Nobody is trying to say that African American lives matter more than White American lives, but they are trying to get the point across that African American lives don't mean any less either. While their tactics are sometimes questionable, there is certainly a legitimate reason for African American people to feel they matter less.

The point and end result of the "Black Lives Matter" movement is to move us out of a "color-blind" society. White America has tried to make society color-blind in culture, laws, the arts, religion, and just about every aspect of American society. They are repeatedly suggesting this, and shooting down this movement, in exchange for supporting the belief that all lives should matter. I, in fact, believe that all lives do matter, but only because life matters.

But in the world that we live in, that is a myth because by action, it is clear that all lives do not matter. There is a significant news media bias toward stories that White America can relate too. When young African American men were dying, prior to the Michael Brown Jr. shooting on August 9, 2014, it was never a big deal in the media because, as I have stated, it didn't affect White America.

If White Americans, in particular, White American women are killed, it is treated as a catastrophic event in the media. African American men die every day, so it is treated as "no big deal." The result is that in our society, we don't pay attention to certain deaths. This is where society is, and we truthfully don't treat all lives with equality.

The phrase "Black Lives Matter" should probably say correctly that "Black Lives Matter Also." It's saying that black lives should also matter. "All" lives matter is White Americans' plan of dismissing the statement and the movement as a whole, because it suggests that it means "only black lives matter." When that is obviously not the case.

"All Lives Matter" essentially says we are going to remain color-blind and have no respect for the individual cultures that exist in the country, and it ultimately sends us back to disregarding the problem of embedded racism in the United States.

CHAPTER 20

PUTTING AN END TO RACISM

Colorblindness never works. Instead we might try becoming culturally aware. At some point people need to become comfortable be uncomfortable.

—*John Parker*

RACISM IS A system where people are divided based on skin color and appearance. It is a belief that race is the primary determining factor of human capacities, and that racial differences produce both an inherent superiority and inferiority of a particular racial group.

Racism is also a prejudice based on beliefs. Racism has transformed and become invisible at certain times. It has embedded itself in every aspect of our lives. Its mask and costume have truly transitioned from white sheets to custom made suits.

Unfortunately, we continue to support racism as long as we divide people according to race. Therefore, it is very easy to end racism, but there has to be a real commitment. All we have to do is to stop dividing people according to these outward features. We should begin to refuse to call ourselves or others "African Americans," "White Americans," "Hispanic American" or other race-related hyphenated names.

Yes, there is only one race, the human race, and yes, all of us belong to one species, *Homo sapiens*, but we have reached a point in evolution where race needs to be recognized less, and culture should be recognized more.

Today, even modern anthropologists and biologists view race as an invalid genetic or biological designation. Neither "race" nor "subspecies" are appropriate ways to describe human populations. Race is not a scientific concept or a medical term, but it is one that permeates throughout society.

Biology does not explain this concept of race. The Human Genome Project, which is the most complex and complete mapping of human DNA known to man, indicates that there is no clear genetic basis to what we today define as racial groups.

History, however, does tell us how it developed. The current concept of race only arose in the seventeenth century. Before that, the term *race* was used to describe nations or ethnic groups. For instance, the Atlantic slave trade created an incentive to categorize human groups and provide a justification for slavery.

In order to change this sense of inequality and oppression, White America must truly understand their *Whiteness,* and its effect on society. Whiteness isn't only an appearance, but a piece of a larger American cultural fabric.

In American culture, Whiteness is the centerpiece of our culture, and in the minds of White America, this makes it the baseline from which differences are measured. This keeps all African Americans (even ones that think they can escape it) on the outskirts of society. It also gives White America an unconscious advantage, while disadvantaging African Americans.

This doesn't mean that all White Americans have it easy, but that they experience certain privileges they are unlikely aware of. These privileges include, but aren't limited to, things like being able to shop without being followed by suspicious clerks, objective representation in the media, and definitely lesser sentences for similar crimes. What they refuse to understand and admit is that all White Americans have White American privileges, although they all experience it differently.

I have grown up in an era where I have heard many White Americans say the phrase "I don't see race!"

Of course, I have to laugh at that person's pompous, know nothing statement. But truth be told, I've met a great many people who believe they truly are "color-blind" and, therefore, unbiased when it comes to race.

These are the sort of people that lean in close, to mouth the word "black," as if noticing and naming race is inherently shameful. I guess they don't realize that it is not. It is what happens after people notice race that is the problem. And I don't mean the moment of racial bias when someone makes a judgment based on another person's skin color. That prejudice, I think that is human and inevitable, based on the society we live in.

Please understand. I am not saying racism is unavoidable or excusable. I mean that whether by nature or nurture (by hook or by crook), human beings are predisposed to make certain judgments and to favor what looks and feels familiar and comfortable. When we watch someone from our own race do something, our brain simulates the action mentally as a form of empathy. But when we see someone of a different race do the same thing, we make much less effort to empathize.

If not part of human biology, racism is embedded in our lives, by the cues we receive from the time we are children. African Americans are all inundated daily with the preferences, of the White American culture.

Most parents of White children prefer a color-blind approach to fight racism. They want their children to grow up never seeing a difference in the different colors of people in this country. But when asked how many White Americans are mean, these same children commonly answered, "almost none," but when asked how many African Americans are mean, these same children will answer with "some," or even "a lot."

All people have natural biases. That really is not the problem. The problem is that these prejudices too often remain like a hair across your cheek. You can't see it, you can't find it with your fingers, but you keep brushing at it because the feel of it is irritating. Understand that prejudice is not the problem, but it is in that thin space between bias and action (or lack thereof) where the trouble lies.

Racism breeds from that place where people fail to recognize their inherent prejudices, and instead act on them as if they were truth. Here is the place where we as a society need to do our work. Unfortunately, America has gotten tangled up in our colorblindness and our mythical post-racial society.

White America has chosen to make bias a moral issue and not a human failing. Many White Americans don't see race. They don't see their own race bias either. And so, they don't see racism, which leads to the work of equality going undone.

In some areas of the United States, the idea of racism as a problem is a remotely scarce concern. That is because in these areas, there tends to be so much diversity that people do not really give it much thought. However, in other parts of the country, racism is still a very near (and dear in some cases) issue that many encounter every day.

That is not to say that it is just African Americans that are discriminated against. It goes both ways. Believe it or not, the good news is that it can be overcome. The question really is, will it ever be overcome?

There truly could potentially be a day when all people are judged by their character. The key to reaching that point is the education of society. We must begin to educate all children, from the point of birth, to not be color-blind to those around us. Society must educate them to become more culturally aware. Then, and only then will race stop being an issue. The way it is now, racism is still a leading prejudice in our society,

First, and perhaps the most important way to move society forward is to be a role model for your children, and a mentor for other children around you. Those with a strong Christian faith already know the importance of letting the light of Christ shine through them.

When you respond to people in a warm fashion, they will usually respond in kind. People around you will also be drawn to you, and you will likely develop friends or acquaintances from many different cultures. Through your example, others might come to change their ways without even realizing it, and children will naturally use you as a role model for how to behave toward others.

With that example, it is important to remember not to spread rumors, or say a harsh words about someone from another culture in the presence of children. It may seem innocent enough, but children pay close attention to what is being said by the adults around them. They take what they hear adults saying, and combine it with what they see and hear on television.

Children absorb things we would never imagine just by being observant. So uttering words or phrases that blame an entire race for the actions on one person, no matter how much you think it may be statistically backed, can leave a lasting negative impression against that race or culture on the mind of a child.

To that end, the media needs to take some real responsibility, because it can leave a lasting impression on the minds of young children as well. Media has the power to either sway people into assuming incidents involving race are hate crime or vice versa. They also have the power to provoke fear of certain races into the hearts of other races.

This is what Fox News has made their living on, by attempting to scare the hell out of White America, with the fear of African American violence and Hispanic illegal immigration.

Our job as adults would be to either not let our children watch these kinds of media pieces, or to be there as they watch, to guide them through what they are watching. You want them to take away the facts of the issues and to judge base on facts, rather than the assumption of others.

This should be the perspective used in everyday situations. If everyone judges base on facts instead of fear, statistics, or past experiences, there would be less prejudice to deal with. The problem is that there are many other psychological aspects that come into play. Though in many issues, these other aspects can be overcome or, at the very least, overlooked.

They can be overlooked because of the influences of positive examples around a person. After all, people learn, they lead, and they even change by example. That example is the foundation that could potentially cause a temporal shift in society.

It causes a change in society by causing a change in the way the judicial and government systems operate. It can change the definition of a hate crime, and it can change the way corporations handle their employees. It would do so because everyone would see people for the way they behaved as individuals, instead of their skin appearance. The racial component would no longer need to be a deciding factor in the hiring process.

Everyone deserves the right to prove themselves worthy for employment at a particular place, based on factors such as experience, loyalty, respect toward others and qualifications. Likewise, employers should be free to fire employees that do not meet their standards, regardless of what race they are without fear of retaliation via lawsuit.

Leading by example can also cause change in society, because the very young begin to learn that although there are differences in appearances, personality, interests, and in the way things are done, these differences are the things that make us special as individuals, and as cultures. Individual cultures and history should be appreciated, celebrated, and studied, but not used as a means of judging people for their actions.

As I stated, we must also remember to watch how we talk about specific groups of people. For example, not all Hispanics are illegal. So when speaking about illegal people in general, be careful not to imply that all Hispanics are illegal, or that just because someone is from Mexico that person has to be illegal. After all, the problem of illegal immigrations is caused by immigrants from all over the world, and not from any one specific country.

People must learn not to immediately resort to race as a descriptive factor whenever there is a problem concerning a large number of people. People must instead learn to speak about others as people that have done a certain action, rather than as an individual of a particular race that has done certain actions.

These targeted individuals must also learn not to assume that all White Americans think the same way, because if they are allowed to become prejudiced toward White Americans, then there is no room left for change to take place. For change to truly take place, every single individual in the country must be the example that does not judge an individual by the actions of other members of their culture.

The real change in American society will come when everyone, of all cultures, learn to celebrate the differences around us, and not jump to conclusions because of race. If everyone is treated as an equal by those in authority, race will eventually become an irrelevant issue.

For now though, we can all set out to be real and ethical examples to the children of society. Our focused mandate should be to facilitate the change for the next generation to come. By these examples, maybe race will no longer be an issue in government operations, education operations, employment operations, friendships or anything else. Maybe, just maybe, there will come a day when racism will be eradicated and become just a distant memory of times gone by.

In the United States, most people who self identify as African American have some White American ancestors, while many people who identify as European American have some African ancestors. Since the early history of the United States, African Americans and White Americans have all been classified as belonging to different races. The consequences are still readily apparent today. The criteria for membership in these races diverged in the late nineteenth century. It was then that increasing numbers of Americans began to consider anyone with even one drop of known African American blood to be African American, regardless of appearance. This is not only absurd but it is illegitimate. Race is one thing that is never mentioned in the Bible.

The Bible does not use the term "race" at all. It does not discuss the color of people's skins. Thus the Queen of Sheba (2 Chronicles 9:1–12) and the Ethiopian Eunuch (Acts 8:26–40) are never described in racial terms. Though there is not even the slightest suggestion of race as the term is understood today, ethnicity is emphasized, but never skin color.

Similarly, the Qur'an does not use racial language to describe people, although such prejudices did develop later among the Arabs for a variety of reasons, especially their conquests and slave trade.

If the Bible and Qur'an do not use such language, then why should society do so? It is high time that we eliminate the word "race" when we apply it to human populations. The word has other meanings, and is still appropriate in other contexts, as when it refers to competitions, but otherwise it should be banned. Recognizing how it has molded our thinking is another way of ending racism.

We define ourselves and others largely in racial terms, and this helps to explain the latent racism that many people have, even among people who say that they are not racists.

At the end of 2014 and well into 2015, a spate of shootings in St. Louis had many people thinking that African Americans are fully responsible. That may be unfair, but it illustrates a commonly held perception of crime in the United States. This is racist thinking, as is racial profiling and, indeed, any discussion about race involving this issue.

There are many ethnic divisions, of course, but these are linguistic and cultural in origin, not biological. When people assert that they can easily distinguish Africans, Asians, and Europeans, as well as many groups within them, they are referring to ethnic differences, not racial ones. Such ethnic divisions can be equally dangerous.

Only recently has Europe become sufficiently united, to be able to rise above the division that dominated European history for centuries, and which had led to innumerable wars. Unfortunately, the United States will probably need significantly more time, probably another generation, to become equally united.

One can hope, pray, and work at it, but ultimately society will have to come together. There have been several stories that reaffirm the extent to which racial bias and anti-African American racism in particular, are real things that happen to real people. Ending racism must become our priority in society.

In addition, there are other divisions of the human species that are objectionable as well, such as age and sex. Ageism and sexism must also come to an end. Society must begin to emphasize the unity of humanity, not the divisions, if this is to happen.

Eradication of racism is to eliminate all race descriptions including any cultural value individual societies have to offer. If we only recognized or only knew the "United States culture," no individual or group could be discriminated against, favorably or otherwise.

Fortunately, we have to begin to value the diversity each culture has to offer, and therefore will always subject society to those who value our differences. We must also allow people the freedom to choose to be a racist or not. It is truly okay to know "what lane someone is in." Freedom comes at a price.

Racist people are allowed to be mean, stupid, or ignorant. Racist people will be judged. A racist will serve his or her own self-sentence of spending their life, without the joy of embracing the variety, or the spice of life in a world of cultural expansion. Society must realize that there is real value in celebrating other cultures that so greatly exceeds the value of feeling you are superior to other races.

Let us change the history of embedded racism. Let us, as a total society, end this mental segregation based on these ridiculous stereotypes. Instead, let us promote our oneness. Above all, we must be motivated by love for our fellow human beings.

Is that too much to ask of society?

INDEX

G

Gateway City, 183, 394
gender, 94, 143, 165, 206, 210, 370
government, 10, 16, 36, 40, 75, 97, 107–8, 120, 167, 176, 250, 262, 264–66, 271, 372
  federal, 108, 344
  local, 175
grace, 36, 90
guns, 211–12, 216, 227, 231

H

hate, 16, 53
hate crimes, 302, 307
hate groups, 35–36, 47–48, 53, 64–65, 68, 308
health care, 75, 163, 334, 339, 344, 346, 351, 369
Hispanics, 36, 383, 388, 404–5
holiday, 50, 341
Hollywood, 128, 135, 137, 146

I

ignorance, 115, 278–79, 342
industry, 51, 129, 143, 146–48, 157–58, 175, 293, 338
  entertainment media, 130, 133
  film, 128, 134–35, 148
  motion picture, 131–33
information, iv, 53–54, 77, 97, 106, 139, 178, 197, 200, 290, 316
Invisible Empire, 39, 47

J

jail, 31, 250, 252, 269, 340
judicial system, 176, 211
  American, 89
justice, 9, 202, 206, 211, 223, 234, 238, 242, 258

K

KKK (see also Ku Klux Klan), 17–18, 24, 29–30, 32–33, 35–36, 39, 46–47, 49–50, 57–58, 67
knowledge, 97, 257, 263, 312, 391
Ku Klux Klan, xv, 15, 18, 22–23, 26, 28, 32, 40–43, 45–46, 51, 53–54, 57, 61, 130

L

law enforcement, 23, 25, 168, 257, 308
Lincoln Motion Picture Company, 131–34
looting, 218, 224, 296, 388
lynching, 22, 24, 39, 47, 56, 67, 273

M

Martin, Trayvon, xvi, 5, 212, 215, 393
media, xvi, 39, 50, 70–72, 95–100, 102–8, 112–14, 124, 129, 141–43, 150–51, 228, 293–96, 396, 403

Edwards Brothers Malloy
Oxnard, CA USA
December 1, 2015